Death of the PostHuman

Critical Climate Change

Series Editors: Tom Cohen and Claire Colebrook

The era of climate change involves the mutation of systems beyond 20th century anthropomorphic models and has stood, until recently, outside representation or address. Understood in a broad and critical sense, climate change concerns material agencies that impact on biomass and energy, erased borders and microbial invention, geological and nanographic time, and extinction events. The possibility of extinction has always been a latent figure in textual production and archives; but the current sense of depletion, decay, mutation and exhaustion calls for new modes of address, new styles of publishing and authoring, and new formats and speeds of distribution. As the pressures and re-alignments of this re-arrangement occur, so must the critical languages and conceptual templates, political premises and definitions of 'life.' There is a particular need to publish in timely fashion experimental monographs that redefine the boundaries of disciplinary fields, rhetorical invasions, the interface of conceptual and scientific languages, and geomorphic and geopolitical interventions. Critical Climate Change is oriented, in this general manner, toward the epistemo-political mutations that correspond to the temporalities of terrestrial mutation.

Death of the PostHuman

Essays on Extinction, Vol. 1

Claire Colebrook

( )

OPEN HUMANITIES PRESS

with Michigan Publishing – University of Michigan Library, Ann Arbor

2014

First edition published by OPEN HUMANITIES PRESS 2014

Freely available online at http://dx.doi.org/10.3998/ohp.12329362.0001.001

PRINT ISBN 978-1-78542-011-5

PDF ISBN 978-1-60785-299-5

OPEN HUMANITIES PRESS is an international, scholar-led open access publishing collective whose mission is to make leading works of contemporary critical thought freely available worldwide. Books published under the OPEN HUMANITIES PRESS imprint at Michigan Publishing are produced through a unique partnership between OHP's editorial board and the University of Michigan Library, which provides a library-based managing and production support infrastructure to facilitate scholars to publish leading research in book form.

MICHIGAN PUBLISHING
www.publishing.umich.edu

O
OPEN HUMANITIES PRESS
www.openhumanitiespress.org

Contents

Acknowledgements

I am grateful for the patience, dedication and support of Open Humanities Press, and Sigi Jöttkandt in particular. For ongoing intellectual stimulus and friendship I thank Tom Cohen, Jami Weinstein and J. Hillis Miller.

Framing the End of the Species: Images Without Bodies

*Society invents a spurious convoluted logic tae absorb and
change people whae's behaviour is outside its mainstream.
Suppose that ah ken all the pros and cons, know that ah'm
gaunnae have a short life, am ay sound mind etcetera,
etcetera, but still want tae use smack? They won't let yae do
it, because it's seen as a sign ay thir ain failure. The fact that
ye jist simply choose to reject whit thae huv to offer. Choose
us. Choose life. Choose mortgage payments; choose washing
machines; choose cars' choose sitting on a couch watching
mind-numbing and spirit-crushing game shows, stuffin fucking
junk food intae yir mooth. Choose rotting away, pishing and
shiteing yersel in a home, a total fucking embarrassment tae
the selfish, fucked-up brats ye've produced. Choose life.*

*Well, ah chose no tae choose life. If the cunts cannae handle that,
it's thair fuckin problem. (Irvine Welch,* Trainspotting, *187-88)*

There are three senses of extinction: the now widely discussed sixth great
extinction event (which we have begun to imagine *and* witness, even if
in anticipation); extinction by humans of other species (with the endan-
gered species of the 'red list' evidencing our destructive power); and
self-extinction, or the capacity for us to destroy what makes us human.
All three senses of extinction require a nuanced conception of climate.
Climate is at once an enclosing notion, imagined as the bounded milieu
that is unavoidably ours, and a disturbing figure, for it is with the recognition *that there is climate,* or that the human *species* is now recognizable as

a being that for all its seeming diversity is nevertheless bound into a unity of destructive power. (This is so much so that geologists are arriving at consensus regarding an 'Anthropocene epoch' where man's effect on the planet will supposedly be discernible as a geological strata readable well after man ceases to be, even if there are no geologists who will be present to undertake this imagined future reading (Crutzen 2000). Climate is not only, then, the surface or terrain upon which we find ourselves, but something that binds us to *this time* on the earth, with its own depletions and limits.)

There is, of course, the standard meteorological notion of climate which increasingly attracts our already over-taxed attention; but this concept of climate is only possible because of a broader thought-event where humans begin to imagine a deep time in which the human species emerges and withers away, and a finite space in which 'we' are now all joined in a tragedy of the commons. I would suggest that just as Darwinian evolution altered the very modes of scientific and imaginative thinking, such that new forms of narrative and knowledge were required to think of man as a species emerging within time (Beer 1983), so global climate change is similarly catastrophic for the human imaginary. It becomes possible to think of climate as the milieu that is necessary for our ongoing life, *and* as the fragile surface that holds us all together in one web of risked life, even if we cannot practically grasp or manage the dynamics of this totality (Gardiner 2006). The concept of climate is also split between knowledge and denial: on the one hand talk of climate draws all bodies (organic and otherwise) into a single complex, multiply determined and dynamic whole; on the other hand, any brief glance at climate change policy and politics evidences a near psychotic failure to acknowledge or perceive causal connections with dire consequences. In this respect we need to embark on a notion of climate change that includes the radical alteration of knowledge and affect that accompanies the very possibility of *climate*. It is only possible to think of climate change in the meteorological sense—with humans now bound to volatile ecologies that they are at once harming and ignoring—if some adjustment is made to the ways in which we think about the relations among time, space and species. A necessarily expansive sense of climate change encompasses a mutation of cognitive, political, disciplinary, media and social climates. The fact that we start to think about climate as a general condition that binds humans to an irreversible and destructive time means *both* that climate becomes an indispensable concept for thinking about the new modes of knowledge and feeling that mark the twenty-first century in terms of our growing sense of precarious attachment to a fragile planet, *and* that climate is an alibi. We talk about climate, ecology, globalism and even environment (as that which environs) even though the experience of climate change reveals multiple and incongruent systems for which we do not have a point of view. We are at once thrown into a situation of urgent interconnectedness, aware that the smallest events contribute to global mutations, at the same time as we come up against a complex multiplicity of diverging forces and timelines that exceed any manageable point of view.

In a recent fable that allegorized the human relation among memory, destruction and the future of life, Nick Bostrom suggests that the human species would remain complacent about its catastrophic history and future as long as it continues to forget that its situation *is* catastrophic. We have taken the catastrophe of human existence as natural and irredeemable: only a counter-narration in which we vanquish destruction will let us see just how death-inured we have become (Bostrom 2005). More recently, climate change scientists have started to play with new strategies for awakening public affect: perhaps the focus on hope needs to give way to mobilizations of fear, whereby we learn to 'hug the monster,' in order to shift from inertia and quiescence to action.[1] How is it that the human species, seemingly so hungry for life and dominance, has conveniently forgotten its own self-extinguishing tendencies? We can only pose the question of human extinction—the fact that humans will become extinct, the fact that we cause other extinctions, and also that we are extinguishing what renders us human—if we locate the problem of climate change inaction in a broader terrain of ecological destruction. The very climates—cognitive, industrial, economic, affective, technological, epistemological and meteorological—that render our life possible are also self-destructive (both destructive of the self, and destructive of climate itself).

There is a widespread lament regarding a trajectory of self-extinction occurring in the human brain. According to Susan Greenfield, in her book *ID*, we are losing identity: where our brains once operated by a synthesizing power of grammar, syntax and critique we are now seduced by a culture of stimulus (Greenfield 2008). We are not just losing one of our critical powers—our power to represent or synthesize what is not ourselves—we are losing our very selfhood. For 'we' are—*as* human, as identities—just this evolved synthesizing power. Greenfield locates her diagnosis of identity within a broader argument regarding the brain and its self-forming capacities. A certain self-loss is required for stimulus and pleasure, but a certain neural extension and order is required for meaning and self. In her earlier work Greenfield had argued for a healthy or normal balance between the capacity for the joy of fleeting sensation (such as the first taste of morning coffee) and the ability to link sensations into some broader network of selfhood and significance (Greenfield 2002). If there were no capacity to enjoy the simple moment we would suffer from depression, or an extreme search for meaning that we may never be able to fulfill; drugs that treat depression enable a release from the grip of significance. But today—perhaps—it is the fleeting insignificance that is taking over twenty-first century neural architecture. The diagnostic dimension of Greenfield's work lies in its lament regarding the new modes and temporalities of visual culture, where the transient ecstasies of video games overtake the sustained focus and pleasure of complex narrative and argument. This lament of human self-loss achieved through the over-consumption of stimulus is not Greenfield's alone. Her work keeps company with Carr's *The Shallows: What the Internet is Doing to Our Brain* (2010), Jackson and McKibben's *Distraction* (2008), Wolf's *Proust and the Squid* (2007), Winifred Gallagher's *Rapt* (2008), N. Katherine Hayles's (2007) theory of the transition from deep attention to hyper attention, and Bernard Stiegler's (2010) lament regarding the short circuits of transindividuation (with humans having lost the orientation of care). Precisely at the moment of its own loss the human animal becomes aware of what makes it human—meaning, empathy, art, morality—but can only recognize those capacities that distinguish humanity at the moment that they are threatened with extinction.

It is possible to argue, as Giorgio Agamben (1998) has done, that there has always been a sense of the human capacity for failing to be human. We can lose ourselves—extinguish ourselves—because we are nothing more than potentiality. If humans were always and already fully human, if humanity were a simply actuality, then there would never be the possibility of failing to realize either one's reason, or to recognize rational humanity in others. This is why Agamben has isolated a last chance for redemption precisely at this point in our history when it becomes apparent that what we are is not something essential that will necessarily come into being: our humanity is not an actuality from which we can draw grounds for action. The fact that we forget our *impotentiality*—that we treat humans as factual beings with a normality that dictates action—has reached crisis point in modernity, especially as we increasingly suspend the *thought* of our fragility for the sake of ongoing efficiency. Both totalitarianism and democratic hedonism are, for Agamben, forms of deadening managerialism. Both act on the basis of *man* as an actuality. It is at this point of exhaustion, when we have become frozen spectators in a world in which images appear as ready-mades, that we can see both that there is no guarantee that we will be human and that it *is* human to forget oneself. For Agamben it is both the modern horrors of totalitarianism (where humans are reduced to so much manageable and disposable matter or animality) *and* modern democratic hedonism (where we become nothing more than the targeted consumers of dazzling spectacle) that demonstrates human *impotentiality*, our essential capacity not to actualize that which would distinguish as human.

Most importantly, this highly human inhumanity seems to center strangely on the organ that organizes the human organism; for it is the same eye that reads and theorizes—that looks with wonder at the heavens—that is also seduced, spellbound, distracted and captivated by inanity. Immanuel Kant already drew on a tradition of philosophical wonder when he isolated man's capacity to look into the heavens as both a source of delusion that would draw him away from grounded knowledge into enthusiasm, and as the necessary beginning of a power of thinking that would not be tied solely to sensation (Kant 1999, 269-70). The eye is geared to spectacle as much as speculation, with speculation itself being both productively expansive in its capacity to imagine virtual futures and restrictively deadening in its tendency to forget the very life from which it emerges. Indeed there is something essentially self-destructive about the human theoretical eye: our very openness to the world—the very relation that is our life—is precisely what seduces us into forgetting that before there is an eye that acts as a camera or window there must have been something like an orientation or distance, a relation without relation. I would suggest that we ought to think, today in an era of climate change, about moralizing laments regarding human reason's self-loss alongside various posthuman theorizations that human reason is constituted by a certain self-forgetting. The human animal or human eye is torn between spectacle (or captivation by the mere present) and speculation (ranging beyond the present at the cost of its own life).

There are two directions this criticism of the embodied eye can take: one is to expand the sense of the body, to imagine a receptive or perceptive power that is not a simple snapshot of the world but a full and expansive openness. Here we might identify a pseudo-Heideggerian criticism of Descartes that was taken up by cognitive science: Heidegger had already diagnosed Western metaphysics with Descartes as a fulcrum: Descartes is able to establish man as the 'subject' (or as that which remains present) because Western thought has always proceeded by forgetting the temporality through which all being comes into presence (Heidegger 1968). By the time Descartes establishes the subject as that which precedes and provides a foundation, 'humanism' has definitively forgotten that there is no such thing as man as a simply existing thing with an essence. For Heidegger what is required is not a retrieval of some pre-Cartesian connectedness to the world, with man and world being co-present; rather, before there is the dyad of man and world there is something like disclosure or revealing. Contemporary cognitive science and certain philosophies of the human have drawn upon this anti-Cartesianism to insist that man is not a camera, not a computer, and the eye is not a window (Wrathall and Malpas 2000; Thompson 2007; Wheeler 2005). Where such contemporary uses of Heidegger differ from Heidegger is in their diagnosis of Cartesianism as an accidental lapse rather than as evidence of humanity's self-forgetting 'essence.' These pseudo-Heideggerian diagnoses suggest that Cartesianism can be overcome by returning man to the richer expansive life from which he has become detached. The subtitle of Andy Clark's book says it all: 'putting, brain, body, and world together again' (Clark 1997). For Heidegger, though, there is a necessary forgetting in any disclosure of being: to experience the world as present for me, and to begin questioning—as we must—from this already given world, relies upon a hiddenness or non-revealing that we must leave behind in living the world as our own. We begin *in media res*, always already thrown into a world that appears as so many natural and separate things. Our tendency to forget, and to live life inauthentically—*not* recognizing Being as the site for all clearing, as though the world were just this way naturally— is not something one can simply place behind oneself as an unfortunate philosophical error. For Heidegger in-authenticity or humanism (where we simply take ourselves to be a privileged thing among things) is not an external and unfortunate event but has to do with the very mode of being's appearance: we see being appear, but do not attend to its coming into being. One mode of phenomenology after Heidegger has, however, taken the form of a correction or adjustment: we should overcome the deep problems of how we know or arrive at having a world and accept that the world just *is* that which is always already given and meaningful for living beings. Phenomenology should be naturalized and tied to a process of embodied knowledge. We are not minds who represent a world, but organisms *from which* the capacity and figure of knowing mind emerged.

But there's another path, another way of dealing with man's tendency to reify himself. This other departure from a restricted subjectivism proceeds not by broadening the self to include emotions, dynamism and the non-cognitive, but by tearing the eye from the body. Rather than restore the human to some unified and expansive vision it might be possible to think of the eye as a machine. This machine would not be a computer, for a genuine machine does not have a central organizing program but is put to work through connections; one could consider synthesizers as computers receiving inputs and turning out data, *or* as machines in their creation and recreation of connections. For Deleuze and Guattari, the reference to synthesizers is *not* another metaphor for thinking, where we substitute one machine for another. Thought *is* a synthesizer: just as musical synthesizers take the sounds of the world and repeat, create and mutate various differences, so thought can maximize rather than diminish the complexity of sensations:

> A synthesizer places all of the parameters in continuous variation, gradually making 'fundamentally heterogeneous elements and up turning into each other in some way.' The moment this conjunction occurs there is common matter. It

is only at this point that one reaches the abstract machine, or the diagram of the assemblage. The synthesizer has replaced judgment, and matter has replaced the figure or formed substance. It is no longer even appropriate to group biological, physico-chemical and energetic intensities on the one hand, and mathematical, aesthetic, linguistic, informational, semiotic intensities, etc., on the other. The multiplicity of systems of intensities conjugates or forms a rhizome throughout the entire assemblage the moment the assemblage is swept up by these vectors or tensors of flight (Deleuze and Guattari 2004, 121)

Before exploring the 'multiplicity of systems of intensities' in detail, we can go back over the relation between the eye and human self-extinction, between the eye that views the world in order to enable survival, and the eye that then becomes frozen or seduced by its own imaging power—to the point where the eye takes in a frozen image of its self. Bergson has argued for an economy of the eye and creative difference: in order to release itself from merely surviving in the world, the human eye organizes the world into conceptualized units, mastering the world by reducing difference. This intellectual process allows for increasing technologies and the furtherance of systems of order: the intellect is at home with technology and matter, or that which remains the same through time and can be mastered though repetition. What is abandoned is intensity—the infinitesimally small differences and fluxes that the eye edits out. For Bergson the problem with this difference-reducing mode of the intellect is when mind turns back upon itself, and fixes upon a static image: thought is no longer intuited (as it should be) as a dynamic creative force, but appears as a brain, representing self, thinking substance or 'man' (Bergson 1913, 196).

This argument for the self as *not* being a substance but, rather, the condition for the organized perception of substance, has a long philosophical and moral history. If Aristotle argued that what distinguished us as humans was not merely perception of the world, nor consumption of the world but the capacity for perception and consumption to go beyond what *is* to consider what *ought* to be, and if Plato also argued that we should not merely perceive but think about that which gives itself *to be perceived*, this moral distinction becomes formal in modernity. That is, Plato and Aristotle concede that man is a biological being but with a capacity for reason, a capacity that distinguishes humans from other beings. But the modern theory of the subject, with Descartes positing a different *substance*—or *res cogitans*—makes a difference of kind and modality with regard to humans and their relation to images. 'Man' is the being to whom the world is given for representation; what man himself is can never be known in itself, but only after the event of perception of the world. For Foucault, it was this shift from a world that possessed its own order and hierarchies to some distinction between ordered world and man as representing being that marked a historical a priori: what shifted was not an event within time but the modality of time itself. In modernity historical time is that through which 'man' both recognizes that he emerges from material conditions, at the same time as the very logic of life that requires him to labor, speak and form social wholes can only be known after the event (Foucault 1970).

If pre-moderns sought to elevate humans among other animals, modernity increasingly rejects human superiority and refuses to see man as rational animal; for man is *pure reason*. Kant does not argue that we have to be more than merely biological or animal beings, he insists that we are not beings at all. Rather, there are only beings because there is something like an organizing or synthesizing power. There is a world because there is a subject to whom a world is given. It makes no sense to strive to perceive or know the self, to try and capture the self as something that might be viewed. In the beginning is a potentiality *for viewing* from which we constitute a viewed world. We then imagine—ex post facto—that there must be selves who would be there to be viewed. Whereas Kant argued that there must be something like *the* subject who existed as this condition for all intuition (even if this subject cannot be known), Bergson (1913) argued that there was no subject who intuited images, just images or perceptions *from which* we posit some thing—the brain—that provides the illusory image that would cause all images.

But if pre-modern philosophy from at least Plato onwards argues that we *ought* not think of ourselves only as appetites, for we are responsible for our organizing relation to the world, modern philosophy argues that we are *only* organizing relations. There is not a self who perceives; there are perceptions, from which something like a self is constituted. We cannot explain the self's relation to images because of the interests and appetites that are its natural base. Desires and appetites are possible only because there is imaging: in the beginning is the relation. We can think of Freud here for whom pleasures are possible because of a prior genesis of a relation between desire and desired; the libido is a force that forms a relatively stable or 'cathected' pool of ongoing equilibrium, relating to the outside world in terms of its own tendency towards quiescence (Freud 2011). The desiring self is possible only because of a prior distribution that emerges from perception; a relation between self and other is formed *through* perception and does not precede perception

Something quite distinct structures modern claims for the relation between mind and image. It is not only the case that the self emerges from organizing perception, but also that perception can destroy the self. In *Beyond the Pleasure Principle* Freud observes his grandson throwing a cotton reel in and out of his cradle, while intoning '*Fort/Da*' (away/here) and it is from this observation that Freud argues that in addition to the self's formation of a stable border between itself and the world, there is also a tendency to want to destroy or annihilate that distance. If pleasure is managing the relation between perceiver and the manageable influx of stimulus, then *beyond* pleasure there lies a tendency towards annihilation of distance, a dissolution of the bounded and perceiving organism.

What if the brain that is supposedly properly (in its human mode) oriented towards synthesis were at risk of falling back, of devolution? For some time it has been noted that there is an anxiety regarding mere images: the society of the spectacle (Debord 1973), a world of simulation (Baudrillard 1994), a world of passive consumption (Adorno 2001) or mere exhibition without aura (Benjamin 2008), a world of hyper attention rather than deep attention (Hayles 2007), at once seems to destroy the brain's evolved powers, and yet also give the lie to a certain destructive illusion regarding the brain as image. If we have lamented for so long—since Kant at least—that man tends to forget that he is a subject and tends to take himself to be just substance, then why are we so alarmed today by the brain's tendency to destroy any image or sense of itself, to be nothing other than the stimulus it receives? After all, this loss of self seems to be the fulfillment of a long modern striving for anti-self-consciousness or pure immediacy (Hartman 1970). Have we arrived, perhaps unwillingly, at Emerson's transformation of the self into a transparent eyeball (Emerson 1982, 39)? And yet this achievement of what was once a Romantic and existential imperative for consciousness to be nothing other than its perceptual relation to the world, a pure process without reifying ground, is being met with mourning and alarm.

First, consider all the ways in which 'we' are now reacting with horror to our own capacity *not* to be ourselves.

This ranges from neo-Kantian claims that without the commitment to some idea of who I am—without some ongoing identification of what I would do if I were to remain true to the idea I have of myself—then 'I' am not a self at all (Korsgaard 2008, 86). There are also neurological claims regarding the importance of ongoing synthesis, ranging from Greenfield's moral anxiety over a culture of mere stimulus, to Antonio Damasio's claim that the self is not, as Descartes would have it, a thing that feels, but a receptive and creative structure of feeling *from which* it might then be possible to have a snapshot attitude to reality. If we lose sight of that feeling self, of the emotional brain, or of the naturally affective, connected and world-oriented self then we risk mistaking mind for mere machine or computer (Damasio 2000).

When today—with horror—we look at young minds, we ask how they have become nothing more than cameras or computational devices. The young brains of today are not affected or world-oriented; they manipulate Facebook numbers with ruthless algorithmic force, and ingest images without digestion or rumination. We watch, with horror, as the human brain reverts to being not so much a reader of Proust as akin to a squid, or mere life (Wolf 2007). This tendency to be nothing more than a screen for images is observed as at once the brain's horrific tendency towards self-extinction (an internal and ever-present threat) and as accidental or extrinsic (something that has assaulted us from without, by way of technology and modernity).

The diagnoses of the brain's and humanity's capacity to destroy itself are persistent and manifold, ranging from a supposed neural devolution caused by spectacle-stimulus culture to various anxieties about over-ingestion (where we glut ourselves on destructive images and various psychotropic drugs that diminish the brain's synthesizing powers). And

yet, at the same time, this release of the intuition of images from the organizing self of Cartesian subjectivism is hailed as redemption from the
rigidity of man: no longer do we enslave ourselves to the notion of the
autonomous, disembodied, affectless and world-divorced subject. One
of the many and varied modes of posthumanism hails an end to human
exceptionalism and cognition-oriented models, and instead begins from
one already integrated, dynamic and connected world. There is no 'really
hard problem' about the relation between mind and world, for the mind
is an effect of relations, not something that has to act in order to represent a world to which it must subsequently relate (Flanagan 2007). It
is not the case that we begin life as observing, representing beings who
then become through receptivity. Rather, in the beginning is a dynamic
and world-oriented receptivity *from which* organized cognition, and the
sense of the self as subject or man emerges. It is from a primary openness
to the world, a primarily sensed world, that there emerges the sense of
one who sees.

This ambivalent observation of the self-extinguishing tendency of the
brain's capacity for imaging does not pertain only to philosophy, theory
or recent theses of the brain. There are also popular accounts of our self-
attrition, with our over-consumption of everything from the internet and
Facebook to empty fats and calories, indicating that the very mechanisms
that led to out expansion are the same that will lead to our demise. Beyond
all the laments and moral proclamations regarding our falling away from
the activity of human reason, and beyond all the posthuman celebrations
that there is no such thing as 'man' and that we are really always already
at one with one web of life, we might ask how it is possible for humans to
have this panicked (or joyous) apprehension of self-loss. If humans really
are at one with the world of which they are nothing more than living and
creative perceivers, why have we felt for so long that we are disengaged
and rational minds? How did 'Descartes's error' take hold? Or, if mind
and reason are our proper self-creating potentialities, how is it that the
spectacle of the world has lured us into destroying ourselves? Why are
our own creations, technologies and desires the very mechanisms that
preclude us from being most properly ourselves? It is as though our
excessive glutting on images—from the seduction by media labels and
visual stimulus to the voyeurism of disaster porn—evidences the brain's

fragility to be nothing more than itself, a mere screen rather than a properly self-organizing whole. The thousands of years of evolved complexity can fall away through overconsumption. Just as the very desire for fats and sugars that propelled the body to hunt and develop technologies for metabolic stability and survival will drive the modern body into obesity, hypertension and an early grave, so the darting eye that stimulated the brain into becoming a reading and interpreting animal, may also be at the forefront of the human species' cognitive atrophy. And does this not say something profound about climate: that the human species' damaging of its own milieu is not an accident that we might otherwise have avoided, precisely because climate—as *our* milieu—is something that our very dependence upon will preclude us from ever really seeing?

Both of these questions—of self-destruction and milieu-destruction—are economic problems. (Both Freud and Bergson argued that the self was an effect of investment, by postponing the discharge of energy and allowing a pool of force that would be relatively stable through time.) The human animal delayed consumption of immediate resources, developed hunting and farming techniques in order to store energy, and so then freed energy and resources for further technical-intellectual-moral development (Ayala 2010). The viewing eye also delayed immediate response, developing concepts and perceptive technologies that enabled greater representational sophistication. V.S. Ramachandran speculates that the self and the notion of mind emerged in a survival tendency to anticipate the actions of others (Ramachandran 2003). The viewing eye becomes a reading and organizing apparatus, allowing 'man' to become a subject. These same replicating technologies, and life-propelling investments—allowing us to fashion cinematic, computational, virtual reality and televisual technologies—would eventually sacrifice the reading brain to the merely stimulated eye.

Apart from the general interest of observing a widespread anxiety regarding the brain's own capacity to destroy itself through the very perceptive power that generated its supposedly proper potentiality in the first place, it is possible to orient this discussion towards the perception of futurity.

Is not the problem of both sides—the dire prediction that we are losing our capacity to synthesize ourselves *and* the posthuman affirmation that we are really, properly, nothing more than a dynamic power to perceive—that there is still (for all the talk of loss) a reliance on a normative notion of the human, whereas what is required today is an inhuman perception? For all the talk of *climate change* we assume that the climate is what environs us, and that change—or the danger of change—needs to be calculated according to the degree to which it enables or precludes ongoing existence of humans (Mann 2009). If biodiversity is a prima facie good then surely *any* ecosystem—even one that emerged after human extinction—would answer the requirement for ongoing life? And if biodiversity is not a prima facie good, and is only good insofar as it offers ecosystem services for humans, then the very reasons why we might finally act in order to maintain biodiversity—in order to continue to live—seem to be hampered by our drive for life. The very eye that has opened up a world to the human species, has also allowed the human species to fold the world around its own, increasingly myopic, point of view. Today, we might start to question the appropriate point of view from which we might observe and evaluate the human viewing eye: from our own greater will to survive, *or* would it not be better to start to look at the world and ourselves without assuming our unquestioned right to life?

Our very narration of the brain and its emergence as *the* properly synthesizing milieu from which all other imaging milieus need to be considered, shelters us from the thought of the inhuman images that confront us at the limits of the embodied eye. We can recall, here, Deleuze's criticism of Bergson, which is technical and counter-vital. Bergson, like so many other early modernists mourned the living and dynamic eye that had been sacrificed to technological expediency. For Bergson the intellect cuts up the world in order to achieve managerial efficiency and then subjects itself to that same technical calculus. The mind starts to operate with an image of itself as some type of viewing machine. Redemption, for Bergson, lies in retracing the path, regaining a vitality that would no longer be that of the bounded organism. Intuition would pass beyond its enclosed self-interests to arrive at the perception of life's duration or *élan vital*. For Deleuze, by contrast, the problem is that the eye remains too close to the lived. (So, today, when we demand 'reality' of television and cinema, or if we criticize cultural production for being too irrelevant or divorced from everyday life, we do so because we think there is such a thing as life and reality to which vision ought to be subordinate.) Rather than asking the eye to become organic once more, and to re-find its place in life, Deleuze asks for an inhuman perception: can we imagine the world without us, *not* as *our* environment or climate? Drawing on Bergsonism, rather than Bergson's concrete example of the fallen nature of cinematic perception, Deleuze calls on philosophy to 'open us up to the inhuman and the superhuman durations (*durations* which are inferior or superior to our own), to go beyond the human condition' (Deleuze 1988, 28). It is the *cutting* power of the eye that needs to be thought: the eye would be approached as a form of synthesizer, but as an analog rather than digital synthesizer. That is: the eye does not need to free itself from imposed distinctions to return to the flow of life, but should pursue ever finer cuts and distinctions, beyond its organic thresholds.

How might we imagine a world without organic perception, without the centerd points of view of sensing and world-oriented beings? Is there such a thing as perception without a *world?* (Think, here, of Heidegger's remark that a stone 'has' no world, which is a way of saying that a stone has no climate, for a stone has no concern for 'its' world or environment.) *This would not be a world without reading, as though abandoning the eye of grammar would return us to an inhuman lifelessness.* Instead, the reading would take a radically different form. After humans have ceased to be present on the planet, their history will remain readable in a quasi-human sense: the earth's strata will be inscribed with scars of the human capacity to create radical and volatile climactic changes. But one might consider a form of reading beyond this quasi-human and discerning mode: if, following Heidegger, the stone has no world, how do we account for the fossil records or archives borne by the stone? What might be thought is the extinction of the climactic eye: can we imagine a mode of reading the world, and its anthropogenic scars, that frees itself from folding the earth's surface around human survival? How might we read or perceive other timelines, other points of view and other rhythms? The fossil record opens a world *for us*, insofar as it allows us to read back from the brain's present to a time before reading; strata will continue beyond human reading, but if inscription continues is it too much of a stretch to say that the earth will remain as a 'reading' of at least one point of the universe? We use this term in literary and art criticism frequently, saying that a certain film offers 'a reading' of a certain event: we do not simply mean that the author is reading an event, for that may not have happened. The earth, after humans, will offer 'a reading' of a species' history, just as we might say that *Robinson Crusoe* offers 'a reading' of race, empire and capitalism, even if neither Defoe nor his readers actually actualized the sense of the reading.

Why have we assumed that reading and readability should take syntactical forms?

Here I want to refer to what geologists have posed as the new anthropocene era, where it is imagined—after humans—that our scar on the earth would be readable for something like a future geologist. Not only do we imagine what *would be readable* for a world without readers, we also have to deploy and imagine (from within geology) a different mode of stratigraphic imaging. Stratigraphy, at present, is a mode of reading past layers, but the positing of the anthropocene era relies on looking at our own world and imagining it as it will be when it has become the past. In imagining this world after humans we are reading what is not yet written or inscribed. We can see, now, from changes in the earth's composition that there will be a discernible strata that—in a manner akin to our dating of the earth's already layered geological epochs—will be readable. This strata or text of the earth does not yet exist; we abstract from the human eye and its reading of the inhuman past, to imagine what would be readable, after humans, in a mode analogous to the human eye. One can only open up to this post-Anthropocene point of view if we start to view this world beyond the bounds of climate, and see climate as one expression—among many—of a broader time and broader (inhuman) life. Perhaps, then, the moral outrage about the death of active and synthesizing vision, or the premature hailing of the world as already posthuman, needs to be tempered by the thought of the seeing brain that looks beyond itself. What we should *not* do is try to retrieve or repair a proper human vision; nor should we think, too easily, that we have abandoned human myopia once and for all.

This allows for a new thought of the brain's self-extinguishing tendency. If there is an anxiety regarding the eye-brain's seduction by images to the point of distraction, is not the figure of the evolved, self-organizing, connected and connecting brain also a lure or figure that precludes us from questioning the worth of the imaging brain? There is a strange torsion operating between the shrill cries lamenting the brain's captivation by spectacle, and the supposedly opposing counter-image of the good flourishing mind-brain. In response we might ask seriously what all these diagnoses of the reading brain and its atrophy amount to for a thought of art and climate change.

First, if the reading eye did have a proper mode—if the human brain had as its proper potentiality the mode of syntactical, synthesizing and world-ordering vision—how would we evaluate the last centuries of aesthetic judgment, which have relied on destroying the brain's capacity for comprehensive consumption? One doesn't have to be a fan of Duchamp and the avant-garde to note that there is something interesting, at the very least, in visual productions that short-circuit recognition. Indeed, one might say that climate change should not require us to return to modes of reading, comprehension and narrative communication but should awake us from our human-all-too-human narrative slumbers.

In Danny Boyle's *127 Hours* (2010), in the film's revelatory final quarter, the central character's voice provides a voiceover declaring that all moments in his life have been leading up to this point. The screen is split into three panels, with one of the panels depicting the depleting battery indicator on his camcorder. At this stage, and for all the character knows, his self-made film and testimony will never be viewed, and yet—even so—he proclaims a moment of destined union between the end of his own life and the earth's history: from the first comet that struck the earth to create life to this final point of self-narration, all this was destined to converge on this filmed present (or so he believes). This temporal point—one of the film's peaks—is at once one of human heroism, confirmed by the final scene where the protagonist and his family are seated on a suburban sofa viewing the cinematic audience the way we have just viewed his triumph. And yet at the very moment that this central character's destiny is related, the film's visual field explodes into a *geological* vision—the camera eye being taken over by the dazzling sun, which in turn dissolves into layers of rock and water beyond human time and perception. This cinematic seduction is quite different in kind from our tendency to be captivated by faces, bodies, objects of consumption and order.

This geological eye operates alongside the lulling eye of the forming human power; it is not the simply destructive eye of the visual avant garde. It is not just the willful assertion of the desire for the human to assert its mastery by freeing itself from instrumental and comforting images. It is a positively geological vision, a seduction not by the light that warms and illuminates but a radiation that moves beyond organicism. This light appears through the cracks of our own survival mechanisms: in Danny Boyle's cinema alone we can see it in *Sunshine* of 2007 (where the sun of light towards which the space mission travels is figured as that which must be viewed but which remains as *not* viewable), and in the sublime scene of the Sydney opera house as a frozen wasteland in *28 Weeks Later* (2007). The very titles of these films—hours, weeks, days—are intensive lived periods in which something like the unlived and unlivable takes hold.

Jacques Rancière has commented on a certain double nature of the image that defines art: commenting on Roland Barthes's *Camera Lucida,* Rancière notes that Barthes (who had begun his career by aiming to strip images of their myth or lure and did so *by reading* what appeared to be enigmatically frozen as actually the outcome of human history and labor) reversed this in *Camera Lucida* by affirming a dazzling power of the *image as such* that occurs when photography becomes an art (Rancière 2009). For Rancière this is not noteworthy because of some interest in Barthes's biography, but because it discloses art's double relation to the image, a doubleness inherent not only in photography but also in the novel. For Rancière, the novel as art at once describes and images, *and* draws attention to (while also destroying) any simple notion that the image is secondary and effaces itself before that which it indexes. Rancière is not as indebted to the French avant-garde as Barthes, or Deleuze, for whom art is the release of affects and precepts beyond the lived, or Derrida, for whom literature is an absolute precariousness that has no referential outside other than that which it traces from itself. But there is a sense in Rancière's notion of art as a release of image from anything other than its own dazzling materiality without reference or relation, of a surmounting of a certain anthropocentrism of the aesthetic image. It as though a release from systems of *human* reference would somehow yield the shining of light in itself.

To this extent all art leading up to the avant-garde would be art and image only to the degree to which it was anti-mimetic, or *other than* any form of reference, as though art somehow were god-like, freed from any necessity to be anything at all, liberated from all constituting relations. This, for Rancière, is the two-sided nature of the image.

I would suggest that something like a third side of the image is prompted by the thought experiment of extinction. By referring to extinction as a thought experiment I want to move in two directions. If we think of the experimental passage to extinction as *thought*—if we imagine thinking as a variation that takes place *from function* but essentially risks all function—then thinking of life as mindful requires thinking of mind as intrinsically destructive. Thought occurs when relations between terms are destructive, when there is a *not* knowing or misprision. Life occurs not with ongoing self-sameness but with an experimental variation that could be construed as *risk,* except that risk implies betting, strategy or even the venturing *of* some being, whereas it is only *after* variation that one might refer *ex post facto* to a mutation that is interpreted as *good for* some being or some environmental fit. And this is also why *environment* (like climate in its narrow meteorological sense) is not such a helpful term, given the notion of surrounding or environing—as though beings varied to fit a world. Extinction—as thought experiment—destroys such notions; there is just variation that is not variation *of* any being. So if extinction is thought experiment, it is because the process of extinction is a variation without a given end determined in advance; thinking possesses an annihilating power.

A certain thought of delimited extinction, the extinction of humans, opens up a variability or intrusion of a different side of the image. This is a geological, post-anthropocene or disembodied image, where there is some experimental grasping at a world that would not be the world for *a* body, nor the world *as* body. This mode of impersonal imaging differs from an avant-garde immanence of aesthetic matters or sensations, for such notions *tend* towards a god-like self-sufficiency. The avant-garde sought to think of the liberation of the image from man, but in doing so it created a heightened subjectivism where 'we' might liberate ourselves from function and become pure perception or pure becoming. In the era of extinction we can go beyond a self-willing self-annihilation in which consciousness destroys itself to leave nothing but its own pure non-being; we can begin to imagine imaging for other inhuman worlds. That is to say: rather than thinking of the posthuman, where we destroy all our own self-fixities and become pure process, we can look positively to the inhuman and other imaging or reading processes.

What happens if one thinks of the vision of no one, of the human world without humans that is still there *to be seen*? What remains might still take the form of 'a' vision or referring eye—the scene of a human world as if viewed without any body. The positing of an anthropocene era (or the idea that the human species will have marked the planet to such a degree that we will be discernible as a geological strata) deploys the idea of human imaging—the way we have already read an inhuman past in the earth's layers—but does this by imagining a world in which humans will be extinct. The anthropocene thought experiment also alters the modality of geological reading, not just to refer to the past as it is for us, but also to *our* present as it will be without us. We imagine a viewing or reading in the absence of viewers or readers, and we do this through images in the present that extinguish the dominance of the present. The figure of a frozen Sydney opera house, a London where Trafalgar Square is desolate, layers of rock distorted through a camera lens that is not the point of view of any body, an underwater Manhattan, or a sunlight so bright it would destroy the eye—all these experiments strive to image a world *as image* (as referential) but not referential *for* any body. These images cannot be sustained, and are unsustainable; they—like the thought of extinction itself—will always be *for us*, and are always co-opted by the narrative lures they fragment. They nevertheless indicate an era or epoch that has begun to sense, if not have a sense of, a world without bodies.

Notes

1.   http://thinkprogress.org/climate/2012/05/07/478984/hug-the-monster-why-so-many-climate-scientists-have-stopped-downplaying-the-climate-threat/?mobile=nc

Chapter 1

Extinct Theory

*Of the Earth, the present subject of our scenarios, we can
presuppose a single thing: it doesn't care about the questions
we ask about it. What we call a catastrophe will be, for
it, a contingency. Microbes will survive, as well as insects,
whatever we let loose. In other words, it is only because of
the global ecological transformations we can provoke, which
are potentially capable of putting in question the regimes of
terrestrial existence we depend on, that we can invoke the
Earth as having been put in play by our histories. From the
viewpoint of the long history of the Earth itself, this will be one
more 'contingent event' in a long series. (Stengers 2000: 144)*

*To the shame of philosophy, it is not uncommonly alleged
of such theory that whatever may be correct in it is in fact
invalid in practice. We usually hear this said in an arrogant,
disdainful tone, which comes of presuming to use experience
to reform reason itself in the very attributes which do it most
credit. Such illusory wisdom imagines it can see further and
more clearly with its mole-like gaze fixed on experience than
with the eyes which were bestowed on a being designed to
stand upright to scan the heavens. (Kant 1991: 62-63)*

If we were serious about considering what theory *after* theory might
mean then perhaps we should push this notion to its limit: not simply
theory after the 1980s indulgence or heyday of high theory—those days
when we could afford to think of texts as such with (some say) little concern for real political conditions—and not simply theory today when
no one could be said to be anti-theory—both because theory has been

thoroughly assimilated and because what is left remains a toothless tiger, legitimating all sorts of positivisms and moralisms. (Evidence for assimilation is everywhere: no monograph in literary studies appears without some cursory footnote to a theoretical concept; no undergraduate education proceeds without some basic overview of 'feminism,' 'post-colonialism,' and 'post-structuralism'; and no graduate student would be advised to avoid theory altogether.) More often than not, being 'after theory' signals nothing more than that one is aware of some textual mediating condition: there is no sex in itself, race in itself, history in itself. This contemporary theoretical astuteness, consisting of acknowledging the provisional status of one's position, then allows for local attention to minute particulars without any consideration of the problems, possibilities and impossibilities of reading as such. The new historicism that supposedly emerged after theory allows for a mode of positivism justified by an avoidance of grand narratives (Gallagher and Greenblatt 2001: 6). Other modes of theory—queer theory, race studies, gender studies, disability studies, digital media studies—seem to be theoretical not so much by a distinct mode of reading but because of a choice of a marginal object. If anything 'theory' as it is now practiced—with its emphasis on the lived, bodies, multitudes, emotions, affects, the political, the ethical turn—is indeed *practiced*; it avoids the problem of theory—what we can say there is, or the limits of existence—by grounding itself in what one ought to do. Recently, and in line with the ebb and flow of critical trends, there has been an anti-anti-theory reaction, ranging from a general contestation of historical and cultural locatedness (or, in Felski's words, 'context stinks') to a profound and wholesale rejection of the Kantian Copernican turn, or the idea that we can only know and legitimately theorize the world *as it is given* (Felski 2011; Bryant, Srnicek and Harman 2011). Quentin Meillassoux argues that it is the Kantian turn, or refusal to know that which cannot be experienced by us, that closes philosophy off from the truth of contingency—and crucial to that thought of contingency would be the imperative to think of the world *not* as it is given to us, including geological statements about deep time and logico-philosophical claims about contingency (Meillassoux 2008). Increasingly the general claims of speculative realism—or the insistence to overcome the Kantian enclosure within the bounds of the subject—seem both to resonate *and*

jar with broader cultural imperatives. On the one hand, there is an efflorescence of cultural production devoted to imagining a world without
humans, beyond human viewing (broadly evidenced in post-apocalyptic
film and literature); and on the other, and often from within philosophy
or 'theory after theory,' there is a retrieval of the world only as it appears
and only insofar as it is a lived world *for* some being (what one might
refer to as the 'naturalist' turn [Petitot et. al. 1999]). The Kantian conception of theory and its project of self-limitation, despite recent refusals of
Kantian finitude, help us make sense of this twin tendency to leap beyond
human limits and yet remain restricted to the lived. Although Kant does
insist that we can only have scientific knowledge about that which can be
experienced *as given* this does allow for a mode of scientific realism, for
it also encompasses that there are also—beyond the given—the forces
from which the given is given to us. What has occurred, since Kant, is
an increasing rejection of an 'in itself' beyond the given, and yet such a
gap should perhaps be thought today—not in order to repair or close the
distance that separates us from the world, but to heighten both our non-
knowledge *and* the imperative to think (but not experience) that which
cannot be known.

Theory, if it is *critical* in the Kantian sense, would need to begin from
Kant's distinction between theoretical knowledge, concerning objects
about which we can speak because they are given *to us*, and practice,
which follows from the absence of knowledge about ourselves. Lacking
anything objective or experienced that might give us a moral law we are
left without foundation. It is because we only know what is given—even
if 'the given' can go beyond the *human* eye to include all the apparatuses through which humans image and project a world—that a strong
scientific realism also creates a unique gap between theory and practice (Langton 1998). Theory is an acceptance of a distinction between
a strong sense of the *in*human (that which exists beyond, beyond all
givennness and imaging, and beyond all relations) and an *un*founded
imperative that we must therefore give ourselves a law. We act in the
absence of knowledge of the world beyond us, and yet knowing *that* there
is a beyond means that practice cannot be reduced to what we know or
feel; nothing we know can ground or determine our decisions. There is a
direct passage from the gap of the undecidable (or that decisions are not

made for us because we do not and cannot know any ultimate ground) to the burden of having to make a decision. Human feeling, or 'the lived,' does not exhaust what there is. Theory follows from being exposed to a world that is *not* ourselves; theoretical knowledge is directed to something that is only given through relations but is also not exhausted by the relations through which it is given. In many respects theory, far from being an academic enterprise that we can no longer afford to indulge, is the condition and challenge of the twenty-first century or age of extinction: 'we' are finally sensing both our finitude as a world-forming and world-destroying species, *and* sensing that whatever we must do or think cannot be confined or dictated by our finitude. Theory reminds us both of the givenness of the world, or that what we know is given to us in some specific way, at the same time as this knowledge and relation exceed us. Theory is at once necessary and impossible, just as its 'relation' to practice is necessary and impossible. Theory, or distance from the real, is necessary: 'we' are faced with an existing world that, precisely because it *exists*, is not ourselves; without that 'outside' world there could be no inner subject, no 'we,' no agent of practice. But this existing world to which we are definitively bound is therefore impossible: the given world is given *to* us, never known absolutely. We are not paralyzed by this distance from the world, for it is the distance that provokes both knowledge and practice (Stengers 2011); but the distance nevertheless entails that practice cannot form the ground for our knowledge ('do what works') nor can knowledge ground practice ('act according to your nature'). To avoid theory and pass directly to practice would require forgetting that the self of practice is only a self insofar as it is placed in a position of necessary not-knowing. Recent forms of Kantianism that conclude from this separation that there is an inevitable ideal of humanity and human normativity (Korsgaard 2009; Korsgaard and Cohen 1996) focus all too easily on the practical side of reasoning—whereby the absence of knowledge forces us to be self-governing—and forget too happily the theoretical problem. This self that gives the law to itself is necessarily exposed to a domain which it must theorize but can never grasp as such. To remain with the theoretical challenge, or accepting the distance from the world as it would be without us, is to face up to the formal problem of extinction. There was a time, and there will be a time, without humans: this provides us with a challenge both to think beyond the world as it is *for us*, and yet remain mindful that the imagining of the inhuman world always proceeds from a positive human failure. There would be two senses in which theory would fail. The first sense of failure is necessary and critical: one must at one and the same time be placed in relation to an existence that is never given as such, and it is this world of necessarily given but distanced existence within which we act. (In an era of encroaching extinction this failing theoretical condition becomes a forceful practical problem precisely because we are obliged, practically, to think not only about the unknowable but also the unimaginable. The world we inhabit is becoming increasingly impossible to know and imagine.) The second sense in which theory fails occurs with its seeming triumph; today, if theory has taken institutional hold it has done so by failing to be theoretical; in various modes of theory after theory, where we have returned to life, affect or 'the lived,' theory feels no qualms about the limits of imagination. Indeed, theory *as* imagination allows 'us' to affirm humanity, the lived, meaning, community, the future and life—precisely when the incoherence of these terms should block any easy praxis.

Symptomatic of this failure of theory (via institutionalization) is theory's complete success, and this can be gauged by considering what is now no longer possible: anti-theory. In the early days of theory to be opposed to theory was to be opposed to textualism; it was to insist that 'everyone knows' that for all intents and practical purposes texts mean what we want them to mean. Theory, by contrast, detached texts from a 'wanting to mean.' Such a distinction is evident in the grand debates of the 1980s, including Derrida's skirmish with John Searle, the latter insisting that context would ground utterances (Derrida 1988). But that Searlean attention to context and practice—the position that was once anti-theory—is today the hallmark of theory, both the theory that still remains of historicism and the newer waves of anti-textualism that affirm life, things, history, intent and bodies.

In 1982 Stephen Knapp and Walter Benn Michaels published 'Against Theory' in *Critical Inquiry* and posed the following thought experiment. Imagine encountering the marks 'a slumber did my spirit steal,' drawn in the sand on the beach; the marks appear to be drawn (by, one assumes, a human) but then a subsequent wave flows and recedes and leaves the rest of Wordsworth's poem. This, the authors argue, at first seems to present intention-less meaning, but this is not so. Once we *read* we attribute intention; any of those supposedly detached, non-referential objects of theory—texts without context, readers or authors—are proven (Michaels and Knapp claim) to be impossible. If something can be read then it has meaning, and therefore intention. What such an insistence precludes is that something might be read, and not be actively or meaningfully inscribed: a geologist 'reading' the earth's layers would not be reading in Knapp and Michaels's sense, and it follows that it would be a mistake to 'read' texts in the way that one might read scars on the earth's surface or fMRI images. One would, supposedly, need to distinguish between reading—seeing the lines waves leave on the shore and discerning some pattern—and reading, where one posits someone who meant to leave marks in just this way in order to say something to someone. It seems such a distinction is easy, but is it? Imagine we find, some hundreds of years from now, remnants of a wall with spray-painted tagging left behind, and then next to the remnant tags would be some paint that fell onto the wall accidentally, and then next to that would be a city-funded community artist's mural. Cities today are made up of such human-inhuman couplings, where graffiti mixes with staining, with randomly posted notices as well as scars from wreckage, damage and animal and technical marking. Knapp and Michaels would claim that our capacity to read marks such as a mural follows from author's meaning: if there were not an author who had painted the work there would be nothing to be read. Other marks, like 'tagging,' one assumes, could also be read—as forms of signature. Random paint stains might indicate that someone or something had existed but—like the natural marks and wear on a wall— could not be read. And yet it is just this hybrid assemblage of marks, stains, signs, tears, human-animal-technical inscriptions that comprises *any* archive: how does one look back and decide to read what was left by a hand, and not read or avoid reading what occurred through inhuman and random processes? For Knapp and Michaels one can distinguish clearly between the rogue methods of theory, that willfully detaches texts from intent-meaning, and reading that relies on texts having a sense which is what an author *wanted to say, and what we must assume he or she wanted to say* for that is what it is to read.

Benn Michaels felt this point still had relevance in 2001 in his 'The Shape of the Signifier,' which was, again symptomatically, an appeal to *the political*. Reading and texts go together to yield intentions and contexts; there are not just signs as such, mere markers of ostensive identity, but historically sedimented and meaningful intentions. In a recent review in *The London Review of Books* Benn Michaels insists again that identity itself cannot bear significance; it makes no sense to say—for example— that race *means* something or anything, for one reads such markers only because of socio-economic and historical semantic horizons. One would not 'read' a body as being of a certain identity, unless that body were located in a broader network of human and meaningful sense. The very markers that allow us to read identity presuppose some understanding of a common humanity that is unfairly differentiated (Benn Michaels 2009). Whereas Knapp and Michaels could articulate this insistence on the necessarily contextual and political production of meaning as an argument 'against' theory in the 1980s, Benn Michaels's position is now exemplary of what counts *as theory*. That is, theory is just this attention to the human, intentional and interested ground of the emergence of texts. This is what theory is and ought to be. What was once anti-theory—a reaction against the detachment of texts from any supposition of human-ity or meaning—is now so mainstream, that the same argument can be rehearsed and become central to a defense of theory 'after theory.'

Theory 'today' is not an acceptance—as it once was, or might have been—that we do not know the political or the practical and that what we are given as objects of theory are both inhuman *and* can be considered rigorously only with something like an extinction hypothesis. But theory, if it takes on the impossibility that is its twenty-first century potential, might be imagined as a radical de-contextualization. Let us not fall too readily into assuming the human, or assuming 'our' intentional presence behind texts; let us short-circuit 'man's' continuing readability of himself in the context of texts *and* his reflexive mode of judgment whereby he sees marks drawn in the sand and immediately recognizes his own ines-capable will.

Theory *after* theory might take a more robust form whereby we con-sider what it might be to think in the absence of theoria. What would be left without the distanced gaze that the thinking human animal directs towards the world? An absence of the look or point of view of theory could take two forms, one of which (I would suggest) is dominant in whatever remains of theory today, and another that represses theory. The first mode was articulated by Hannah Arendt in *The Promise of Politics*. Politics—being in common, speaking in common, living as a multitude—has always been repressed, Arendt argues, since Plato at least, and has been subjected to the ideal of *bios theoritikos* (Arendt 2005: 85). The contempt for labor and for the multitude has meant that political philosophy has always been oriented towards contemplation rather than action, a privileging of theoria over praxis.

> [S]ince Socrates, no man of action, that is, nobody whose original experience was political, as for instance Cicero's was, could ever hope to be taken seriously by the philosophers [...] Political philosophy never recovered from this blow dealt by philosophy to politics at the very beginning of our tradition. The contempt for politics, the conviction that political activity is a necessary evil, due partly to the necessities of life that force men to live as labourers or rule over slaves who provide for them, and partly to the evils that come from living together itself, that is, to the fact that the multitude, which the Greeks called *hoi polloi,* threatens the security and even the existence of every individual person, runs like a thread throughout the centuries that separate Plato from the modern age. (Arendt 2005: 83-84)

Since Arendt that targeting of theoria for the sake of life and praxis has intensified, particularly in the work of those whose redemptive *political* theory has seemed to save theory from the cartoon characterizations that consigned the irresponsibly formalist and textualist modes of 'French' thought to a past that was not yet properly attuned to the politics of life. I will consider this retrieval or saving of theory later. For now I want to suggest that there might be another, diametrically opposed, sense of theory *after* theory. This would not be a return of theory to life, and certainly not a return of theory to the body, to affects, to living systems, living labor or praxis. One could create an exhaustive and exhausting list of all the ways in which theory has been re-territorialized back onto the lived, all the ways in which a radical consideration of force without center, without life, without intention or sense is continually relocated in practical life, in *doing*. One diagnostic point, for example, would concern the migration of certain terms, such as 'performativity,' or 'difference,' which harbor the potential to think an act without an actor, but which have actually oper- ated to reinforce the practices of self-formation. Although Judith Butler insists on there being 'no doer behind the deed' in her theory of perfor- mativity (Butler 1993: 142) one might observe that performance was nevertheless for Butler that which, ex post facto, produced a body who would recognize itself as human (Butler 2005). This aspect of human recognition, with a specific focus on the face, comes to the fore in her later work (2006). Whereas theory might be approached beginning from estrangement and distance, considering a world that is not ourselves and a force that cannot be returned to the human, theory is moving precisely in the opposite direction to being nothing more than the expression of praxis, nothing more than relations of recognition. Antonio Negri insists that 'living labour' and the self-producing body of 'homo homo human- ity squared' opens up a world liberated both from the centralizing exploi- tation of capitalism *and* freed from any position of knowledge and cogni- tion outside the collective body, and he appeals to the master thinkers of theory (Derrida and Lacan) in order to generate this 'genealogy of vital elements.' How, we might ask, is a Lacan whose corpus was devoted to the necessarily alien and inhuman fact *that there is system,* and a Derrida who began by considering genesis as 'anarchic,' read as modes of vital liv- ing expression?

> [T]he living expressions of our culture are not born in the form of synthetic figures but, on the contrary, in the form of events; they are untimely. Their becoming is within a geneal- ogy of vital elements that constitute a radical innovation and the very form of the lack of measure. Some contemporary phi- losophers have set off in pursuit of this new expressive force of postmodernity, and they have attempted to characterize it. Already Lacan had pointed to the absence of measure in the new; for Derrida, the productivity of the margins as it seeks new orders as it disseminates; as for Nancy and Agamben,

>we find them picking the flowers that grow in these extreme
>fields. (Negri 2008: 66-67)

This joyous affirmation of the living, of the multitude, of productivity, of the other, or of pure potentiality and futurity is but one way of reading theory. But is this the best mode of thinking and reading when we are at a moment when there is no shortage of information about life and its temporality—no shortage of data bombarding us daily with the inevitable end of the human organism—and yet are all the more insistent that whatever else it is thinking and theory are primarily organic? Does not one of theory's earliest gestures towards a force without production, or a potentiality without actuality or presence, at least suggest that one might consider relations beyond life and creation? How would theory confront the absence of theoria: 'life' without the human look? Life without praxis, life without meaningful action, life without production or labour: such would be theory *after* theory, or theory that opened itself to the thought of extinction. Hints of such a theory were articulated at theory's very genesis: not only explicitly in texts such as Derrida's 'No Apocalypse, Not Now: Seven Missiles, Seven Missives' (1984) or Gilles Deleuze and Félix Guattari's suggestion that one might need to think of the world beyond or before the gaze of the organism ('becoming-imperceptible'), but also in theory's most scandalously 'apolitical' moments, such as Paul De Man's suggestion that theory begins when one reads a text as if there were no readers, no contextual life that would be its site of emergence, and no living horizon that might maintain or animate its sense (De Man 1972). More recently, hints of a surviving or nascent theory occur in extensions of Alain Badiou's promising 'theoretical antihumanism' that push theory beyond Badiou's own decision of the subject (Badiou 2001: 5). Ray Brassier (2008) takes up Badiou's antihumanism, along with Quentin Meillassoux's insistence that it is possible to think beyond human knowledge (Meillassoux 2008), to move further into a world without cognition. Graham Harman has also taken up phenomenology, *not* to insist that the world as given is always given *to* some subject or body, but to demand that we think of relations of givenness beyond self-present thinking (Harman 2005). Despite the fact that Kantian philosophy defines 'theory' as that which is given to a necessarily presupposed subject, we might say that these gestures are theoretical insofar as they begin from what is not immediately present to a subject of action.

One might want to go further than these suggestions from within philosophy to consider what *literary* theory might offer to a present that is dominated by information calculating the end of time, alongside a range of cultural productions striving to witness such an end—however paradoxical such an end might be. That is: how would theory approach the influx of data regarding irreversible threats to the human species—an onslaught of evidence that is met at one and the same time by increasing climate change denial, a resurgence in 'theories' of human praxis, and a widespread cultural production that intimates the end of human life? How would a theory that was *literary*—or that considered the remnants of the letter—'read' the spate of films of the last decade or more that have been witnessing the possible end of all human life? Such films include, especially, redemption narratives where the potential extinction of the species is averted by a popular or ecological victory over techno-science: James Cameron's *Avatar* (2009) would be the most recent example. But for all their redemptive and re-humanizing work, post-apocalyptic films and novels also open up the thought of literary theory, where the 'literary' would signal something like Benn and Michaels's enigmatically inhuman traces. One can think here of texts as remaining, unread, dead objects without authors or audience. Would readers fifty or one hundred years from now who found random copies of *Glamorama* or *Finnegans Wake* be secure in attributing intent and meaning, or would not such texts be more likely encountered as marks or traces without animating hand? A literary theory would not assume that texts or letters were the work of a living body, and yet would be theoretical as well as literary in asking what sort of reading, viewing or look such texts or marks might open. Imagine a species, after humans, 'reading' our planet and its archive: if they encounter human texts (ranging from books, to machines to fossil records) how might new views or theories open up? Such a literary theory would not, as Derrida suggested concerning literature, be an opening to democracy insofar as literature is a right to 'say anything' (Derrida 1997: 58). Rather the 'text' would operate as an 'anarchic genesis' or 'mal d'archive': a force or disturbance not felt by the organism but witnessed after the event in its having always already occurred.

Leaving those suggestions aside for now, I want to begin by address-ing the question of why such a strong sense of theory after theory ought to be entertained. First: one might consider the current terrain of theory as a reaction formation. In response to a world in which 'the political' is increasingly divorced from meaningful practice (whatever that would be) theory has insisted in ever more shrill tones on the grounding of theo-ria in meaningful, practical, productive and human-organic life. Second: our context or life is one in which a radical sense of '*after* theory'—the non-existence of thinking beings—is all too obvious, despite the fact that the one area theory has failed to address is what it might mean in this (literally posthuman, or after-human) sense to be 'after theory.' That is, one might ask why it is just as the world faces its annihilation, or at least the annihilation of something like the organic life that was capable of *bios theoretikos,* that 'theory' turns back towards productive embodied and affective life? Third: if popular culture is dominated by a genuinely post-theoretical meditation—by a constant, obsessive and fraught imagi-nation of a life or non-life beyond the gaze of the organism, and by the literal image of extinction—why is this the one mode of post-theory that 'theory' has failed to consider?

The twentieth century witnessed several waves of extinction threat or catastrophic risks coming in various modes with various temporal inten-sities: the sudden nuclear annihilation of the cold war was perhaps the only potential extinction threat that has abated. Sudden nuclear catastro-phe is perhaps the only event that would produce apocalyptic annihila-tion; all other possible extinctions would be gradual, allowing for a mini-mal 'human' presence to witness the slow and violent departure of the human. Indeed, two of the senses of post-apocalyptic lie in this indica-tion that there will not be complete annihilation but a gradual witnessing of a slow end, and that we are already at that moment of witness, living on after the end. Indeed, this is what an ethics of extinction requires: not an apocalyptic thought of the 'beyond the human' as a radical break or dissolution, but a slow, dim, barely discerned and yet violently effective destruction. Since the cold war, other threats to human species survival have succeeded each other with the public imagination being turned now to one human extermination menace, now to another. It is almost as though there is a global and temporally myopic attention deficit disorder:

we can imagine as other and as 'our' end only one threat at a time. If post-9/11 culture seemed gripped by the threat of terror, then more recent fears of systemic economic collapse have overtaken the focus on the war on terror. One might note that although the threat of AIDS—the initial figuration of which was highly apocalyptic—has hardly gone away, little mention was made of viral disaster once other concerns such as climate change began to attract attention. After 9/11 and the shift from a war on drugs to a war on terror, various viral disasters have deflected 'attention' from bio-weapons, nuclear arsenals and suicide bombers, 'focusing' instead on SARS, bird flu and the H1N1 virus. Interspersed among those surges of panic have been waves of other threats (including the threat of panic itself, for it may be the case that it is the fear and chaos of terrorism and viral pandemic that pushes the system into annihilating disorder). Before the financial meltdown of late 2008 the 'era of cheap food' came to an end (due partly to the shift in production towards bio-fuels), with food riots in Haiti presaging intense global aggression from the hungry. This was eclipsed by waves of lawlessness and violence that followed the stringencies caused by economic chaos, which in turn would lead to a fear of disorder that would be both precipitated by diminishing resources while also exacerbating the increasing fragility and incompetence of systems of social order that would suffer from widespread uncertainty and confusion.

These terrors—viral, political, economic, climactic and affective—have not failed to dent the cultural imaginary. In addition to quite explicit texts about viral disaster, from *Outbreak* (1995) to the more recent *The Invasion* (2007), *28 Days Later* (2002), *28 Weeks Later* (2007) and *Contagion* (2011), other disaster epics have focused on spectacular catastrophes prompted by global warming (including Danny Boyle's *Sunshine* in which a space mission to reignite the dying sun is thwarted when the space travelers fail to resist the desire to stare directly at the source of the light that would have saved the earth, so drawn are they to light's blinding intensity). Like *The Invasion* in which humans are infected by a virus that robs them of all affect and thus annuls their capacity for violence and emotion, fiction and documentary culture have repeatedly asked the question that theory has failed to ask: why should the human species wish for or justify its prolongation, and what would be worth saving? (Exceptions to this investigation of species-worthiness would be David Benatar's *Better Never to Have Been* (2006), Thomas Ligotti's *The Conspiracy Against the Human Race* (2010), and Ray Brassier's far more questioning *Nihil Unbound* (2009).) But beyond asking the worth of the species, we might ask why and how such questions are both possible (given that they are implied in so much contemporary fiction) and yet impossible, given that the human species seems to have defined itself as a will to survive? How might the human race imagine its non-existence, and how would we humans of the present adopt a relation to those whose miserable future will be 'our' legacy? (In *The Day After Tomorrow* (2004) survivors taking refuge in the frozen-over New York Public Library decide not to burn the works of Nietzsche, choosing an economics text book for some final warmth.) Other texts have passed judgment on a self-extinguishing humanity, with the recent remake of *The Day the Earth Stood Still* (2008) featuring a dead-pan Keanu Reeves informing human-ity that it has no right to live given the waste and violence of its history. Such worlds are *after theory* in a quite banal and literal sense. There are no theorists.

This era of theory after theory has been considered by 'theory,' if at all, either in the mode of mournful despair (by an Agamben who wishes to retrieve the political in the face of the hedonism of spectacle) or re-humanizing emancipation, (by a Hardt and Negri who regard liberation from any external point of judgment as the consequence of living labor no longer subjected to spatial fragmentation or material production). These new trends in theory are accompanied by a series of returns or relocations of the previous generation of thinkers to their less threaten-ing philosophical fathers. Derrida is returned to Husserl in order to avoid the radically disembodied and inhuman forces of writing; Deleuze and Guattari are returned to Bergson in order to re-affirm the boundaries of the organism; the machinic potentials of digital media are located in the bodies of meaning-generating audiences (Hansen 2000; Hansen 2003; Hansen 2004). A Merleau-Ponty whose concept of 'flesh' bore the pos-sibility of taking the body and even 'life' beyond the sense of the lived has, for theorists of biopolitics, become a way of positing vital norms (Esposito 2008) or, even more alarmingly, a re-grounding of thought on embodiment (Gallagher 2005).

More specifically still: if theory after theory has any meaning, should it not refer to a hyperbolic *and* minimal theoretical condition in which we consider not simply the formal absence of a population but an actual disappearance? Theory is constitutively distinct from practice precisely because theory relates to that which is not ourselves; theory is the consideration of that which is given to us (while practice is the law one gives to oneself in the absence of knowledge). Hyperbolically, then, theory ought to relate to cultural production *not* in terms of bodies, affects, multitudes and identities, unless these too were also considered not as self-evidently familiar and living but as strangely dead to us. This would also give us a minimal approach to an ethics of extinction, which would also be a counter-ethics. We would not assume an ethos, a proper way of being, community, 'we' or humanity that would be the ground and value of literary or other objects. Just as Foucault's counter-memory sought to consider all those forces that had some power in the present but were not present to living history (Foucault 1977), a counter-ethics would be theoretical in beginning from the condition of the present—looming extinction—without assuming the ethos of the present. That is, one would—as the world after theory ought to compel us to do—consider what is worthy of concern or survival, what of the human, the multitude, or the living would enable an ethos that was not the ethos of the present.

We can return again to the question of theory after theory, today, and ask why it has so focused on an empty tomorrow—a future of open creativity, and unbounded possibility—that it has not considered the tomorrow of its own non-existence. Given even the minimal assumption that reading theoretically requires some necessary distance from any actual audience, and given the now-literal threat of the absence of the human species, why has theory survived, after theory, in a mode of increasing humanization and organicism? Why, when events and timelines would seem to demand just the contrary, does theory takes its current self-englobing form? As an example of the ways in which theory has, just as Arendt suggested it ought to do, retrieved a politics of living in common (a polity of the multitude with no outside), we might consider three dominants. First, a deconstruction that now mourns Derrida does so precisely by insisting on a dimension of deconstruction oriented towards hospitality (Royle 2009: 137), and towards a future whose radical openness defies all calculation (saving justice and democracy to come) (Naas 2008: 67-68). Such a mode of deconstruction would survive at the expense of a Derrida who suggested an 'untamed genesis' that would be neither living nor dead, neither before nor after the human but nevertheless disruptive of any mode of good conscience. Second, a turn to life or naturalism insists that the world is always the world for this or that living system, always embedded in a milieu given as a range of affordances: this ranges from the retrieval of phenomenology and the embedding of mind in life (Petito, Varela, Pachoud and Roy 1999) *against* an anti-organicism or textualism that would draw attention to forces beyond the lived, to the celebration of bio-political production and the multitude against a bio-power that is seen as extrinsic and opposed to life (Hardt and Negri 2000). Finally, one might cite a return to the aesthetic, whether that be an aesthetics of language that separates man as a speaking being who gives himself his world from animality (Agamben 2004), to a re-affirmation of literature (Joughin and Malpas 2003; Attridge 2004) or art in general as grounded in the human organism's sense-making capacities of its world. It would be far too obvious to add to this list the affirmations of identity politics or, worse, subjectivity, that would posit a self that is nothing more than the negation of a world in itself (knowable, measurable and presentable) precisely because the subject is that which gives a world, law and norm to itself.

Theory might have both interest and worth—if we accept the thorough contingency of such worth—only if it is as destructive of the imagination as our milieu of possible extinction allows. We might need to abandon the grounding of ecology on nature (Morton 2007) or consider modes of deconstruction in which the future were not radically open, hospitable and affirmative (Clark 2010). There is no shortage of data regarding the possible or inevitable absence of humans: terror threats are calculated meticulously by government think tanks; climate change protocols and negotiations require detailed prediction and scenario plotting, and popular news is dominated by economic, climactic, viral and political 'updates' regarding a range of intruding violences (Grusin 2010). Such information, far from indicating the location of texts in a polity, suggests just the sort of approach deemed to be horrifically absurd in Knapp and Benn Michaels's miserable summation of theory. Let us imagine texts as lines drawn without any preceding or ideal community. Let us also, more importantly, be aware (insofar as we can) that the text of the current 'multitude' includes information regarding climate change, terror, destruction and extinction expressed in a vocabulary of mitigation, adaptation, viability policy and sustainability, none of which can figure the non-existence of the human. If theory were to operate as it might then it would be destructive of such an imaginary; it would be theory after theory.

Chapter 2

The Sustainability of Concepts: Knowledge and Human Interests

Climate change studies—a burgeoning field prompted by government research initiatives and academic opportunism as much as by the impending crises associated with global warming and resource depletion—is, in general, formed by combining the 'hard' sciences (geography, geology, physics, biochemistry, biology and genetics) with the social sciences (geography again, psychology, political science, demographics, sociology and economics). As a consequence of most major research institutions having produced some type of climate change research network the humanities, too, are beginning to contribute to understandings of the problems presented by climate change. Before considering why any simple *inclusion* of the humanities in climate change studies needs to be questioned, I would like to open a series of considerations.

First, the combinations of the hard sciences and human sciences that make up climate change studies—even though *inter*disciplinary research networks bring these sciences together—keep the disciplinary borders of various fields in place. There are, of course, some sciences—geography, psychology—that are in part both hard and social sciences, but even this division within the subject presupposes something like the idea of a *human science.* That disciplinary distinction, as Michel Foucault argued in *The Order of Things,* is not simply a division of labour that takes a single subject such as nineteenth-century natural history and then divides the same practices of gathering information into different disciplines: what counts as true or false alters dramatically, with the very idea of a distinction between hard science and social or human science creating 'man' as a distinct object of knowledge (Foucault 1970). Foucault argues, for example, that we cannot see natural history as simply preceding biology or the science of life. Nor can we read Adam Smith's theory of wealth as leading seamlessly to economics; nor can we see theories of grammar as similar in type to the social science of linguistics.

To understand how these new disciplinary distinctions create a curious new object of knowledge—man—we can take our lead from the present. Even popular economic theories, such as *Freakanomics* (Levitt and Dubner 2005), or the Chicago school theories that directly influence government policy (Overtveldt 2007) presuppose a certain concept of man. Either—as *Freakanomics* theories posit—we constantly miscalculate the effects that our 'choices' will have on our well-being (by being lured into paying more for our daily coffee if only we can be seduced by a special offer that will create a habit); or, we are naturally competitive and self-interested animals who, if left to themselves, will allow the most efficient players to rise to the top while the muddling remainder of the population can benefit from economic prosperity in general. What economics as a social science assumes is a 'subject of interests' (Montag 2009): it is not sufficient just to look at relations among goods and prices but also to have some notion of human behavior, especially if the operations of human behavior are not immediately apparent to humans themselves.

Questioning the extent to which capitalism presupposes normative concepts of the self is hardly new. C.B. Macpherson's 1962 classic theory of possessive individualism is perhaps now widely accepted, with the concepts of the free individual or the level playing field now recognized as being barely veiled assertions of liberal market norms. What is slightly more nuanced, and not so widely acknowledged, is not the critique of liberal normativity but the shift from the normative to the normal. If behavior is based not so much on (even implicit) regulatory ideals regarding the proper life that one ought to live, but more on some preceding and determining *life*, then the mode of decision or axiology shifts from self-determination to alignment—bringing human existence into accord with the life of which it is an expression. We tend to explain human actions by appealing to some prior logic of life from which they emerge. There is a shift from assessing human action according to its manifest sense to regarding 'man' as a strangely doubled animal who is the outcome of a longer history of life processes that he can only dimly discern. And yet man is also able to read and interpret the life of which he is an effect. In this respect certain historical theses—ranging from MacPherson's claim that the supposed neutral individual of capitalism is in fact the outcome of a specific politico-economic historical period, or Louis Dumont's argument that modern *homo economicus* needs to be explained anthropologically—rely on some ultimate horizon (history, anthropology) that would gather and explain human positivity. Foucault (1970) agued that Adam Smith's *Wealth of Nations* of 1776 explained how human interaction produced commodities, how these could be exchanged, and how a system of circulating goods produced an overall stability and system that benefited all concerned (Smith 1976). When Karl Marx forms a theory of labor the life or species being of the human animal is added to the way questions are posed: why, we might ask, do human beings labor and enter into exchange? For Marx the answer presupposed *man's* species being: we must labor, collectively and with the help of technology, in order to meet our needs. This, in turn, explains the existence of ideology for there are forces that determine the relations we establish to each other—forces of production that place some bodies in greater servitude to production than others. The very concept of ideology in its Marxist sense—not what we believe but belief as grounded in a preceding and hidden life—relies upon situating the human species in a collective history that originates from an initially life-serving aim. These initial forces determine our social being, even if they are not directly experienced, and are capable of being interpreted only after the fact. Marx's theory of ideology, in a manner shared by social or human sciences more generally, relies upon *interpreting* the way in which we live our social relations: what we experience as natural—that I go to work for an employer who pays me for my time—needs to be understood as the outcome of a historical process whereby those in command of the means of production that will ultimately reduce human effort (factory owners, for example) are capable of buying the labor of other individuals from whom they profit (Foucault 1970, 257). The human sciences, such as economics, do not just chart the circulation of goods (as did Adam Smith's theory of wealth) they presuppose something like human interests that can explain systems of exchange.

Second, this production of 'man' in the human sciences would also yield the possibility of the humanities. Not only would we have social sciences looking at the mechanisms of 'life, labour and language' (Foucault 1970, 345) through which social systems are effected, we can also have human-ities disciplines that would be interpretive in their examination of human cultural production, and would also presuppose 'man' as an historical, social and productive animal. Anyone working in a literature depart-ment today may well recognize that Foucault's notion of literature—a mode of human production *not* grounded in purposiveness or a theory of human function—has well and truly been overtaken by logics grounded on a normalizing theory of man, whether that be a theory of literature as ideology (allowing for smooth social functioning and the reproduc-tion of capitalist social relations) or a theory of narrative and story-telling as a human survival mechanism (or so literary Darwinism would claim). Foucault, referring to the knowledge practices of his own day, was critical of some of the key discourses that made up the humanities, such as phe-nomenology, structuralism and psychoanalysis (Foucault 1970, 355). These approaches would examine cultural production while presuppos-ing what Foucault referred to as man as an 'empirical-transcendental' double. Man is empirical—a being whose language, social relations and bodily habits are determined by the material relations he must take up in relation to his environment and others; but man is also a being who can analyze those material forces and thereby 'read' the ways in which he has come to be the specific social being that he is. Psychoanalysis, for example, will argue that we can only exist and live if our desires take on some acceptable, socially-sanctioned form; we can, however, always read these socialized forms to discern something like *desire as such*. (Other less humanizing or organic forms of psychoanalysis would not ground desire in the function of man as a social animal, but Foucault's target was a psychological form of psychoanalysis, one grounded on a desire that would be explicable according to the human animal as a self-furthering and survival-oriented being). Phenomenology, also, insists that we exist only insofar as we make sense of ourselves and our world; we need to see all that we do—from daily habits to great artworks—as a mode of world-production. Structuralism, too, regards language, culture and social rela-tions as a product of a transcendental need for ordering: the specific forms of social ordering are empirical (or to do with how this or that social formation comes into existence); but the requirement that there be some mode of ordering is necessary or transcendental—characterizing any and every culture.

We can pause and look at how these first two considerations—both involving normalizing theories of man—open up questions for climate change studies. For it is not just that we address questions of climate on the basis of certain values, including assumptions regarding market viability and social fairness; it is also the case that we adopt normalizing forms of reasoning and calculation, both assuming that individuals may act more benevolently towards the climate (and future others) if narratives can be formed that are sympathetic and coherent, and that the values of survival and the future are shared by all humans here and now. There is also division of labor between the predictive hard sciences concerned with climate change research and data, and the interpretive projects of the humanities.

How does the distinction between the physical sciences and moral sciences not only alter the way we approach climate change (as something with a physical base that may affect different humans differently) but produce the very concepts through which we think about ways of tackling climate change? First, as long as we assume something like the possibility of a social science, in its distinction from hard sciences, we will not only have a bifurcation between data (such as the evidence yielded by the earth sciences for global warming) and social impact (such as the work done by social geographers who gauge how gender, class and race produce disproportionate and unequal impacts of climate change); we also presuppose a subject of interests. That is, it is assumed that there is a physical world of material forces and constraints and that this physical world is the milieu, environment or climate within which we are located. The concept of *climate* may be the most telling of all, deriving from concepts of surface and habitation, when in fact what 'climate change' indicates is that there is not a distinct milieu that we can observe and manage but a mesh of overlapping, divergent, interconnected and dispersed systems with certain factors such as clouds and even human hope itself, operating in two directions at once: too much hope and we don't act, not enough hope and we don't act; clouds may both increase and lessen global warming, trapping or deflecting. But rather than consider the dispersed, diverging, multiple and incongruent forces of multiple planes (where economics, politics, technology, knowledge and industry operate by divergent timelines and logics) the concept of climate reinforces the sense of 'a' milieu or habitus. *Climate change* would therefore refer to a material and physical locale that may be treated as material resource for goods and data (by the physical sciences) or as a restraining and determining condition that will alter how we produce our world and our polity (by the human sciences). The word 'climate' originally refers to a specific region, indicating different modes of human life, but once we refer to 'climate change' and have something like *the climate,* we also generate the concept of something like humanity in general. That is, if we now have something that is not a specific 'clime' or territory but a single condition for all living beings then there is also something like a general concept of life that comes to be threatened.

Second, this leads to the specific possibility of the humanities. This possibility might seem, at first glance, to produce something quite distinct from either the physical being of the hard sciences or the social systems of the human sciences. If political theory, economics and sociology can examine the impacts of climate change and climate change policy on different nations, social groups, ethnicities and gender—and if these social sciences can also explain non-physical aspects of climate change, such as the needs of developing nations and peoples to maximize production without being able to afford strategies of mitigation—what they cannot do is examine the meaning of climate change: how it is lived by 'us' and what modes of understanding and cultural production led to climate catastrophe and disdain for the environment upon which we depend and which also produces us as the beings that we are. This is where the humanities may, and has, entered climate change studies. One might even argue that the humanities has *always* taken the form of climate change studies: has always asked what humanity or 'the human' *is* such that it may have come to treat its own milieu as so much raw material for profit, consumption and energy maximization and not as a body worthy of care. The humanities, we might say, has always considered the earth as climate or environment—the home of our being, or our unavoidable terrain and surround—and never as mere stuff, matter or potential energy. The humanities originates both in a unified sense of the human, *and* in a commitment to the cultural, historical and textual variability of humanity across time and space. In a humanizing mission, reacting to the disenchantment of the world by the supposed 'hard' sciences, the humanities open a space for human variability. This humanizing motif occurs as early as the first formulations of English Studies in the late nineteenth and early twentieth centuries, concerned to develop a moral framework in an increasingly secularized and disenchanted world, and is reiterated—today—in various calls for the humanities to be led by life and praxis against the mechanizations of globalization and capitalism (Baldick 1983; Bérubé and Nelson 1995). By the time the humanities *explicitly* take up these concerns of eco-criticism or environmental philosophy it has a wealth of material to draw upon that would demonstrate that we are, primarily, ecological beings. The humanities could not do without the ecological motif, or the commitment to historical cultural variation across a comparative and meaningful plane. By the time universities form explicit networks for climate change studies there is already a demarcated niche for the humanities: neither assuming the brute facts of the world, nor dealing with humans statistically in the manner of the human sciences, the humanities nevertheless presupposes a ground of life that expresses itself in human self-creation.

On the one hand environmental philosophy—even though generalizing this area covers over many complexities—reacts critically to the fundamental concepts that are deemed to constitute Western metaphysics. The idea that we are self-determining 'subjects' whose relation to the world is one of representation (knowledge) or use (with the world as mere raw material) needs to be supplanted by a relation of care, concern or respect. The humanism and anthropocentrism that have marked Western thought need to give way to a new relation to the environment. This would not be a shift in the value we attribute to the planet and atmosphere that is our home; it would not be a question of valuing the environment *more, or of granting it greater worth, importance or significance.* We would require what Nietzsche referred to as a transvaluation of values (Nietzsche 1968). Rather than generating values on the basis of instrumental reason or utility—rather, that is, than assuming that the worth of an object or action is gauged by how much it furthers our own purposes—we would criticize means/ends rationality. We would not assume that all valid means are justified if they serve to maintain humanity in its current mode. We would, at the very least, consider values *as if from a point of view different from that of 'man.'* This would occur if, for example, we granted non-humans (animals, trees, ecosystems) rights, or if we questioned the concepts of rights and entitlement and instead developed values of mutual care, concern and deep ecological connectedness. On the other hand, while insisting upon the need to alter the very structure of our thought away from instrumental (or use-oriented) and cognitive relations to the world in which we live, eco-criticism has already uncovered an implicit and long-running awareness of a complex relation to nature that might be unearthed in canonical literature (Bate 1991; Bate 2000). Despite a manifest assumption that humans are given the world as so much available property, eco-critical readings can show the ways in which there has always been an awareness that the earth is not mere matter, but an environing and meaningful place that is as much constitutive of our sense of self as we are of the significance it has for us. Again, like environmental philosophy, eco-criticism cannot be reduced to a common set of principles. What can unify both these ways in which the humanities disciplines have anticipated current attempts to approach our climate differently is both their target and some of their key concepts. What is targeted is the notion of human beings as self-sufficient and primarily rational agents whose relation to the world is ideally one of disinterested or disenchanted knowledge; the use of key concepts, ranging from environment and ecology, to the privileging of place over space, along with concepts of care, concern, indebtedness and most importantly *life* also serve to move from a philosophy based on individuals and matter to a mode of thought that is more relational, more sympathetic and ultimately more concerned with meaning. That is to say, there is never a world as such, in itself, that we then have to manage and quantify, for 'we' exist and have a sense of ourselves only insofar as we have a specific place that is always embedded in, and generative of, an entire world of possible futures (which involve other timelines and potentials beyond ourselves).

Perhaps the strongest mode of this critical relation to Western knowledge takes the form of James Lovelock's *Gaia* hypothesis, where he insists that not only is it not a question of taking up a different attitude to nature, it is also imperative that 'nature' no longer be seen as a distinct object that would be more worthy of our care. On the contrary, the Gaia hypothesis presents the world as a single organism, so that human life would not be placed within the world, or in relation to the world, for human life would be just one aspect of an intricate, complex, dynamic, interacting and homeostatic system (Lovelock 1979). The Gaia hypothesis was formulated to challenge conventional ways of thinking about humans and their relation to the environment. It suggests that any adequate response to climate change would require a radical reassessment of our conceptual terrain.

We might, then, consider some of the key terms that orient climate change policy, ranging from 'cap and trade,' adaptation and mitigation to sustainability and viability. These terms remain managerial and instrumental. Cap and trade is, of course, an explicit adoption of a calculative framework. Policy and negotiations focus on a single variable (carbon emissions) despite the volatility and complexity of factors that the physical sciences have consistently demonstrated to make up the problems of climate change. The very notion of *trading* carbon emissions—that as long as a payoff is made somewhere or by someone then further destruction can be sanctioned—not only (again) places human response in the mode of *homo economicus*, it also precludes any genuine thought of the future. If carbon emissions can be managed, traded, and held at 'acceptable' levels then we fail to confront the scientific evidence that indicates that even a halt in current carbon emissions would leave a tailing effect that would continue to wreak havoc; continued trade in emissions presupposes that the future will be different in degree, or a continuation of the present, and not different in kind. There is something anaesthetizing in the idea of *trading* carbon emissions and allowances: as though something like an economy were at work, an enclosed system of more and less, and not—as is becoming apparent—a future that will be unmanageable and have entirely different terms. One might make a similar remark about the concepts of sustainability, adaptation, mitigation and viability. Sustainability assumes the value of continuity: if one changes it is only insofar as is required in order for human life to continue, an implication that is less subtly contained in the strategy of mitigation. Not only do all these terms accept that humanity exists as something that has the right to continue, and that it must do so now only in the mode of damage limitation; they also have a primarily calculative conceptual base (where the calculations are arithmetical, concerning more and less, rather than differential). Climate change is perceived as a problem of disturbance, precluding us from continuing life in the same manner; and it is only for that reason that changes need to be made. Such changes will not be global in the full sense of the word; they will not alter the fundamental or entire system within which we are imbricated. They will rather occur as responses to a predicament. Life may have continued unperturbed—had we been wiser and more cautious, perhaps less profligate and wasteful—but unfortunately we plundered nature excessively and with short-term thinking. Our response is therefore to *extend* our calculative approach to the future to include not only our maximal efficiency here and now but our ongoing existence, our sustained existence.

All these terms are aligned with what Gilles Deleuze referred to as extensive multiplicities: certain multiples have their units determined in advance, and are composed of equivalents (Deleuze 1994). In general we might say that the very possibility of the social sciences is built on calculations of extensive multiplicities: in relation to climate change studies one can look at how different members of populations respond to, or are affected by, policies or climatic disasters. More importantly, the timelines take the mode of more or less: what practices do we need to adopt to live longer? How might 'we' adapt? Can we use less? Can we be more like developing nations? How much suffering and sacrifice will be demanded from our future generations? All such questions assume that the future would be a continuing time of *more or less*. Such extensive calculations also presuppose a general underlying substrate—human life—that may vary culturally and historically, that may have to *adapt,* but will have nevertheless have some mode of continuity. Rather, then, than continue a late Romantic project of re-enchanting the world, following a science of calculation that disenchanted the world, I would suggest that what is required is a more intensified disenchantment and evacuation of meaning, or what Timothy Morton has referred to as an ecology without nature. As long as we regard the world as our lived world, as an organic and meaningful whole that is the milieu of our being then our approach to the future will be bifurcated: split between an increasingly multiple and intensive mode of scientific calculation, concerned with positive and negative feedback loops and multiple timelines, and an englobing environment. In intensive quantities it is not a question of equivalent units of more or less, but of speeds and thresholds that have the capacity to produce differences in kind. Climate change calculations, models and scenarios have long been characterized by quantities that are not those of a single unit (beneficial or detrimental) but will alter in kind and relation depending on speed and quantity; not only are there tipping points (or thresholds where one more degree of heat will alter the entire system) there are also unpredictable feedback effects and incalculable productions of disequilibrium. Had the social sciences taken on a similar complexity they would have to consider the possibility that the units with which they work—humans, societies—would alter in kind, beyond recognition, at certain speeds and thresholds. This could be seen positively, whereby one might say that climate change will not simply disturb human life, requiring it to sustain itself in a more viable manner, but will alter the very unit of 'the human.'

Here, one would have to rethink the very being of 'man' that was produced by the division between hard and social sciences: there could no longer be this animal blessed with language and history, who produces himself socially and technologically, but who can also study and read himself as an object of historical and cultural production. For there would no longer be man (historically and socially determined and determining) but a species tied to rhythms that were geological and beyond the historical and familial imagination. This would require us to consider that the question of the humanities and the human is not something that might be *added* to the problem of climate change, as though the environmental and policy problems could benefit from an examination of some concepts. Here is where we might return to how theories of ecology, environment and—of course—climate as terrain or habitation have already been considered by the humanities. For perhaps what may need to be rethought is the very concept of the human as it subtends the humanities.

Returning to Foucault's genealogy of the emergence of the human sciences in modernity, we can recall that 'man' becomes possible as an object of knowledge only with the strict distinction between the hard sciences of matter, and the social sciences that chart man as a socio-historical cultural production. If we accept that construction of man that is coterminous with a normalizing ground of life, splitting the world into the hard sciences of matter, and then the temporal-cultural expression of man in the social sciences, then it follows that the *discipline* of the humanities forms both an enabling condition and presupposed axiology: for discipline is both a set of conditions of knowledge and an art of formation. In the disciplines of the humanities 'man' not only studies himself as determined, in part, by his climate, for he can also reconfigure his intellectual climate, rewrite his concepts and vocabularies. He can alter himself from within his own history, sustaining himself, and rendering himself more viable by becoming more attuned, more sympathetic, less instrumental in relation to what will always be his climate and his environment. Indeed, in theories such as the Gaia hypothesis, man can project his organic being onto life as a whole. No longer would he be fragmented from a climate that is unfortunately not bending to his will and knowledge; he would, rather, be part of a living form that in its dynamically self-sustaining manner would guide him away from self-seeking politics to a naturally forming politics of the whole. Ethics and politics—what 'we' ought to do—would follow directly from the natural and vital norms of the one living earth. Lovelock's Gaia hypothesis, like any theory that assumes a natural or proper connectedness (however occluded), reinforces what Foucault referred to as the specifically modern nature of bio-power (Foucault 1978), and maintains an extensive and bourgeois approach to values. That is, despite the recognitions of ecology, environment, climate and biosphere, it is man who will read the conditions of this system, discern its proper order, break free from merely instrumental attitudes and arrive at a proper mode of self-regulation.

The alternative to this privileging of climate, environment, ecology and biosphere as continuations of self-sustaining life was already prefigured when Foucault spoke about the possible erasure of man. Here, one would not assume that the future would only need to be altered in degree in order for life to continue: one would ask whether the future would be one of life. That is, would all those disciplinary norms, including a distinction among hard sciences of data, human sciences of self-management, and the humanities as self-interpretive, not be fragmented following their dissolution and failure in the face of impending catastrophe? If we did *not* assume that life (as it is) were self-evidently worth sustaining, if life were not viable, could not be adapted, then we would no longer be reading and managing the human, via the humanities, but would be asking how we might think in the absence of sustained human life. This would lead, in turn, to thinking climate intensively—and this, in turn, would require not only adjusting concepts but creating new concepts, or even thinking beyond concepts. At its simplest, climate change 'policy' would have to shift from being *political*—the coming together of bodies in common via a common language of sustaining and adapting—to become *impolitic*. What ways of speaking would fragment, disturb and destroy the logics of self-maintenance that have always sustained humanity as an animal that cannot question its existence? (Humanity has, of course, always questioned the *essence* of its existence—who is man?—but it has rarely questioned the actuality of its existence: that it may *not be*.) To consider the future *intensively* we would at least begin with the possibility that an event might occur to 'us' that would create a mutation of such a force that 'we' would no longer exist. What we have known as human life, supposedly marked by instrumental reason, self-maintenance, risk-assessment, management of resources and exchange with a view to relatively short-term futures, would give way to a being *that does not have a future*.

As long as we calculate the future as one of sustaining, maintaining, adapting and rendering ourselves viable, the future will differ only in degree; this would mean of course that there would be no future for us other than an eventual, barely lived petering out. If, however, we entertained the erasure of the human (especially as defined through the discipline of the humanities, whereby humanity is that fragment of a self-maintaining nature that can sustain itself through reading itself) then there might be a future. This would not be a future of the *climate*, of a terrain or habitation, and certainly not of an environment—as that which environs or encloses. For if the experience of climate change were to be experienced it would disclose that there is no climate, biosphere or environment. There is not 'a' world, existing in the manner of an organism, that maintains and sustains itself.

Chapter 3

A Globe of One's Own:
In Praise of the Flat Earth

Questions, today, of climate and climate ethics—and even concerns regarding the sustainability and viability of this life of ours on earth—appear to present a new imaginary for political questions. One might say that it was only in the late twentieth century, with events such as the picturing of the earth from space, the possibility of nuclear annihilation of earthly life or the increasing speeds of new media allowing for the possibility of global audiences (such as the entire world viewing 9/11), that something like the problem of a global ethos would emerge. If there had always been a silent presupposed 'we'[1] in any ethical theory, then this virtual universalism would always struggle alongside moral valorizations of specified communities.[2] How do we, from the particular world we inhabit, begin to think of life as such? It is the present sense of the planet as a whole, as a fragile bounded globe that might present us, finally, with the opportunity and imperative to think a genuine ethos. Now that we have a notion of *climate* that seems to break with the etymology of this specific inclination or latitude *of the earth* , and does so by gesturing to something like a sense of the earth as *a* region or inclination in itself, this might open a new imaginary of the globe. We might think of ethos as no longer bound to a territory within the planet; instead there might be the ethos of this globe of our own, that has no other region against which we might define ourselves or towards which we might direct our fantasies of another future. If there is something like climate change, perhaps it takes this form: not only a mutation of this climate (warming, depleting, becoming more volatile) but an alteration of what we take climate to be. One might want to suggest that as long as we think of climate in its traditional sense—as our specific milieu—we will perhaps lose sight of climate change, or the degree to which human life is now implicated in timelines and rhythms beyond that of its own borders.

The figure of the globe appears to offer two ethical trajectories: on the one hand an attention to global interconnections and networks would expand responsibility and awareness beyond the figure of the isolated moral subject. Ethics may have to be considered beyond discursive, human and political modes (especially if one defines politics as the practice of a polity). On the other hand, the figure of the globe—considered as a figure—is intertwined with a tropology of interconnectedness, renewal, cyclic causality and organicism. This traditionally theological series of motifs, with the globe's circularity reflecting a divine intentionality, is maintained today in many of the most profound and seemingly secular ecological theses, including the Gaia hypothesis and the global brain.

It is the possibility of extinction or the end of human time that forces us to confront a new sense of the globe: far from being an unfortunate event that accidentally befalls the earth and humanity, the thought of the end of the anthropocene era is both at the heart of all the motifs of ecological ethics and the one idea that cannot be thought as long as the globe is considered in terms of its traditional and anthropocentric metaphors.

The word 'globalism' along with the word 'biopolitics' suffers from a curious double valence. As a descriptive term globalism can refer to the lost autonomy and destroyed difference among worlds: the formation of global media, markets and communications eliminated what was once a panorama of difference. Once upon a time the globe enjoyed divergent timelines and worldviews. Even if it was central to the colonialist imagination to romanticize the extent to which 'other' worlds were exotically untranslatable, mystical and embedded in a non-linear time, there is nevertheless a very real sense in which globalism has created an earth of a single time, single market and single polity. Globalism would be a mode of homogenization, disenchantment or rendering quantifiable that one could lament as having displaced an earlier world of distinct places for the sake of one quantifiable space. This reduction of distinction has significant material consequences; today, any particular country's environmental or wage policies will directly alter the day to day life of bodies elsewhere on the globe. But global inclusion and simultaneity also trigger a series of imaginary ramifications. In positive terms this has been described by Michael Hardt and Antonio Negri in terms of a new multitude. Liberated from nation states and physical locales there can now be a humanity as such, a self-creating living labor that has no body other than that which it gives itself through its own immaterial productive powers (Hardt and Negri 2004).

Thought less optimistically, one might say that the physical ability to occupy converging and synchronized worlds and times is coupled with a cognitive paralysis to think of any future that would not be one more chapter in a familiar collective narrative. This is evident in the terms that are used to describe the predicament of the globe. It is not only the case that events are materially and systemically linked, so that the volatile economies of even the smallest countries may precipitate global crises; it is also typical today to see all of financial history as similarly continuous and interconnected. This occurs both in short-term and long-term thinking; recent events have prompted the publication of a series of histories and genealogies, including the histories of debt, of money, of corporations, bonds and markets: all suggesting that the present is an expression and extension of a single history of something like 'the' globe (Ferguson 2008; Cashill 2010; Graeber 2011; Coggan 2012; Bakan 2005). Economic events are considered in relation to a past that we have been unable to think as anything other than differing by degree. Despite the new global conditions and linkages the 2008 cascade of economic crises were gauged to be either as bad as or worse than the great depression, while terms such as 'recovery,' 'recession,' 'depression,' and 'crisis' place the current state of play as a continuation of a past, a past that varies and recovers always in terms of one easily comprehended cycle. The lexicon deployed to assess and gauge the environment is similarly comforting in terms of its linear temporality and delimitation: Australia still refers to its condition as one of 'drought,' even when the period of insufficient rain and increasing desertification exceeds a decade; climate change policy refers to 'mitigation,' 'adaptation,' 'sustainability' and 'viability'—all of which enable one to think of management (however difficult) rather than cessation, rupture or incomprehension. One might say that the imaginary is, indeed, *global*. A literal globalism—the stark reality of there being no escape, no outside, nowhere else to flee now that the earth has been forced to yield ever more to the human desire for life—is coupled with an incompatible global figuration. Things will cycle back to recovery. The globe can be taken and assessed as an object and managed, saved, revived or given the respect and care that it deserves. If where we are is a *globe*, then it can be imagined as delimited, bounded, organically self-referring and unified.

Perhaps—given the advent of globalism as a concrete event where there can now be no time, place or body that can live outside a certain destructive force field of events (such as the possibility of viral, political, economic and climactic terrors)—now is the time to think non-globally. The usual figures of the bounded earth, the ideally-self-balancing cosmos, the interconnectedness of this great organic home of 'ours' are modes of narrative self-enclosure that have shielded us from confronting the forces of the present. It is not surprising that 'globalism' is at once a term of mourning, signaling a world economy and politics that has taken every space and timeline into its calculative, cynical and rigid systematic maw at the same time as it signals a redemptive potential. We are, so various environmental and ecological imperatives remind us, always interconnected across and through this one living globe, this living world that environs us. The maxim, 'act locally, think globally,' should be reversed: there can be no encompassing global thought, for insofar as we think we are fragmented by various locales, figures, lexicons, disciplines and desire, but we nevertheless are caught up in a globe of action where no intent or prediction will be enough to secure or predict the outcome of any action.

It was the great contribution of Lacanian psychoanalysis to point out that the visual figural unity of the human body—the bounded organism we see in the mirror—serves as a captivating lure that precludes us from confronting that ex-centric predicament of the speaking subject whose desire is never given in a living present but is articulated and dispersed in a time that is never that of a self-comprehending and self-affecting whole. Just as the spatial unity of the human body covers over the temporal dispersion of the speaking and desiring subject, so the delimited material object of the planet enables a misrecognition of the multiple systems, forces, timelines, planes and feedback loops that traverse what we imagine to be the single object of the globe. The advent of globalism—or the intensification of the world's various modes of systemic interconnectedness and hyper-volatility—should, if anything, have prompted a destruction of the figure of the globe. And yet the opposite appears to be the case: even in the genre that is apparently most devoted to global catastrophe—the disaster movie—the globe is strangely reinforced and consolidated. A typical instance is *Independence Day* of 1996, in which an invasion of earth is initially viewed from the contained space of a US government control room, as though we will be able to have advance vision of 'our' end and limit from the point of view of a single screen and panel of experts.

Perhaps today we might note that it is the physical image of the globe that serves as a reaction formation, precluding a thought of the consequences of globalism (if globalism remains the correct term for the increasingly evident and non-human complexities that are precluding any possibility of a global or comprehensive vision). If capitalism could once have been thought of as 'a' power imposed upon the globe then this is no longer the case. As the recent economic crises demonstrated capitalism is not a system, cannot be attributed to a body of interests, and is less a transcendent structure imposed upon organic life than it is just one of the many ways in which local, ill-considered, barely intentional forces of consumption and acquisition exceed the comprehension of any body (be that a physical, political, national or economic body).

Marxist theory's attempt to locate capitalism within history and within a theory of interests can be compared to a whole series of localizations and narrative therapies. Popular culture has for decades been giving a face and/or body to a series of diffuse and essentially 'unglobable' threats. Despite a series of calls for thinking in terms of distributed, de-centered and dispersed cognition, where we acknowledge that institutions, cultures and even organisms are not governed by a central organizing brain, the political imaginary remains wedded to organic figures. Popular culture has presented viral invasion more often than not in terms of an isolable and intruding body: conquering such threats can then be placed in a standard narrative of good and evil, self and other. Terrorism, too, is given a specific face in media culture (either the named Osama Bin Laden or an ethnically specified other). But it is not only popular culture that has been unable to confront a temporality and politics that is no longer that of contesting agents waging a war for the sake of a determined end.

Lamenting the fall of modernity into a bio-politics that manages populations according to a general and quantifiable 'life,' Giorgio Agamben argues that it will be possible to arrive again at a genuine politics only by considering what Foucault failed to confront: the problem of sovereignty in modernity (Agamben 1998). That is, whereas Foucault was critical of the sovereign model of power, or power as an external and imposed body, Agamben's critical concept of bio-politics wants to resist a modernity of diffused or capillary power, focusing again on how power establishes itself *as a body*. Agamben refuses the notion of the political and the polity as a universal or a given; the polity is constituted in and through human potentiality's realization that it lacks any determined end. For Agamben, what needs to be recalled is the genesis or emergence of the political fold, the opening of something like a political space that then enables a distinction between that which is interior and that which is exterior to the polity. What counts *as political* is, for Agamben, itself not a political decision, and this is because 'the polity' or the opening of a space of what will become 'our' concern is an event, and one to which genuine thinking ought to (constantly) return. Today's losses of commonality, or the absence of something like a global community, should prompt us to address that the global community or horizon is neither given nor guaranteed, but is nevertheless urgently required if we are not to lose sight altogether of our potentiality *to be political, to open a political space.* What bio-politics and its terrors force us to acknowledge is that our defining potentiality—for speaking together and opening up a political space— discloses itself most fully when it is not actualized. For bio-politics, too, bears the same double valence as globalism. It is precisely in the era of the bio-political, when all decisions regarding what we ought to do are grounded on maximizations of life that the passage from life to polity, and the political constitution of what counts as political life is forgotten. It is Auschwitz, modern hedonism, and the bio-political absence of a genuine political space of speech and decision that evidences the true nature of politics. Politics occurs not when bodies located in a world then decide to speak together, for politics is—through the event of speaking—the opening out of a world. Here, then, in this confrontation with a modern bio-politics that is criticized and lamented for being insufficiently political—insufficiently oriented to the opening and manifestation of a political space—Agamben gives the contemporary term 'bio-politics' a force that relates directly to the imaginary hyper-investment in the globe. Agamben, unlike the Foucault whom he criticizes for not confronting the relation between bare life and sovereignty, regards bio-politics in its various forms—both totalitarian managements of populations and democratic aims to increase a society's happiness—as a *loss of the political*. As long as politics is focused on bare life, or the calculation of a living substance we will have retreated from the question of the potentiality of the political: man is not born as a political animal but becomes one, and he does so by creating a political space through speaking, opening up a world that is always *his* world.

The Greek distinction between *bios* (or a life that is formed, bounded and oriented to what man might make of himself) and *zoe* (or mere bare life that, in modernity, becomes so much disposable waste *and* that increasingly becomes the subject of politics) is, for Agamben a difference that needs to be re-thought and re-inscribed. It is *bios—created, formed, bounded, delimited life*—that has been lost and that entails a loss of the political. How does this relate to globalism? Both Agamben's critique of biopolitics and the reaction against globalism express a traditional and theological mourning for a loss of form. Globalism's evils follow from its ravaging disrespect for limits and difference, its tendency to consume all previously distinct and specified nations and cultures into one vast calculative system without definition or limit. Not surprisingly the response to both globalism (seen as an inhuman, mindless and unbounded system) and to biopolitics (seen as a loss of the self-defining polity) has been the reaffirmation of the figure of the globe or bounded form. Agamben, for example, posits a series of positive manoeuvres that would ameliorate the biopolitical ravaging of the man of poiesis; these include a return to the active creation of man as a political living form as *bios* rather than *zoe*, as a being whose political nature has little or nothing to do with his mere life but requires creation. Not surprisingly, then, Agamben also wishes to retrieve a more authentic aesthetic encounter, where art is not passive spectatorship of an artist's private invention but an opening out or disclosure of a created world. Here, art as *poiesis* or putting into distinct form would not be disengaged from collective *praxis*.

Hardt and Negri, reacting more explicitly to a globalism that has precluded any active and intentional formation of a polity, call for the creation of a single, self-producing, self-aware and self-referring open whole of humanity: a single, continually re-productive body of man:

> In addition to envisioning revolution in ethical and political terms, we also conceive of it in terms of deep anthropological modification: of *metissage* and continuous hybridization of populations, of biopolitical metamorphosis. The first terrain of struggle is, from this point of view, the universal right to move, work and learn over the entire surface of the globe. Thus revolution, as we see it, is not only within Empire but also *through* Empire. It is not something which is fought against some implausible Winter Palace, but something which extends against all the central and peripheral structures of power, in order to empty them and subtract the capacity of production from capital. (Negri, Hardt and Zolo 27)

We can pause here to note that what underpins Agamben's call for a new politics and Hardt and Negri's manifesto for a self-productive multitude is a figural globalism that is a variant of a traditional and theological organicism. That is, the figure of the globe—the ideally bounded sphere in which each point is in accord with the whole, and in which the whole is a dynamic and self-maintaining unity—harbours an axiology that privileges *bios* over *zoe*. What must be asserted as dominant and proper is a whole or bounded form that has no external or transcendent principle, no ordering that is given from without or that would elevate one point or term above another.

Literal globalism, perceived as humanity's alienation from itself and its earth through dead technical systems (such as the market, mechanization, computerization and speculation), is to be cured by figural globalism. Life as *zoe*, the mere life that lives on without a sense of itself, without a world and without form, is to be combated by life as *bios*: a properly political life of self-formation and speaking in common. Politics ought to be of, by and for the polity: thus, the call to immanence, whereby a body is not deflected by any power other than that of its own making is yet one more refusal to consider the predicament of a palpably non-sovereign power. Recall that for Agamben Foucault failed to consider the relationship between biopolitics and sovereign power, between power as instituted law that creates the border between law and non-law, or between governable life and the merely living. For Agamben the problem with biopolitics is that it is insufficiently directed towards *bios*: both totalitarian governments and democracies focus on well-being and happiness rather than confronting the problem that mere life does not proceed without some sort of gap or decision towards its proper world and end. If one were to recall the Greek attention to *bios,* or formed life, one might be able to retrieve something of the proper political potentiality that is covered over in modernity.

Foucault, however, suggests an opposite path. The problem with biopolitics is not its inattention to bios or self-making but, rather, its maintenance of organic—or what I will refer to here as 'global'—thinking. One could be misled by reading Foucault's corpus backwards, concluding that his final thoughts on Greek and Hellenistic arts of the self would be the natural consequence of a theorization of biopolitics, leading to a retrieval of a poetics of the subject. But there are other possibilities indicated in his earliest criticisms of the concept of life. The problem with this concept, or more accurately this *problem,* is that its manner of folding an inside from an outside, or of producing a relation through which something like knowledge is possible, is—to use a Deleuzian term—its reactive reterritorializing quality. It is the concept of life as such, the life from which bounded beings emerge and against which they maintain themselves, that leads to a certain structure of ethics. Man becomes that being who is nothing more than a reflective structure, a being whose only law is that of giving a law to himself. The three concepts analyzed by Foucault that constitute the modern empirical-transcendental episteme are life, labour and language. It is because there is something in general called 'life' as a process of striving, self-production and self-maintenance that language and labor become the means through which man creates himself as an historical being.

On the one hand Foucault suggests that this is in quite a specific sense the consequence of a refigured globe: the pre-modern space of knowledge had distributed beings in relations of analogy, such that the universal order of things was reflected in each living being. In classicism this book of nature, or experience of the earth as possessing its own sense that could be unfolded in various ways in each living form, gives way to an order that appears in representation and tabulation. Man, in classical thought, is not yet that being produced through the act of speech and labour that forms him in relation to a life in general that is only known after the event of its formation. In modernity the globe is no longer the book of nature or scene of readable order, becoming a site of 'life' that is now known as the enigmatic progression through which organisms and systems emerge: life is a process that can be read after the event of its ongoing acts of formation. Critically, then, this would suggest that with the politics of life itself something of the globe is lost or occluded. And this, indeed, is how ecological and anti-globalist theory understands both biopolitics and globalism more generally. What is lost is any sense of the earth as a living whole, as bearing a life and temporality of its own, within which human beings are located and towards which they ought to pay due respect and care. Yet despite the sense that globalism as a political event has erased all traditional and enchanted senses of the globe as a living whole that harbors its own order, the appeals to the figure and normativity of englobed life have become more intense than ever. If Agamben seeks to retrieve a sense of the world as that which man gives himself through speaking in common, and if Hardt and Negri aim to catalyze the self-expressing multitude, then they do so in thorough accord with a tradition and spirit of the self-evident beauty and worth of the organic globe.

First, we can note the theological nature of this figure of the self-referring, self-creating living form that has no end or determination outside its own existence.[3] Not only is this how the Christian God of monotheism was defined (as a potentiality that has no essence other being in pure act, never deflected from pure self-forming), it is also the case that theological poetics used the figure of the bounded sphere to express a divine intentionality of perfect accord, balance and (most importantly) self-reference. Such a form has its own temporality which is at once linear, organic and circular; it is a time of increasing creation and fruition, in which beings arrive at their proper form and in which the end concludes and discloses the reason of the whole. As an example we can think of Milton's frequent references to the pendant world or balanced globe, contrasted with the boundless, formless and time-deprived chaos. The divine meets the human in John Donne's frequent references to globes, circles, circumference and recovery, as though the earth's form is that of the soul:

> Then, soul, to thy first pitch work up again;
> Know that all lines which circles do contain.
> For once that they the centre touch, do touch
> Twice the circumference, and be thou such
> (Donne 2000, 229).

Second, this divine, organic and perfectly bounded form of immanent self reference can take the form of philosophy itself: that activity through which human reason refers back to, and redeems, itself by circling back and recognizing its own constitutive conditions. One could include here Heidegger's hermeneutic circle, Hegel's philosophy of absolute self-reference, and more recent and supposedly scientific claims for 'human' understanding, such as Robert Wright's recent claim that the monotheistic figure of God will, organically, evolve to become nothing more than that of human nature understanding itself as the origin of all the figures to which it was once enslaved (2010).

Third, and finally, when current ecological theorists continue to refer to the environment—as that which environs or encloses—or call for a due reverence to an earth that bears its own balance and self-ordering, it is once again a figure of bounded form or *bios* that is maintained against a life that would be a force without sense of itself, a time without disclosure of fruition.

The problem with this anti-globalization global tropology is twofold. First, it is inefficacious when one considers the nature of modern power. The twenty-first century is marked by an intensification of diffuse and destructive forces. The cold war and its threat of nuclear annihilation had already troubled the motif of life as a war of interests among bodies, for it was clearly possible that the trajectory of man for survival and dominance was the same path that would lead to his disappearance. The subsequent wave of annihilation threats, from the AIDS awareness of the 1980s, followed by increasing anxieties about global warming, food shortages, viral panics (SARS, bird flu, swine flu), terrorist organizations that no longer concerned themselves with a worldly survival, and then economic crises that exposed an absence of any centered or commanding viewpoint: all these serve to show that the image of the globe, of an inter-connected whole, is a lure and an alibi. We have perhaps always lived in a time of divergent, disrupted and diffuse systems of forces, in which the role of human decisions and perceptions is a contributing factor at best. Far from being resolved by returning to the figure of the bounded globe or subject of bios rather than zoe, all those features that one might wish to criticize in the bio-political global era can only be confronted by a non-global temporality and counter-ethics.

Second, it follows that far from being an ecological figure that will save us from the ravages of globalism, subjectivism and bio-politics, it is the image of the globe that lies at the center of an anthropocentric imaginary that is intrinsically suicidal. Of course, extinction and annihilation lie at the heart of all life. But accelerated and self-witnessing extinction can only be achieved by a global animal, a 'man' whose desire for survival and mastery is so frenzied that he consumes his own milieu. And he does so because his milieu is a globe. If, as recent 'returns' to phenomenology insist, the thinking and living being always has a world, and if that world is always a world of meaning—defined in terms of potentialities and the organism's timeline—then we are truly global. We are bounded by our own living form, with a world of our own folded around our sensory-motor apparatus (Thomson 2007). But does not the phenomenon of a violent, life-annihilating and globe-destroying globalism present us with another possibility? Perhaps what we need is a zoopolitics: not a lament for the ways in which politics has taken hold of human populations as mere life, but a critique of the ways in which political thinking remains human all too human—repressing the utter contingency of life by insisting on the meaning and form of bios. Rather than criticize bio-political modernity for rendering mere life as formless, calculative, and void of meaning and mindful creativity, we should cast *both* bios and zoe on the side of figural lures, and strive to think beyond all forms of life. Neither the mere life of animality nor the formed life of political man, our attention would be better directed to a multiple and divergent network of times and matters. That is, bio-politics ought to be criticized *not* for seizing upon bare or mere life—*not* for forgetting the human forming power that enables politics, not for regarding man as bios rather than zoe. Rather, the biopolitics that is hysterically and morally regarded as destructive of well-bounded life would still be captured by bios, by the good form of self-producing man and would be better directed towards forces beyond the human, beyond the organism and beyond the globe. The globe or earth as the planet that was blessed with the contingency of life, including the human species whose global imagination has done so much to create destructive systems beyond its own power and comprehension, cannot be saved. Insofar as it is imagined as a globe or living whole with its own order and proper potentiality that might be restored, the earth will continue to be sacrificed to the blindness of an organic thinking that can only insist upon its own self-evident value.

One final feature of globalism that needs to be noted, and that might suggest a new counter-global temporality is that of information. There is no public sphere, no bordered polis in which circulating data may be reflected upon, and incorporated; there is no transcendental and procedural ideal of consensus that would emerge as an aspect of an all encompassing life-world. According to Habermas, and other theorists of discourse theory, insofar as one speaks or even insofar as one claims to know, an intersubjective claim is presupposed (Habermas 1991, 378); it would be a performative contradiction to say something that one did not also claim to be true (Apel 2001, 47). Insofar as one speaks one is already with an ideal domain of recognition that is procedurally, if not actually, intersubjective and global. But the actual fact of globalism destroys global inclusion, consensus and recognition. There is a glut of speech and a deficit of both recognition and the demand for recognition. The more global citizens seek and demand inclusion the less attention and media space becomes available: every tweet, blog, Facebook post and text message places more and more pressure on the bloated domain of available consumable information. Individual speech acts are not fragments of one grand communicating globe; rather, the excess of production is utterly destructive of any possibility of (even ideal) reception. Indeed, it is the surfeit of information, especially information regarding the limits of the globe (such as data about global warming, resource depletion, new speeds of viral mutation, terrorist cells without traceable command centers) that requires a micro-politics (if that term could be freed from the notion of a polis) and demands some mode of schizo-analysis. The latter would refer to a tracking of splits in forces, of divergent systems and incongruous fields. One may never free oneself from the figure of the globe, or even the globe as the notion of *figure*—the notion that 'we' give a world to ourselves through our own recuperating imagination. But if the present has the capacity to teach us anything it may be this: only a shattering of the globe, with an attention to forces that resist recuperation, incorporation and comprehension—forces that operate beyond intentionality and synthesis—only this radical destruction can save us from ourselves.

Notes

1.   In his commentary on Husserl's vision of the task of phenomenology, Derrida notes that any consideration of universal truth, or truth in general, must presuppose a subjectivity that would transcend any specific or determined cultural norm; this would yield humanity as a horizon within which located norms would function, a 'silent presupposed we.' Derrida notes, though, that this freeing of humanity from any determined and concrete image of 'man' occurs with Husserl's modernity and the vision of phenomenology as uncovering the transcendental presuppositions of Western thought (Derrida 1978, 61).

2.   Michel Foucault argues that in modernity only *ethics* is possible, only a negotiation of the forms of arguments, and that morality—or the practical judgment of specific forms of life—is no longer possible (Foucault 2002, 357).

3.   '...this amounts to thinking time and movement on the basis of the *telos* of the *gramme* that is completed, in act, fully present, that keeps its tracing close to itself, that is, erases its tracing in a *circle*.' (Derrida 1982, 60).

Chapter 4

Earth Felt the Wound:
The Affective Divide

We are suffering, today—here and now—from hyper-hypo-affective disorder. We appear to be consuming nothing other than affects; even the supposed material needs of life—food, sex, sociality—are now marketed affectively. Branding relies on irrational attachments or 'lovemarks,'[1] while politics trades in terror and resentment. Affects themselves are marketed: one can purchase games of horror or disgust, and even the purchase of a cup of coffee is perhaps undertaken less for the sake of the caffeine stimulant and more for the Starbucks affect.[2] This is what led Michael Hardt to theorize a new era of affective labor.[3] But this over-consumption and boom of marketable affects is accompanied by affect fatigue, as though there were an inverse relation between the wider and wider *extension* of affective influx and the ever-diminishing *intensity* of affect. It is not surprising then that cultural diagnoses of the present observe two seemingly incompatible catastrophic tendencies: a loss of cognitive or analytic apparatuses in the face of a culture of affective immediacy, and yet a certain deadening of the human organism (ranging from Walter Benjamin's observation of an absence of experience in an information age to Fredric Jameson's claim for a 'waning of affect' in a world of over-stimulation, in which there is no longer a distinction between experiencing subject and external object, no other person, for whom one might feel empathy[4]).

On the one hand there is a widespread consensus and diagnosis that the human sensory motor apparatus has departed from an informational-cognitive or even image-based mode of immaterial consumption to one of affect. (Such a turn to affect has been both lamented and celebrated, seen either as a retreat from judgment *or* as a liberation from overly calculative modes of reason.) N. Katherine Hayles has referred to a shift from deep attention to hyper attention (2007). Bernard Stiegler, working critically from Hayles, has diagnosed a widespread cultural attention deficit disorder. He rejects Hayles's suggestion that this shift or loss might be ameliorated by different pedagogic strategies; more is required than—as Hayles proposes—simply intertwining Faulkner with computer games. Stiegler places the turn to mere stimulus within a broader *fault* or potential deficit of the human brain, which has always required (and yet been threatened by) inscriptive technologies that extend its range beyond its organic boundaries. For Stiegler, the loss of deep attention is also an atrophy of trans-individual networks: the script technologies that had always supplemented the brain's power and had also always threatened to weaken that power through externalization and alienation reach new levels of risk. Without extended circuits connecting the reading-writing brain to logics not its own we face the perils of a new infantilism (Stiegler 2009). *Techne*, for Stiegler, no longer opens the brain onto broader circuits but produces short-circuits. Flickering screens now leave the eye-brain within itself. In a more popular mode, closer to the more panicked tones of Nicholas Carr's *In the Shallows: What the Internet is Doing to Our Brains* (2010), Susan Greenfield (2008) argues that we are no longer developing the neural networks or habits that allow us to read with a connecting grammar. We are more oriented to the flashing stimuli of detached intensities, not so much meaning as sensation. In a contrasting celebratory mode Mark Hansen, whose signature maneuver has been one of returning texts to lived bodies ('correcting' Deleuze by way of Bergson, 'correcting' Stiegler by way of Husserl), argues that digital media's simulation of faces has the direct affect of re-engaging the viewer—consumer's emotive responses thereby redeeming art history and 'high theory' from the errors of its inhuman ways:

> Insofar as the confrontation with the DFI functions by triggering affectivity as, precisely, a faculty of embodied heterogenesis, it operates a transfer of affective power from the image to the body. Instead of a static dimension or element intrinsic to the image, affectivity thereby becomes the very medium of interface with the image. What this means is that affectivity actualizes the potential of the image at the same time as it

virtualizes the body: the crucial element is neither image nor body alone, but the dynamical interaction between them. As the digital artworks discussed at the end of this article propose, if we can allow the computer to impact our embodied affectivity directly, our communication and our coevolution with the computer—and along with it visual culture more generally—will enter a truly new, 'post-imagistic' phase.[5]

Before we launch into too simplistic a notion of a historical break or fall into a myopic culture of affect we need to note that there has always been an affective component of cultural production, and that this has always been acknowledged and theorized (going back to the 'doctrine of affects' [Lenneberg 1958]). It would be more accurate to say that we are witnessing a shift in the cultural dominant. Just as the affective component of cultural production has always been present, so has a suspicion or denigration of the *merely* felt. The anxiety regarding a dominance of the merely affective or visually captivating in the face of a weakening of cognition has often been tied to a concern regarding the externality of technological and mnemonic devices that supposedly deflect the brain from its proper potentiality. There have always been fears regarding the capacity for technology to weaken cognition, reducing the brain to mere automaton of stimulus interface. This is why Stiegler's reading of the history of techne as *pharmacological* is so important: he neither simply adopts Derrida's history of metaphysics in which writing technologies have always been unjustifiably purged as parasitic, nor celebrates a post-human digital culture in which illusions of the brain's autonomy would have been overcome. For Stiegler, any brain-extending system, including the brain's own mnemic networks, at once enables more complex relations *and* precludes the brain from ever having a law or propriety of its own. What Stiegler laments is not alienation, technology and loss of internal integrity per se, but the historical loss of *individuation* where systems would not be general and mechanistic but would enable 'a' singular time to be read for all time. It is not technology's takeover Stiegler laments so much as its reduction to localized stimuli at the expense of broader and more complex circuits, not so much the liberation or tyranny of digital culture as its over-simplification. To read Plato's dialogues, Stiegler argues, requires a highly sophisticated writing-reading system that enables a sense to be intuited that is not that of my present world, and that also allows something like 'a' Plato to be reactivated by future generations (generations who can nevertheless read a past time for the present). What the present threatens to do is break those very individuating modes of reading that have created the circuits that have taken individuals beyond the range of their own isolated psyches. This is why, perhaps, Stiegler attributes an individuating potential to social networking sites, such as *Facebook* (Stiegler 2010, 134). *Here,* the screen I encounter is not a simply stimulating prompt for rule-bound response but an opening to other speeds and networks.

So while it would be too simplistic to create a pure divide between cognition and affect, and similarly inadequate to posit a straightforward historical break between an early era of slow reading and a present of immediate reactions, it is possible to notice within *any* artwork two tendencies or temporal economies: the connective delays of cognition versus the immediacy of affective stimulus. There is nevertheless, today, a contraction or weakening of grammars and syntaxes of cognition in the face of the instant gratification of affects. Computer games, and the cinematic and tele-visual cultural products that are inflected by game culture may have narrative and teleological components, but the dominant experience is that of intensities. A culture of shock and awe allows us to sit before a screen and enjoy the affects of horror, terror, mourning, desire, disgust, fear and excitement without *sense.* This has been one of the long running criticisms of the visual temporality of pornography, in which bodies and movements are displayed without any narrative framing, and certainly without the individuating temporal circuits of care that Stiegler regards as crucial for modes of becoming that would not weaken the human psychic apparatus. The distinction between cognitive-semantic and affective-stimulant aesthetic modes is not purely historical and operates in any recognition of an artwork *as art* or any text as true. Approaching a text as art requires that it become detached from its functional or communicational mode, at the very least allowed to survive in part as some sort of material monument. *The Prelude,* while perfectly capable of being translated can nevertheless never be fully translated without remainder. By contrast, a formal equation *if true* can be true only if its sense can be circulated regardless of its mode of inscription or articulation. If a text were to offer itself as 'pure' truth then its affective dimension, though possibly present, would (or should) be immaterial; by contrast, if one grants an object the status of *art* then one attributes some monumental quality to its materiality, some sense of an affective component that is that of the art object itself.

This dependence of artworks on an autonomous materiality that is essential to the work (whereas pure cognition or logic would aim to be 'substrate neutral') would still apply to digital or mass-produced media, for it is digital culture that manages to create an infinitely divisible matter. The digital codes that enable the continual repetition of a materiality, such as a sound, color or text generated by codes, may be purely formal and substrate neutral, but the outcome of digitalization is the capacity to reproduce matters without any loss or division of the original. It is the clarity of color, sound or resolution that gives digital culture its force, intensifying the capacity to experience sensible qualities in the way that it was once able to transfer semantic content alone. Digital culture could therefore be *either* purely formal and cognitive, with the manipulation of digits and empty variables, *or* predominantly affective with digital technologies enabling the simulation of stimulating matters. What is significant is digital culture's tendency towards a far more strict retraction to the digit or the circulating unit: even when visual culture is not digital in the sense of being digitally rendered into codes for computer replication, there can be a restriction of attention to the already established digits or units of communication. If one laments the waning of a culture of reading and the loss of deep attention in favor of hyper-attention then this may also count as a mourning for analog modes of reading, whereby there was not a direct passage or translation between stimulus and response but a delay in assessing what counted as a unit of information or input. The very history and possibility of reading relies on a complex relation between digital and analog. All reading operates by way of digitalization, or—as Bergson noted—a capacity to reduce differential complexity to already established units of recognition; without that reduction of differential complexity perception would be paralyzed precisely because the influx of intensity would be too complex to master or recognize (Bergson 1912). Concepts enable generality and reduce the experienced world to recognizable form to enable action: the simpler the digit, the higher the speed, and therefore the greater the efficiency. What appears to be operating today is a high degree of digital distinction and accuracy, precluding the need for interpretive delays. Digital culture would include not only computer digitalization in the narrow sense, but a culture of speeds whereby stimulus circulates without translation or transfer, where there is a single circuit of relay. This would begin to explain why attention deficit is actually the need for *more* stimulus—precisely because there is increasingly less delay or depth that requires decoding. We are at one and the same time constantly bombarded with new intensities, and yet the simplicity of the codings enables quick consumption, and then the demand for more.

The various diagnoses of attention deficit, which descry an over-consumption of affect, often rely upon a historical narrative regarding the dialectic between cognition (or reading *as*) and affective pleasure (or stimulant vision). The eye-brain is abandoning or self-extinguishing one of its evolved powers, and one sees this exhaustion of the power of *sense* and the hypertrophy of sensation not just in the proliferation of new media but in the invasion of new media speeds into traditional media.

Non-digital forms of production are altered, now, by digital speeds; 'high-brow' novels (such as David Mitchell's *Cloud Atlas*) are composed from bite-sized chunks assembled to yield multiple and dispersed viewpoints. Even seemingly slow and manifestly human-centered cultural productions, such as the unstructured reality television events of *Big Brother* or *Jersey Shore,* rely not on plotting and character development so much as the capacity to pick up or leave the screen at any point. Such works are unsigned or devoid of sense precisely insofar as they are less events of production, created to stand alone or possess a certain force, as events of consumptive immediacy: the camera simply takes up whatever is there to be passed on and viewed. It would be too easy and inaccurate to align cinema and television with immediacy and stimulus, and reading with grammar and deep attention. Cinema and visual culture can be both narrative-semantic and stimulant-affective, just as literary forms can start to emphasize episodic affects rather than narrative coherence. Perhaps the success of *Fifty Shades of Grey* lies both in its claim to be erotica, offering sexual stimulus, and in its repetitive and episodic form—small chapters that repeat phrases and described affects. (There is, of course a distinction between stimulus and affect: the former is neutral and pre-semantic, and could either be read as information or merely felt. But affect is often associated with the merely, solely or simply felt as though it were only stimulus; this conflation is at the heart of hyper-hypo affective disorder. For if affect could be distinguished from cognition and yet still have a non-informational or non-semantic sense then one might find a way of overcoming the deep mourning for a culture of meaning and deep attention without celebrating the brain's self-extinction. That is, there might be something like affect that would *not* be feeling, and that would not be reducible to the organism's stimulation. Something of this isolation of affect is being sought, I would suggest, in Deleuze and Guattari's (1994) idea of art as the production of affects that stand alone.)

Any historical divide or paradigm break can be intuited only by distinguishing tendencies within mixtures; there are no hard and fast lines, but there are dominants and distinct inflections. The capacity to reflect upon the relation between felt stimulus and conceptual order was long ago placed within the artwork in Kant's aesthetic: one feels the influx of sensation but not as bodily pathos. Rather, it is because the sensations are not yet conceptualized, and yet conducive to conceptualization or thinking, that the subject feels her own forming power. This feeling is not pathological—not a bodily sensation, and not emotion—but the feeling of the relation between the world that is given in sensations, and the subject's capacity to synthesize sensations. Lyotard, writing on Kant, referred to this process as tautegorical: it is not the imposition of the subject's categories, but the subject feeling itself feeling: 'Tautegorical: this is judged absolutely great because the thought that judges this feels itself to be great absolutely' (Lyotard 1994, 81). The feeling is not individual, but individuating, for it gives me a sense of myself as a forming power, as capable of being a subject. The experience of beauty is the experience of that which ought to find its way to some communicable sense, not the sense of what this object *is,* but a sense of how this sensation *would feel*—*sensus communis*. The Kantian concept of *sensus communis* anticipates what Stiegler (following Simondon) refers to as trans-individuation: technologies create networks that allow the reading-viewing brain to be invaded and constituted by signatures and speeds not its own. For Stiegler selves develop through the memory systems that at once expand circuits of thought beyond any individual brain and body, even though those very same technologies that inscribe a supra-individual circuit of thinking and reflecting may—as in the case of modern media technologies—become short-circuited, reducing the cognitive and affective range of the embodied brain. What is important in Stiegler's critique of current media technologies is that he regards media in all its sense not so much as mediation, or the means through which thought is communicated, but as constitution: selves thing, live, feel and remember through the inscriptive and affective networks of their time and milieu. For Stiegler affective force and range is diminished the more bodies are turned back and inward upon sensation and stimulus.

Closer to the Kantian legacy there has been an art-critical tradition of considering affect not as bodily feeling but as the sense of a work, where sense is an orientation prompted by perceived relations. What this implies is that viewed objects, or relations of viewing, have distinct promissory temporalities: reflective judgment, enabled by art, offers the sense of a feeling of humanity in general, what 'one' would feel. It is in this tradition that Deleuze draws upon Worringer's (1953) art-historical work to place the relation between cognition and affect within art history: early art is geometrically abstract, giving order to the world; but this is superseded by empathy or the depiction of organic forms that one might perceive and feel. Deleuze then places this historical problem *within* the work of Francis Bacon: how can one paint the body not as an organism one *feels* but as a figure emerging from forces not its own? Deleuze and Guattari also write a pre-history of the reading eye that is directly political: the eye moves from being a collective organ, *feeling* the pain as it sees knife enter flesh, to being a privatized reading machine, viewing the cut of the knife as a *sign* of a punishment for a transgression committed and a retribution to be paid. The eye becomes organized as a reading and memory machine:

> the voice no longer sings but dictates, decrees; the graphy no longer dances, it ceases to animate bodies, but is set into writing on tablets, stones, and books; the eye sets itself to reading. (Deleuze and Guattari 2004, 223)

This formation of the reading eye occurs also as the organization of the body, which becomes an organism in which seeing, hearing, speaking and touching all fold in on the private body who can now view the world as a single matter determined from 'a' point of order. (This organization is an event of deterritorialization, for a term outside the system of relations now determines relations from some privileged point).

With that Deleuzo-Guattarian work in the background it is not surprising that there has been a celebration of affect, as though affect would release us from the 'despotism of the signifier' (or, more broadly, the tyranny of Cartesian and computational paradigms). And yet it is the event of privatization, with forces or pure predicates being referred back to the single organizing living body that is celebrated by the 'affective turn.' Much of what passes as Deleuzian inflected theory champions precisely what Deleuze and Guattari's projected future would go beyond. While Deleuze and Guattari chart the genesis of the organized body from affects, and then describe the organization of those affects (now as lived) by way of the unified organism of the man of reason, this does not imply that they want to return to the site of genesis, return to the embodied lived affect that has been alienated by the axiomatics of the single system of capital. On the contrary, the problem of affect—the *truth of affect, which would be something like force as such*—cannot be retrieved by a return to the body. Rather, for Deleuze and Guattari, capitalism is not axiomatic enough, not inhuman enough. It suffers from an anthropomorphism that can also be tied to contemporary hyper-hypo-affective disorder. Capitalism, if pushed to its maximum potential or 'nth' power, would open the relations among forces to produce multiple differential quantities. As long as everything is organized according to consumption and production (in terms of the digits of the private organism) the potential for forces to be produced—such as affects—will always be grounded upon affections. The visual production of the affect of horror or terror will be oriented to horrifying or terrorizing (as in many horror films or political campaigns). As long as affects are confused with affections, or feelings of the lived body, then nothing will ever be felt; the body will only re-live itself.

An element that has always been present in any work—the degree of lived bodily stimulus—has now become the focus not only of consumption and production but also of criticism and 'theory.' The 'affective turn' accounts for the emergence of language, music, morality and art in general by referring to the lived body's desire for self-maintenance. (In a similar manner the ethical turn was also a turn *back* to social relations, feelings and duties: and we might ask why this turn back occurs just as humanity is facing a world where there may be an *un-lived*?) Deleuze and Guattari offer a complex history of the relation between brain, body, intellect and affect, and follow Bergson in arguing for a history of thought's different powers, with technologies of concepts and artistic methods allowing at once for organic *unity* (the sensory motor apparatus that reduced all to efficiency) *and* for another tendency to think time as such or difference as such. Concepts, for example, reduce complex differences to generalities so that thinking can proceed efficiently, in the service of action. But there could also be concepts that destroyed expediency and action—such as the concepts of justice, democracy, humanity—but that opened thinking to a future. What might justice be? The same might be said of affects: it would only be by destroying affections—the ready and easy responses craved by our habituated bodies—that one might enable affects. If Deleuze's work has seemed to license a return to lived and bodily affections this should alert us to the constant tendency for relapse and re-territorialization in the brain's relation to its world. Deleuze and Guattari were critical of a historical tendency of paranoid capitalism: the tendency to read all events through the scheme of the individual set over and against of world of differences that can be felt and lived as his own. Any supposed private affection, they argued—including parental love—opens up to all of history, and ultimately the 'intense germinal influx.' We need to turn back from organized units and feelings, not to the lived body, but to the quantities and relations of forces from which identifiable bodies and sentiments emerge. The mother arrives as already organized, racialized and historicized, and (similarly) the love between any couple carries all of history and politics with it. In the beginning, Deleuze and Guattari argue, is not the body and its affections, but the affect. There is the force of knife and flesh, or the dazzling light of the screen; bodies become organisms through the affections composed from these potentialities.

So what can we say about both the 'affective turn' in theory, and the addiction to affections at the expense of affect, especially if we do not want to fall too easily into a joyful historical break or mournful nostalgia?

It is not new to diagnose an epoch. Freud placed modernity at the neurotic end of the spectrum, suggesting that an over-fixation on symptomatic displacements needed some release. Our desires, he suggested, did require some form of social organization for the sake of civilization, but with the stringent requirement to love all of humanity it would not be surprising if aggression would then be unleashed in the form of total war. For Freud, culture had become overly neurotic, investing unreasonably in what (for Freud at least) was a dispassionate (inhuman or overly ideal) figure of humanity. Today, we might think the pathology of collective desire differently. Perhaps we have swung towards psychosis—not so much tied to libidinal containment and repression as lacking all sense of order, generality, universality or transcendence. If Deleuze and Guattari appealed to schizophrenia they did so against what they saw as the paranoia of modern capitalism—the over-attachment to a single system in which any event or affect would be the sign *of* one single system of life, a life that becomes nothing other than the interaction and exchange of quantifiable force (a simple digitalism of a single axiomatic). Deleuze and Guattari's schizoanalysis would split or de-synthesize forces, not reducing all flows to a single system of exchange. And this splitting would give force a 'stand-alone' quantity, creating it neither as felt-stimulus *nor* recognized generality. It would short-circuit hyper-hypo affective disorder: the over-stimulated appetite for consuming affects alongside the hypertrophy of the capacity to think affectively. Whereas affect-empathy and abstraction-cognition have been noted as opposing historical and formal tendencies, the present's diagnosed retreat into affect-sensation evidences not a tipping into one of these modes or the other but their indistinction; it is as though there can be no abstract conceptual thinking that is not confused by 'feelings,' and no experiencing of affects that is not already generalized or pre-marketed and 'branded.' So we need to note first that there is a growing market in pre-packaged, already-consumed-consumable affections. And yet it is for this reason that there is no affect.

We need, I would suggest, a far more nuanced understanding of affect that distinguishes it from affections. If art and art theory have always had some orientation or sense of affect this was never that of a simple bodily response or lived feeling; what was attended to was not an affection but a force that *would yield* an affection. Affects would be 'stand alone' powers, possessing a certain autonomy. One would need to distinguish affect— such as the terror of tragedy—from the affection of being terrified, and these tendencies would have different temporalities. Affect would have to do with the artwork's capacity to create circuits of force beyond the viewer's own organic networks.

The notion of the autonomy of affect—or affect being corporeal but non-cognitive—was theorized by Brian Massumi, who argued for a range of bodily responses that bypassed conceptual or emotional sense (Massumi 1995). Antonio Damasio (2000) also argues that there is, in addition to the feeling of what happens in the body, another dimension of the organism's response that is not attended to. For Damasio this unattended proto-self is the ground and condition for the more conscious self, while for Massumi this non-cognitive dimension has a political force that needs to be considered today precisely because it is barely registered. But we might, given the contradictory celebratory turn to affect, alongside the mourning of the human loss of more sophisticated responses, want to ask about the contemporary specificity of this range of the non-cognitive affective body. If we are suffering from hyper-affective disorder this is because a potentiality of the body for undergoing stimulus but without conceptuality and attention is now no longer a background condition but accounts for the desiring structures of contemporary culture *tout court*. The social and political organization of bodies does not occur by way of ideas or beliefs—the imposition of semantic content or structure—but by way of affective addiction, either to the diverting stimuli of personal screens and headphones, or to the bodily stimulants of caffeine, sugar, tobacco or other widely ingested and publicly legitimated substances. If the constitutive human condition was once deemed to be *Angst*—a sense *that* there might be some event, without any fleshing out of just *what* that event would be—or if the dominant mode of politico-economic affect was once that of speculation (a paranoid control of all events into a single system [Colebrook 2012B]), then we can observe a new and possibly posthuman affective order. Rather than *Angst*, or the channeling of attention and investment into an overly mapped and determined future, we have perhaps become psychotically detached from any object domain, 'experiencing' the immediacy of affects without any sense that we are being affected by a world of which sensations would be signs. We may well be in an era of a new self-enclosed narcissism, each 'individual' being nothing more than a privatized bubble of instantaneous intensities.

Or, more accurately, rather than lamenting a narcissistic enclosure, what might be wanting would be narcissism: we are no longer entranced or motivated by a better image of ourselves. There is an absence of self-image, a supposed liberation from the figure of myself as a beautiful or worthy 'member of humanity;' yet it is just such an image that would release me from being driven by the immediacy of sensations. (Is not the popular refusal of stereotypes, along with a certain academic critique of normativity as repressively normalizing, indicative of a refusal of anything other than the self as pure performance, an affirmation of active immediacy and a horror of any element that would not be included in the dynamism of life that is always already the self's own?) Many of the celebrations of affect today, directed as they are against the linguistic paradigm or intellectualist or Cartesian accounts of the self, valorize a model of life in which the self is not really a self at all. There is not an enclosed individual who then represents the world; in the beginning is the relation or affect, from which some relatively stable responsive center emerges. Jeremy Rivkin argues not only that we are presently driven by affect and that affective bonds precede the formation of individuals and competitive aggression but that empathy is the human civilizing drive *tout court* (2009). Antonio Damasio, along with Joseph LeDoux (1996) and Maturana and Varela (1987)—and many supposed Deleuzians continuing their emphasis on embodiment and living systems—have turned theory and analysis away from the cognitive, conceptual or reflective dimensions of experience towards embodied, distributed and autopoietic selves. Damasio argues that the background self is largely unnoticed, and that 'Descartes' error' consisted in taking the fragment of the responsive self that came to attention as some sort of center or representing 'theatre.' Maturana and Varela, insisting on the embodied nature of the mind, reject the notion of 'a' world that would then be pictured or known by a distinct self. There is no world in general, no subject in itself; the world is always given *for* this or that living system and *as* this domain or horizon of possible affects to which bodies would respond. The Cartesian subject is not only a philosophical error; it is embedded in a tradition of Western individualism in which minds are set over against a world that they quantify and master. A more mindful tradition, closer to Buddhist models of selflessness, would not only be more correct, but may help us in domains as diverse as artificial intelligence and management studies (Flanagan 2007).

All these turns in theory are, I would suggest, *both* expressive of and reactions against hyper-hypo affective disorder. That is, it is precisely at the point at which we have become glutted with affect—so consuming of affects in a blind and frenzied manner—that theory insists upon the intelligence and profundity of affect. This complex reaction formation is similar to the three sides of the obesity epidemic: we stuff ourselves full of food at indiscriminate speeds, cannot taste or discern anything outside its pre-branding (for we have to be alerted to a food being 'chicken-fla-vored') and yet all this is accompanied by a new genre of food porn: master chef competitions, the spectacle of celebrity chefs, restaurant menus that require literary criticism and the migration of artful food depictions from the genre of still life to advertising. Similarly, we gorge on affections yet cannot get the sense of any affect, and all the while live in an age of theory that wallows in the autonomy of affect. Whether we regard the predominantly affective self as a loss of a subject whose identity would yield greater social responsibility and awareness (mourning cognition and grammar in the widespread loss of attention), or whether we see the Cartesian tradition as something better left behind, there seems to be agreement that there has been some affective turn (Gregg and Seigworth 2010; Clough and Halley 2007). This occurs not only at the level of theory, where we recognize the error of the linguistic paradigm or the cognitive or computational models of the self; it also occurs in a widespread shift in perceptual mechanisms and relations.

It is possible to say that that we are indulging in affective over-consumption and that cinematic and marketing devices have responded by remaining constantly innovative: the genre of 'torture porn' both reflects and reflects upon this hyper-affective addiction trend. On the other hand, if it is possible to note a deterioration of the traditionally bounded and individuated subject, alongside an atrophy of the narrative or novelistic imagination of a life lived as a trajectory towards wholeness, recognition and social meaning—whereby I consider myself from the point of view of the better self I would like others to see me as being—it is also possible to note a contrary tendency towards waning of affect. I would, though, want to give this notion of affective hypertrophy a different inflection from Fredric Jameson's criticism of a postmodern subject who, deprived of historical connectedness and any broad political sense, becomes nothing more than a schizoid field of intensities, caring little about social trajectories or class consciousness (Jameson 1991). In many respects hypo-affective disorder occurs alongside a strongly informational, if not narrative, attentiveness. There is no shortage of information about the dire threats posed not only to the future of the human species, but also to the current financial, ecological, political and bureaucratic systems upon which present generations rely in order to survive. Predictions regarding catastrophic economic disorder, imminent resource depletion, viral devastation, chemical warfare, bio-terrorism, rogue states in possession of nuclear weapons or unforeseen disasters brought about by various genetic technologies seem to have had little effect on behavior and decision making *despite* their widespread narration and imaginative rehearsal. In addition to explicit thought experiments such as Alan Weisman's *World Without Us* or the television series *Life Without Humans,* or one-off documentaries such as *Aftermath,* cinema of the last decade has intensified and multiplied a long-standing tradition of disaster epics entertaining the possibility of the annihilation of the species. Whereas these were once imagined as exogenous events (usually the invasion of alien species), climate change and viral threats now dominate the cinematic imaginary. Novels such as McCarthy's *The Road* or Atwood's *Oryx and Crake* begin in a world in which devastation has occurred; just what event led to such a situation can quite easily remain unstated precisely because the idea of a near-posthuman world is today utterly plausible. To call such novels or films post-apocalyptic misses their significance, for there is not only no apocalyptic revelation or dramatic disclosure, there is also no real sense that there need be a radical intrusion or disturbance for such worlds of depletion and posthumanity to appear. Yet, despite all this information and narrative entertainment regarding humanity's probable end, there is neither panic nor any apparent affective comportment that would indicate that anyone really feels or fears the sense of the end. Climate change denial is one thing, and possibly more rational than climate change awareness coupled with minor delusory negotiations (such as cap and trade, mitigation, adaptation or any of the other bargaining strategies).

The affective turn is not then a solely academic or theoretical correction to the supposed linguistic paradigm of high theory; it is also a pathology of the populace (which is certainly not a polity, for it has nothing to do with bodies assembling to speak, deliberate and communicate in common). There is a passion for affective consumption that is *extensive*—more affective input please!!!—but inversely devoid of *intensity*. There is nothing effective or affective about affections; and this includes the fact that we constantly remind ourselves of the primacy of the affective and insist that in the beginning is the emotive attachment, and then proceed to act as if the same old cognitive rules applied. We recognize our affective core, repair our theory and then proceed with argument as usual. Our response tends to be pharmaceutical rather than pharmakological: that is, just as we deal with ADD by providing the brain with chemical stimulus (because ADD sufferers fail to focus because nothing is stimulating enough) so we have dealt with our affective hypertrophy (our inability to sense) by over-consuming and over-producing affects.

How then might we assess the seeming dominance of or addiction to the intensities of affect—including the direct marketing of affects in 'feel good' experiences or the horrors of torture porn—alongside the no less apparent atrophy of affective response to an overload of information regarding genuine threats to organic life? Perhaps the way in which affect itself has been theorized might indicate a peculiar structure that would go some way to accounting for this divide.

What if the *concept* of affect were potentially a formation that would shatter the organism's emotive enclosure?

It is possible to see affect as a *concept* in Deleuze and Guattari's sense: it would not be extensive—referring to an already lived and actualized set of phenomena—but would be intensive, creating new relations and lines of thought, opening different mappings or potentials among what is, what is lived, and what might be thought. Affect can be thought of *not* as the influx of sensation that prompts response or engagement, for it is in the *not acting*, or in the receptivity without responsiveness or relation that affect occurs. Affect becomes a genuine concept when it poses the possibility of thinking the delay or interval between the organism as a sensory-motor apparatus and the world that is (at least intellectually) mapped according to its own measure. If we do tend to conflate affect with emotion—if we do not mark a distinction between the feeling of what happens and a whole domain of pulsations and fluxes beyond the perceptions of the organism—then this is symptomatic of the tendency to reduce the force of concepts to the lived. And is it surprising that the concept of affect with its potential for thinking of forces detached from the lived, from the organism's responses, from feeling and from emotion would be reduced to an association with thoroughly humanized notions of meaning?

Such problems are particularly important today when the distinction between affect and emotion may go some way to allowing us to envisage life beyond the organism. For it is life beyond the organism—both an actual world in which organic life has been extinguished and a virtual world of potentialities that are not lived—that has become increasingly unthinkable. Such a world may exist (dimly) at the level of affect but not at the level of feeling and the lived. On the contrary, what is presented as potential affect (a world without us) is reduced to affections—feelings of horror that are resolved ultimately as redemption narratives. That is, there is an industry today built on the affective lure of humanity's and possibly life's non-existence: this would include high culture installation pieces that feature machines, mechanized robotic humanoids, lost objects and automated sound productions (something like Thomas Mann's camera without person at the end of *Death in Venice*) to popular visions of a life without humans, such as the sublime opening scene of Danny Boyle's *28 Days Later* of 2002 (or the conclusion of Matt Reeve's *Cloverfield* (2008) (where a supposed department of defense filming of the last humans to have suffered from a violent viral intrusion plays out to the film's end). There is a widespread circulation of the image of life without life, of witnessing without vision. Or, at least, one might begin to note that there is a disjunction between affect and the lived and that what might at first appear to be differences in degree—such that affect would be a response in the body's systems that would only partly be lived or felt—might eventually become a difference in kind, such that there would be affects that 'stand alone.' Now might be the time to begin considering affect not as the base or ground from which cognition has been abstracted, nor as a primarily embodied and *barely lived* near phenomenon, differing in its intensity from fully fledged and conceptualized experience, but as a power or force with a tendency to persist or endure.

When Brian Massumi wrote about the autonomy of affect he was referring to somatic responses that not only exceeded the cognitive but also the level of feeling and emotion. (His examples included a melting snowman and President Reagan. Images of both produced bodily responses that could not be mapped onto cognitive values of affirmation or negation, and were not felt as emotions that would then prompt action or belief. In the case of the melting snowman, the children who reported on their felt responses were at odds with their bodily responses; what they described as memorable and pleasant was—when measured physiologically by heart-rate and galvanic skin activity—of a certain intensity rather than to do with content).

> [T]he primacy of the affective is marked by a gap between *content* and *effect:* it would appear that the strength or duration of an image's effect is not logically connected to the content in any straightforward way. This is not to say that there is no connection and no logic. What is meant here by the content of the image is its indexing to conventional meanings in an intersubjective context, its socio-linguistic qualification. This indexing fixes the *quality* of the image; the strength or duration of the image's effect could be called its *intensity.* What comes out here is that there is no correspondence or conformity between quality and intensity. If there is a relation, it is of another nature. (Massumi 1995, 84-85)

The disjunction between quality and intensity may, in the case I would like to conclude by considering, be one of disjunction or reaction formation. That is, the higher the degree of threat to the organism, the more the quality of affect is that of terror or sublime annihilation, the more disengaged the intensity appears to be. 'We' late near-extinction humans appear to be addicted to witnessing annihilation, to the *feeling* of near-death or posthuman existence, and yet have no intensity: it does not prompt us either to action or to any sense of what a posthuman world would be. On the contrary, the more evidence, imagery, feeling and 'experience' of a world without humans is displayed, the less affect or intensity occurs.

In fact, both theory and experience become increasingly organic: with thinkers ranging from Maturana and Varela, to philosophers such as Evan Thompson and Andy Clark insisting that the world we are given is exhausted by the world as felt or lived (Clark 2003; Thompson 2007). 'We' are now living a world of popular, academic and 'high' culture in which scenes of human and organic annihilation are repeatedly and obsessively lived, and yet at the cognitive level we continue to affirm the primacy of the world for the embodied, emotional and living organism. Man is no longer *homo economicus* or *homo faber*, defined by enterprising activity or production, but by feeling. What is occluded is the *unlived*, that which occurs both at the level of somatic responses that fail to be registered (other than by their negation at the level of reaction formation, with the shrill affirmation of emotion). What is also occluded is what Deleuze and Guattari theorized in *What is Philosophy?* as the definitive capacity of art—an art that occurs outside the human and beyond the organism: affects stand alone, exist in themselves and cannot be reduced to the lived.

On the one hand this appears to be an example of a privilege accorded to high modernist aesthetics, in the assumption of an art object that breaks with the bourgeois banalities of consumption and enjoyment. On the other hand, though, there is a sense in which Deleuze and Guattari's distinction among art, philosophy and science—and, in turn, their geneses of these potentialities outside the organism—also breaks with the high modernist aesthetic of art as cultural revivification. That is, if modernism separated the art object from feeling and emotion in order to break with social codes and conventions of consumption, it nevertheless re-humanized or re-vitalized affect: that is, art restored *thinking to life and returned life to thinking*. There was a sense that critical art might return thinking to the sense of *its* own emergence. A debased form of this aesthetic occurs today with many of the wars on the banality of images (including the myriad of denunciations of the internet or mass media as dehumanizing—for such denunciations seek to restore individual perception, autonomy and feeling).

What Deleuze and Guattari suggest in all three of their potentialities for thinking—creation of concepts in philosophy, of functions in science, and affects and percepts in art—is a locus of production outside the organism and outside the lived. Brian Massumi, separating intensity from quality, nevertheless located affect entirely within the living system:

> Both levels, qualification and intensity, are immediately embodied. Intensity is embodied in purely autonomic reactions most directly manifested in the skin-at the surface of the body, at its interface with things. Depth reactions belong more to the form/content (qualification) level, even though they also involve autonomic functions such as heartbeat and breathing. The reason may be that they are associated with expectation, which depends on consciously positioning oneself in a line of narrative continuity.' (Massumi 1995, 85)

For Massumi affect occurs as the *event* or disruption into social coding of the newness of a (not-yet narrated or linear) disturbance.

Deleuze and Guattari, in their chapter on affects and percepts, give a relatively clear instance of the autonomy of percepts—prior not only to human, but also to animal life. They describe the stagemaker bird, organizing coloured leaves to assemble a territory. The bird is only able to move and self-organize because there are expressive matters that enable processes of assembling: in the beginning is neither the doer nor the deed but the matters to be dealt with (Deleuze and Guattari 1994, 184). The coloured matters precede and are followed by the bird, with the bird becoming a functional and defined organism through this assemblage of autonomous sensory qualities. When art captures sensations that stand alone—as though the perceptions of organisms would only be possible because of these autonomous potentialities of percepts—then this is relatively easy to understand, as though a Mondrian or Cezanne drew upon, rather than produced, the vibrations of colour. But how could we say the same of affects, render them autonomous, inhuman and inorganic, in a way that would render them distinct from affections?

There is some indication in Deleuze's book on Francis Bacon of how art might capture affect in its autonomy—not simply its distinction from symbolic orders and cognition (as in Massumi) but in its inorganic or incorporeal moment. Deleuze refers to Bacon's painting of the scream—not the feeling of horror, felt by the body, but a depiction through the body of the forces that seize it:. Unlike a viewing of *A Nightmare on Elm Street*, the viewer is not horrified—the work does not cause horror—but we are capable, supposedly, of witnessing affect, not as felt or lived but as force beyond the organism and its meaningful responsiveness:

> If we scream, it is always as victims of invisible and insensible forces that scramble every spectacle, and that even lie beyond pain and feeling. ... Bacon creates the painting of the scream because he establishes a relationship between the visibility of the scream (the open mouth as a shadowy abyss) and invisible forces, which are nothing other than the forces of the future (Deleuze 2005: 43)

But are these forces really affects, or the forces from which affects are composed? And is their depiction by Bacon, via the screaming body, really akin to the pure sensory qualities that we can think of in the use of colours or expressive matters? Some provocation is given by Deleuze's phrase, 'forces of the future,' for it is here that we might think affects beyond the era of humanity, both in traditional modes of literary expression and in recent genre shifts. How are affects created by art if they are not expressions of some artist's or character's psycho-physical organism? How could affects possess that stand-alone inhuman inorganic quality that percepts seem to do when they provide potentials for assemblages (rather than being derived from them)? There would be no easy answers to this problem; it should not be easy to distinguish between art that makes us feel joyous—tapping into our sensory motor apparatus—and art that *is joyous*, that intimates a joy outside humanity and organisms. (What, for example, is trance music: a drugging sound that detaches us from meaning and the traditional temporal lines of chord progression and development, or a physical pulsation that operates directly at the level of sensory motor response rather than thought?)

Canonical literature gives us some indication of an autonomy of created affects that are not those of the organism, as though art could give body to that which exceeds the lived. Adjectives such as Kafka-esque, Dickensian or Lawrentian and Orwellian refer to affective assemblages that are not those of characters. Nor do such affective complexes prompt us to *feel* absurd bureaucratic torpor, oppressive urban paternalism, phallic atavistic passion or nightmarish social surveillance: it as though these worlds offered affects as such, there *to be lived,* as if they existed as potentialities for all time, even if captured through the depiction of a certain time. Such expressions pass into common parlance and refer not to a style of writing so much as the potentiality of that writing to seize on forces that it manages to assemble. If we travel through middle America we might view certain scenes *as if* captured by a David Lynch or Raymond Carver. Beyond canonized art there are today many attempts to capture affects beyond the lived and humanity: books (and television series) such as Alan Weisman's *The World Without Us* or cinematic scenes such as the opening of *28 Days Later,* along with a vast range of unremarkable nature documentaries do not only depict worlds and life beyond humans, but can also suggest (perhaps) a melancholy or joy of a world without living witness. It would be telling, then, in the face of this tendency to imagine or contemplate joys, depressions, horrors and screams outside the lived—and right at the moment of possible human self-annihilation—if *theory* were unable to think affects beyond the lived world of the bounded organism.

Notes

1. http://www.fastcompany.com/magazine/38/roberts.html

2. Dan Ariely, *Predictably Irrational: The Hidden Forces that Shape our Decisions* (New York: Harper, 2008.)

3. Michael Hardt, 'Affective Labor,' *boundary 2,* 26.2 (1999): 89-100.

4. The very concept of expression presupposes indeed some separation within the subject, and along with that a whole metaphysics of the inside and outside, of the wordless pain within the monad and the moment in which, often cathartically, that 'emotion' is then projected out and externalized, as gesture or cry, as desperate communication and the outward dramatization of

inward feeling. Fredric Jameson, *Postmodernism, or, The Cultural Logic of Late Capitalism* (Durham: Duke University Press, 1991) 438.

5.   Mark B.N. Hansen, 'Affect as Medium, or the `Digital-Facial-Image" *Journal of Visual Culture* 2.2 (2003): 205-228, 208.

Chapter 5

Destroying Cosmopolitanism
for the Sake of the Cosmos

What would the value of cosmopolitanism as a concept be? How might it work and what problems might it resolve or transform? Today the term intersects with globalism, offering itself as a mode of connection or collective resistance that would enable a thought of some political totality or 'open whole' irreducible to the forces of the market. The problem appears to be posed, from Kant to the present, as a way of thinking beyond human to human conflict—seeking a higher order beyond interests of individuals and polities.

Cosmopolitanism appears to be a self-evident good: is not the very concept of the good oriented towards that which would be or could be a good for all? Insofar as we rationally will anything at all we seem not only to be claiming something for ourselves as particular persons, but also to be appealing to some ideal or idea as such that could be agreed to by any subject whatever. Cosmopolitanism is at once in line with a purely formal or procedural liberalism, but also has the benefit of appealing not only to that which 'we' here and now agree to be good, but beyond that to some virtual humanity not yet present: 'Cosmopolitanism ... starts with what is human in humanity' (Appiah 2006,134). If cosmopolitanism is a universalism that is also *not* the assertion of one's actual goals as the goals of all, but indicates an ideal of maximal inclusion and self-critique, who would assert the contrary? And what would the contrary thesis be? That we are all, inevitably, bound up with local attachments incapable of truly transcending the particular? No, even that suggestion is already incorporated in a good cosmopolitanism. We are all culturally embedded, and cosmopolitanism cannot be a naïve or violent assertion of a single and uniform humanity. Cosmopolitanism is not the reduction of all differ-ence to a single model of citizenship; it is, rather, an *Idea* of a polity—a gathering of bodies for discussion, decision and determination—that would not be that of this or that nation but of the cosmos. We might say that the cosmos is an Idea in the Kantian sense: we require the notion of the cosmos in order to think the relations among different localities, and this Idea generates a task for future thinking, but such an Idea can never be fully actualized or presented. Perhaps, today, this cosmopolitan idea is more urgent and more possible than ever. Surely it is the advent of (increasingly evident) threats to this cosmos—resource depletion, rising sea levels, global heating, desertification, species extinction, viral apoca-lypse, violent fundamentalisms, bio-weapons—that impel us to free the polis from the nation state and imagine a greater cosmos.

For is it possible to say any more that politics occurs at the level of the state or nation? If decisions are made in the name of national polities, such as recent decisions to put environmental policy on hold in the face of economic imperatives, or of the compromise of claims for rights to life and universal health care because of a need to sustain fiscal responsibility and corporate structures, then what one appears to lose is not only the space of the cosmos but also a certain modality of the future. Decisions based on polities of the nation state are enslaved to a temporality of com-peting interests, whether that be the political terms of opposed parties or—if one is dealing with nation to nation negotiations—calculations regarding markets, future flows of capital and investment and *Realpolitik*. A cosmopolitical imperative would not only expand horizons spatially—to think beyond the geographical boundaries that create political, cul-tural and imaginary borders—it would also necessarily alter temporal limits. Globalism as an economic phenomenon in which territories once external to the nation state are included in ever-expanding and mutating markets would need to be supplemented or transcended by a cosmo-politanism[1] that imagined modes of sympathy, recognition and respect beyond the terms of the market.[2] If cosmopolitanism were truly to distin-guish itself from globalism then it must not do so merely in a spatial and extensive manner (being more inclusive) but would need to differ inten-sively.[3] The cosmos would differ from the globe only if it were not simply the spatial unit of this planet earth with its already identified resources, organizations and geographical borders (all included in the systems and networks of globalism); the cosmos would, in its new mode, include a virtuality.

Traditionally the cosmos signifies an orderliness, suggesting that the actual globe as material entity is placed within, or expressive of, a broader harmony (a cosmos of the planets and heavens). In contemporary forms of cosmopolitanism such appeals to divine or eternal harmony give way to an imaginative supplement: whatever the world is here and now, with all its global networks, markets and power structures, there can also be the figuration of *ethical* territories. Above and beyond physical and political borders there might be affective or immaterial communities, such as Michael Hardt and Antonio Negri's redemptive positing of a humanity united by ties of immaterial labor (Hardt and Negri 2000).

> The political times and the mode of production have changed. We have to construct the figure of a new David, the multitude as champion of asymmetrical combat, immaterial workers who become a new kind of combatants, cosmopolitan brico-leurs of resistance and cooperation. These are the ones who can throw the surplus of their knowledge's and skills into the construction of a common struggle against imperial power. This is the real patriotism, the patriotism of those with no nation. (Hardt and Negri 2005, 69)

These territories would not be extensively spatial (a portion of the globe) but intensive—a space of infinite hospitality without limit, a city of refuge that occupies a virtual space, a community that is not grounded upon a common soil or even a normative notion of the citizen (Derrida 2001, 8).

Such a virtual or spiritual humanity (that could no longer be reduced to man as an organism) was already imagined by Bergson in his *Two Sources of Morality and Religion*. Bergson's work on the distinction between morality and religion was part of a broader project that aimed to intuit, from the actual world's present state of complex phenomena, the *tendencies* that had enabled the emergence of the current state of things and that would indicate possible futures. If we have, today, a complex mixture of morality and spiritualism—of closed self-interest and open altruism—this is because there are two tendencies or speeds that produce opposing (yet coupled) forces in the groupings of human bodies. Morality is an extension of the organic and material need for survival; it makes sense at the level of our merely biological or instinctual existence to gather into localized units, establish basic order, defend ourselves from others and imagine others to be rather like ourselves. If *instinct* is the tendency that enables organisms to act for the sake of their own preservation, then basic morality is instinctual. If intellect is another tendency—this time allowing for generalization and abstraction beyond individual survival—then this, too, would account for more complex social groupings—such as the nation state, or even 'man': such groupings would be based on a calculation of the present for the sake of a future that is akin to the present. I might die for my country, my children, or even act somewhat selflessly by consuming fewer resources for the sake of future generations that I imagine to be an *extension* of the present. Morality, Bergson argued, would proceed from social groupings and recognition: the intellect would not be limited to animal self-interest and immediate gratification of needs but would imagine a life beyond the present, and bear sympathy towards individuals beyond itself and immediate family. Morality sacrifices the demands of present pleasure for the sake of future security and the formation of a public good. But Bergson posited another tendency that was also a different mode of temporality: spirit, unlike intellect, was not generalizing and extensive (creating categories that would reduce minor differences for the sake of inclusiveness and efficiency). Spirit would slow down the speedy and manageable reduction of complexity and instead begin to intuit differences, rhythms and perceptions beyond its own purview—beyond the range of ready-made concepts. Religion is different in kind, not degree, from morality. It would be a mistake to see something like Pauline universalism as the extension of sympathy to include all of mankind, creating a 'family of man.' It would similarly be mistaken to see an *evolution* of monotheism as a movement of increasing abstraction and universality (Wright 2009). It is Bergson's claim that a truly spiritual religion is not more and more inclusive, but moves beyond inclusiveness and single groupings of 'man' and instead imagines that one might act and feel for what is not yet present, represented or imagined. For Bergson the spirit of religion has an annihilating rather than self-preserving or self-furthering quality. One may form moral frameworks for the sake of man, for the sake of those other organisms that I imagine to be like myself and towards whom I feel some (however distant) sympathy. Bergson's examples of Christ and Socrates, by contrast, do not extend sympathy to yield a greater inclusiveness or broader definition of the human. Their actions and teachings are not directed to some normative or general figure of the human. The intellect that will sacrifice the present of pleasures for the sake of long-term gain, efficiency and stability is surpassed by a spirit that can liberate the temporalizing and creative power from any body. Whereas the intellect uses the imagination of a future to calculate more efficient self-interests, expending more energy in the present for the sake of a greater deferred good, spirit can embark upon *deferred action as such*. This would not be for the sake of any already imagined, figured or felt good—it would be a saintly, Christ-like, Socratic and dynamic spiritualism that did not rest with any object.

Bergson is explicit that for the most part the forces of matter tend towards inertia: the intellect may break with immediate organic self-interest but will then be seduced by the moral image of man or humanity as a stable object with properties. It takes an *anti-social* and *anti-moral* impulse to break with norms, pleasures and habits of communication: 'Shaken to its depths by the current which is about to sweep it forward, the soul ceases to revolve around itself and escapes for a moment from the law which demand that the species and the individual should condition one another' (Bergson 1977, 230). Nature (by way of moral obligation) builds 'man' for stable and closed societies—akin to the ant in the ant-hill—but there is another impulse that is distinct from man's organic being and distinct from moral humanity. This creative dynamism is destructive of the closed figures of man, tearing the intellect from its forms and figures; spirit bears a supra-rational force, especially if we think of moving beyond rationality as the surpassing of any single ratio. There is something essentially malevolent in Bergson's passage beyond moral humanity. Bergson notes that such an individual reaction against collective moralism not only tends to close back on its own figures and myths; the creative impulse always works in conflict with the tendency towards inertia. There must have been a time, Bergson suggests, when there was not a split between an explosive tendency and matter exploded, when differential force occurred as such, without resistance. But those days are over, and moral man—global man with all his delusions of existing as a being with a closed nature—can never be fully surpassed by the dynamism of spirit. All one can aim for practically is some ever-expanding and ever-creative figure of humanity that would be relatively open.

Bergson's thought therefore anticipates the current predicament of cosmopolitical desire in an age of globalism. On the one hand political relations, geographical distributions, market forces and the residues of imperialism already include and anticipate all human organisms as a unified whole. On the other hand, a new cosmopolitics would allow every event of inclusion to have a destructive force on the very humanity that appropriates all others in its name. Bergson makes a distinction between static and dynamic religions, the former creating stabilizing myths and figures, projecting its own organic image of itself onto life as a whole; the latter draw upon already given figures but do so in order to recreate and open the image of what counts as ethical life. The former tend towards self-satisfaction and the rewards of pleasure, the latter towards a selfless and mystical joy. Both are results of the creative or differential force of life, which works against the closed and fixed forms of matter—destroying the actual for the sake of a not-yet present end. Following Bergson, though, we can mark a difference in kind, and not just degree, between globalism and cosmopolitanism. The former tends towards measuring its own movements according to the actual world: striving to achieve greater profits or even human rights for more individuals, improved conditions for more individuals, inclusion of more individuals (all the while maintaining the standard figure of the moral individual as rational consumer blessed with rights and moral judgment). Cosmopolitanism, by contrast would be oriented to the virtual: hospitable (as Derrida suggests) to an other who is totally other, who does not answer to or accord with already given notions of human dignity and whose possibility (rather than presence) is destructive of any supposed good conscience (Derrida 2001).

We are left, then, with a politics of the virtual that seems remarkably similar to a politics of the Idea. Kant had also, in one of the key texts on cosmopolitanism, argued that as a being of nature man could only regard himself as bound up with physical causes and passions. But natural being does not exhaust man's nature. The human species, though seemingly acting in a lawful manner when considered historically, is neither governed by pure animal instinct nor a rational law. Kant assumes that if we could separate man as he is *in himself* from the manner in which he *appears* then humanity would follow a prearranged plan in the manner of 'rational cosmopolitans' (Kant 1991, 41). Why would the 'rational cosmopolitan' be the figure that Kant opposes both to an animal nature that is instinctual and man as he appears historically? A preliminary answer would draw upon what Kant says elsewhere about the pure forms of moral law that we are capable of thinking but not knowing. If I were to act *as if I were a rational cosmopolitan* then my individual and worldly being (with all its pleasures, calculated interests, possible pay-offs from good actions and other motivations) would be surpassed by the imagination of myself as a member of humanity in general. I would not be a specific historically located and culturally defined self, but a pure will who could act *as if* my actions and desires were those of all wills for all time. Cosmopolitanism, then, is for Kant an idea that we cannot avoid; it is the duty to think of how one might act for all and for all time. If we can *think* such a will (despite the impossibility of knowing or actually becoming a 'rational cosmopolitan') then we ought to act in accord with such a possibility: 'Nature only requires that we should approximate to this idea' (Kant 1991, 46-7). The first manoeuvre of Kant's essay is, then, to place cosmopolitanism out of this world. It is an Idea, something that we can not see evidenced in history other than afterwards, via reflection, when we can look back on collective past actions that seem to tend towards increasing order. Because we only know human actions, and ourselves, in terms of natural consequences of cause and effect, and within a nature of physical laws, any seeming 'rational cosmopolitan' may, for all we know, be acting from local interests. As in personal morality, one never knows whether one has acted from duty. One can know that one has acted according to duty. Similarly at a global level, one can never witness benevolent humanity as such—one is presented with antagonisms, violent usurpations, wars, disputes over honor and recognition—and this because man is a divided being. Unable to remain in a state of animal inertia and security he struggles to conquer those others without whom he would not receive recognition but with whom he cannot live peacefully. Even so, something like cosmopolitanism will emerge: not through material and empirical calculation (which can only be a question of more or less sophisticated brutish self-interest) but through a nature that we assume, on reflection, after the event, opens to a human concord beyond that of our merely animal natures. Kant's idea of cosmopolitanism is not the result of calculation within this world, but intimates another ordering power liberated from the finite point of view of man whose world is only known as it is given to him, not as it is in itself:

> Wars, tense and unremitting military preparations, and the resultant distress which every state must eventually feel within itself, even in the midst of peace—these are the means by which nature drives nations to make imperfect attempts, but finally, after many devastations, upheavals and even complete inner exhaustion of their powers, to take the step which reason could have suggested to them even without so many sad experiences—that of abandoning a lawless state of savagery and entering a federation of peoples in which every state, even the smallest, could expect to derive its security and rights not from its own power or its own legal judgement, but solely from this great federation (*Foedus Amphictyonum*), from a united power and the law-governed decisions of a united will. (Kant 1991, 47)

Where Bergson's dynamic religious or mystical impulse differs from Kant is in its suggestion of the positive power of the virtual, and this may well mark its distinction from anything *cosmopolitical*. That is to say: Kant, like contemporary cosmopolitical approaches, distinguishes between a calculative, conflict-based, self-interested and antagonistic global warfare (even if that global war is one of market competition and political expediency) and the idea, beyond that, of a humanity that can imagine itself beyond any of the natural figures that have grounded its specific communities. The problem—despite the distinction in kind between a managerial globalism and an open ethical cosmopolitanism—is whether one can ever do more than *think* this potentiality as a negation of the actual.

This, indeed, seems to be the issue that exercises writing on cosmopolitanism: is not the aim for a plural world inclusiveness just one more way in which one reduces the world's differences to one's own ideas of humanness? Acting in accordance with duty is not the same as acting dutifully.

I may appear to have effaced self-interest, nationalism, global capitalist assimilation and predation and yet who knows whether this benevolent outcome is not the consequence of a will oriented to particular calculations? For Kant, one cannot *know* such a thing, but that is beside the point. We can, at least, aim to act *as if* we were rational cosmopolitans; we can imagine what such willed maxims would be. Whether any of the actual decisions we make would actually be executed solely with the view of 'humanity in general' (liberated from any determination of locality or history) would not alter our attitude towards how we think about what a good principle would be. Cosmopolitanism of this nature—as an Idea or infinitely receding horizon—characterizes the post-Kantian tradition that ranges, however diversely, from Habermas's ideals of ongoing critique to Derrida's infinite hospitality (even though Derrida distinguishes his city of refuge from Kantian Ideas precisely in its lack of a human normative dimension and its orientation to the wholly other). Positive approaches tend to locate the cosmopolitan intention not in a necessarily impossible 'beyond' but in the real, in the bringing into actuality of an already given potentiality. In the case of Hardt and Negri's *Empire,* it is humanity itself, in its laboring activity that yields a multitude that is no longer delimited by a normative image of humanity but creates from itself, for itself, nothing other than its own collective being. But it is just the language used by Hardt and Negri—'homohomo humanity squared,' the Christian love of St Francis or *agape* (therefore not confined to bourgeois normality)—that ought to give us pause (Hardt and Negri 2000, 204). Such an appeal to immanent potentiality avoids the crippling effects of what Deleuze (1994) referred to as the 'thermodynamic' nature of bourgeois ideology, whereby one recognizes the force of a moral ideal and yet also resigns oneself to knowing it only in its diminished and finite mode. One recognizes a call for justice, democracy, hospitality and cosmopolitanism but always in the deferred form of a 'not yet.' On the one hand I know that cosmopolitanism requires the surpassing of any given or particular norm, and yet I know that such an ideal will always be marked by a particularity from which it emerges. Life is deemed to be nothing more than the compromised actuality that we are already given.

Can cosmopolitanism find a way beyond standard balancing acts between feelings of liberal guilt and liberal self-satisfaction? Hardt and

Negri discern a potentiality not just for *more* justice, or even the intrusion of an Idea of justice, but of a revolutionary rupture from the present and within the present. The conditions of the present, such as immaterial labor and the networks of globalism, are precisely those that can inaugurate a new commonwealth that transcends localities, nations and state forms. Hardt and Negri's debt to Deleuze is by no means direct, nor straightforward. One of the clearest distinctions between Hardt and Negri's approach and some of the philosophical sources upon whom they draw is their sustained commitment to figures of humanity. Their call for an immanent politics remains wedded to the anthropomorphic tendencies of global, commonwealth or cosmopolitical figures and the residual archaisms of man that such figures bring in train. First, for Hardt and Negri the bringing into actuality of the new commonwealth is liberated from static and transcendent ideas of the state that would impose order and justice from without; but the image of a man who makes himself from himself and who exists, not as an isolated being, but as a creative component of a multitude that has no being other than its ongoing dynamic creativity transposes theological axiology into a supposed secular immanence. It is now not God who expresses his being through a creation capable of returning and recognizing itself in its divine and immanent origin; it is the human creative spirit. This much, also, was suggested in Bergson's dynamic religion that, like Hardt and Negri's multitude, tended to figure the future in Christian terms. Bergson defines mysticism as the creative spirit liberated from practical affairs and inertia, and it is because of its mystical component that Christianity had the potential to remain active, not simply resting with a negation of the world but proceeding to bring forth a new world *of life's own creativity, a creativity feeling itself in its own creative joy.* For Bergson such a power of creative life partaking in its own creativity—no longer stalled by meeting the needs and pleasures of the organism or society—found its end in man, and especially in the Christian man of dynamic religion:

> the ultimate end of mysticism is the establishment of a contact, consequently of partial coincidence, with the creative effort which life itself manifests. The great mystic is to be conceived as an individual being, capable of transcending the limitations imposed on the species by its material nature,

thus continuing and extending the divine action. (Bergson 1977, 220-221)

So, here, we arrive at a problem that is not at all extrinsic to cosmopolitanism. How do we conceive the virtual or futural domain that is irreducible to the ties of global capital and interest? Must it take the form of humanity imagining itself, of a city of refuge, of the divine? Bergson, via a thought of the divine, at least raises the idea of a life that cannot be identified with the organic or global, even if he then falls back upon an already given notion of the divine. As long as we think the surpassing of competing self-interests and organic expediency as being transcended by the cosmopolitical we still remain at the level of difference in degree. First, the cosmos, even if it is not a spiritually ordered or harmonious whole is nevertheless distinguished (by Kant) from the wars of competing social bodies or (by Hardt and Negri) from the globalism of merely material forces that do not yet bring to full potential the immaterial lines of affection, labor and communication. Kant will argue that the cosmopolitical order is the result of a reflective equilibrium: we do not positively engineer political harmony but can discern the tendency towards cosmopolitical peace after the event. This discloses a certain reason in nature, suggesting that human discord, war and aggression ultimately tend towards a higher stability above and beyond human-to-human conflict. This is truly, then, a cosmopolitics: human historical life takes on a cosmological dimension irreducible to the forces of the polity. This cosmpolitical reason does not emerge from political relations directly, but opens out onto another plane.

Even so, while distinct in order, Kant—like those after him—nevertheless sees the potential for a passage from polity to cosmopolitanism. The former achieves order among bodies (as a polity) but is then placed in warring relations with other bodies. The *cosmo*political is therefore a version of the polity—equilibrium achieved among bodies—that layers over the political: no longer sympathy, affinity and legitimation at the political level, but the same concord from discord manoeuvre taken one level higher. Order from disorder, equilibrium from disequilibrium, increasing generality: all this occurs at the point where the cosmopolitical other is not a distinct other (with traits different *from* mine) but is wholly other—human in general. Second, the increasing generality of abstraction of the cosmopolitical order becomes a way of *extending* the forces of globalism: either one argues that global economic, marketing and communicative lines can yield to a new commonwealth by being freed from strictly economic codes (Hardt and Negri) or one posits a critical cosmopolitanism where the economic violence of globalism is reflected upon by a cosmopolitical perspective that never frees itself from, but is also irreducible to, the economic.

Despite Bergson's reliance upon (Christian) humanity as the means through which the creative force of life might create a new potentiality of dynamic spirit, he nevertheless suggests a different way of approaching the cosmopolitical problem. Consider, first, how the problem is posed, invariably passing from relative order to greater order: man as an animal creates polities—relations among similar bodies striving for ongoing stability of their kind or species—but these polities become warring bodies in turn. The problem is posed as one of passing from the political man to man in general, from the generalized and grouped to the higher groupings of a higher generality, from radical difference to increasing indifference. And this passage to the indifferent is disclosed in the ultimate formulae of a new cosmopolitanism in which I need not recognize any traits in the other apart from pure and formal otherness. This is at once an extension and fulfillment of liberalism, from Kant's imperative to act as a member of the kingdom of ends and Rawls's 'veil of ignorance' to Derrida's hospitality towards the wholly other and perhaps even notions of a 'community without community' that would signal the pure form of relation without being governed by any normative term. As long as the problem is posed as one of *cosmopolitanism* it seems that the passage towards greater abstraction, formalism or generalized humanity—Hardt and Negri's 'homohomo humanity squared'—would be the only option.

But is cosmopolitanism a genuine concept of the future that might help us to think twenty-first century horizons? I would suggest that it is not, and this for several reasons. First, for all the laments today regarding the loss of 'the political' (supposedly vanquished by managerialism or biopolitical bureaucratic calculations of mere life), is the polity the best way to think about relations of force? Beyond the political—the gathering of bodies on common for the sake of decision and determination—now is the time to think non-anthropic relations, potentials and forces. The cosmopolitical, after all, is an extrapolation of the polity: a mode of harmony, order, humanity or citizenship that transcends, extends or emerges as the pure (or purer) form of the polity. The problems we encounter today, ranging from a global financial system without center, accountability, rationality or future to a planetary destructiveness that has resulted directly from the inflation of human sustainability at the expense of other rhythms cannot be achieved by granting a greater ideality and range to the political, and certainly not by positing a cosmic (or higher order) harmony that would supplement or override human conflict.

Second, if we accept that the cosmopolitical imperatives of hospitality, community, humanity or refuge occur as a passage from necessary conflict—what Kant refers to as 'childish malice and destructiveness' or what Bergson describes as the enclosure within the organism—towards a higher order equilibrium, then the cosmopolitical would always have as its basic terms the already formed and bounded units of the aggressive individual. Politics and order, even when stretched to its highest ideals, would be a question of negotiating the degree to which the forces of these individuals could be combined to form some higher order individual. In Kant war is defined as a consequence of the human species' strange threshold condition: neither governed by animal instinct nor capable of intuiting the rational cosmopolitanism that would be their pure ideal, humans live with each other for the sake of recognition, yet cannot abide each other because of their competing desires. For Bergson, however, the situation is slightly different: there is a conflict or warring power in the impulse of life as such. Creativity is at once explosive—pulverizing inert and closed forms—and yet always coming up against its past created forms. It is intellect, after all, that frees the human organism from the self-interests of animal instinct (by calculating on a more efficient expenditure of deferred energy), and yet this same intellect maps the future according to already determined units. Perhaps this is one way of understanding contemporary globalism, at once extending itself to all territories in an all inclusive manner but—in reaching the limits of its coherence—failing to adjust its measurements of profit, efficiency, expansion and enterprise. One might say the same about any form of cosmopolitanism that wanted to redeem globalism by reaching a greater or more open humanity; it would only be an extension by degree, not a difference

in kind. But if life itself in its creative dynamism is, on Bergson's suggestion, already at war with itself, creating the very obstacles to its own forward movement, obstacles that in turn require a greater creative 'thrust,'
is there another way to think the passage beyond global war?

This leads to the third, and final, objection to cosmopolitanism already
hinted at earlier. The very nature of the politics of cosmopolitanism is
bourgeois and thermodynamic: calculating the relation among forces in
terms of management of degrees, or more or less, and of compromise.
Yes, we want an all inclusive humanity, but not one of the market. Yes we
want equality, but not the reduction of all human cultures to one standard. Yes, we want multiculturalism but not the narcissism of small differences. Yes, we want the rights and freedoms of the enlightenment but
should be wary of universalizing specifically modern Western values. In
criticizing bourgeois ideology as thermodynamic Deleuze was drawing
attention to the crippling and self-important nature of notions of political
compromise: on the one hand I maintain certain norms and values—this
gives me the individual identity that allows me to be a moral individual.
Yet, on the other hand I am aware that those values are provisional, culturally and historically specific and never fully universalizable.

Deleuze signals an alternative mode for thinking 'political' concepts
(although it needs to be borne in mind that all his and Guattari's political terms—including *micro*political and *schizo*analysis—decompose
psyches and individuals into forces and relations). If one began, not from
models of mediation, more and less, or greater and expanded models of
hospitality, but from *differential calculus* then forces would not be forces
of bodies and the cosmos would need to be considered beyond the polity.

In the plateau of *A Thousand Plateaus* that deals, however fleetingly,
with the cosmos, Deleuze and Guattari achieve two conceptual manoeuvres. Before one can think of the cosmos as a deterritorialization of the
earth or territory, one also needs to see earth and territory as themselves
assembled from forces of chaos (with their attendant autonomous qualities): 'The forces to be captured are no longer those of the earth, which
still constitute a great expressive Form, but the forces of an immaterial,
nonformal, and energetic Cosmos' (Deleuze and Guattari 1987, 342-
343). That is, any world, earth, territory or globe (including the globe of
globalism) is assembled from powers that are not those of the organism.

On the contrary, it is from the assembling of expressive qualities that something like an individuated body can emerge. Deleuze and Guattari here (and in *What is Philosophy?*) cite the stagemaker bird, whose turning over of leaves to display their lighter side creates a territory of found qualities; it is this formation of assembled qualities that creates individuation. There is a selection *from chaos* of materials that are not indifferent but that possess various potentials for relations and distinctions. Thus any earth or territory has already resulted from the assembling of qualities. Today's figure of the globe, for example, is not arbitrary and relies on the selection of qualities—such as the spherical planet, the generic image of the human being as a communicative, universalizing, enterprising and communal animal—from which something like the concept of globalism is formed. When these qualities are 'deterritorialized' or extended beyond their already actual form to consider virtual variations we get the cosmopolitical citizen: a man blessed with speech (but no language in particular), a sexually differentiated and culturally specified individual (but with no culture or gender in particular). We might look both at the ways in which a supposedly generic humanity draws upon a range of expressive qualities—from the figure of face and voice to the motifs of family, sexual difference and skin color—and at how the composed 'family of man' then allows for extension (or deterritorialization) to a cosmos that is always *cosmopolitical*. That is, the cosmos is always an extension of the composed polity, an abstraction or idealization of man englobed in his world of human others.

If the first feature of Deleuze and Guattari's concept of the cosmos is that it is not cosmopolitical—for the cosmos can occur as the deterritorialization of *non*-human forces—the second is that (at least in this plateau) it bears a direct relation to music. But this is the case only if music is defined as the relations of qualities and differences, the power to form inflections and rhythms *from which* something like the human practice and culture of music emerged:

> The T factor, the territorializing factor, must be sought elsewhere: precisely in the becoming-expressive of rhythm or melody, in other words, in the emergence of proper qualities (color, odor, sound, silhouette...).

Can this becoming, this emergence, be called Art? That would make the territory the result of art. The artist: the first person to set out a boundary stone, or to make a mark. Property, collective or individual, is derived from that even when it is in the service of war and oppression. ... The expressive is primary in relation to the possessive; expressive qualities, or matters of expression, are necessarily appropriative and constitute a having more profound than being. (Deleuze and Guattari 1987, 316)

There is a pre-human and pre-organic music that is generated from the differential relations among expressive qualities: the beating out of a rhythm establishes a pulse or band of time from which something like a meter might be organized. There is an articulation of sounds into tonal inflections that provides the condition for something like a scale or melody (or phonemes). Before there is something like a language— a repeatable and formalized set of relations—there must be the formation of qualities and the creation of differences. (One can think here of Freud's example of his grandson establishing a pulsation of *Fort-Da*, opposing two sounds across space and time, securing a territory that then enables the forming of a body and its world.) And it is here that we can tie Deleuze and Guattari's plateau on the refrain (where cosmos is conceptualized) with Deleuze's idea of a differential mode of thinking. Deleuze and Guattari insist that there is an autonomy or differential power in expressive qualities. Relatively stable terms or beings are formed from pure predicates or qualities. One might say that 'man' as a rational animal who is defined through the speaking-seeing-eating figure of the face and voice has a *political* composition (for it determines relations among human bodies) but this occurs *after* the entering-into-relation of certain qualities. Man is an animal assembled through the speaking-seeing face (itself composed racially of skin colors), the commanding voice (again enabled through the composition of a phonematic spectrum) and the organized body (effected by bringing the hand-eye-brain complex into relation.) There is, in this respect, nothing *political* about the cosmos as long as we take politics to be the relations of the polity. On the contrary, the most important events are micro-political: how did this figure of political man (with the eye of judgment, voice of reason and body of labor) come to be composed from the forces of chaos? Such a determination would have been enabled by certain expressive qualities—the potentialities of sound in the voice, of light in the seeing eye, of conceptual configurations in the reasoning brain. Such qualities are synthesized and coordinated to produce the man of politics. To define the proper destiny of man to be that of a cosmo-political animal is to contain thinking within the already formed bounds of the organism. A differential politics, by contrast, approaches the cosmos as a radical *deterritorialization,* freeing expressive qualities from a human-all-too-human composition:

> For there is no imagination outside of technique. The modern figure is not the child or the lunatic, still less the artist, but the cosmic artisan: a homemade atomic bomb—it's very simple really, it's been proven, it's been done. To be an artisan and no longer an artist, creator, or founder, is the only way to become cosmic, to leave the milieus and the earth behind. The invocation to the Cosmos does not at all operate as a metaphor; on the contrary, the operation is an effective one, from the moment the artist connects a material with forces of consistency or consolidation. (Deleuze and Guattari 1987, 345)

How might we think this meditation on the limits of cosmopolitanism in concrete terms? What would Deleuze and Guattari's suggested cosmic release of matters mean, or—more accurately, since it is no longer a question of meaning or symbols—how might such deterritorialization work? Consider one of the problems of the twenty-first century: water. At once crucial to life, water is also one of the elements whose relations to human organisms and polities exposes crucial fragilities, including water borne infections, floods, drought, rising sea levels and melting ice caps. Water has, of course, been politicized. In the 2008 documentary *Trouble the Water* Hurricane Katrina was an event that could not simply be referred to as a natural disaster but exposed political distributions: the absence of decisions, intentions, attention and sympathy that affected a certain geographical region of America that was also, of course, a racial and sexual region. More broadly, and also in 2008, *Flow: For Love of Water* charted the various ways in which corporations sold, channeled, marketed, restricted and managed water sales and supplies—rendering this most basic of *human* elements into a key political weapon and structuring cause. Such cinematic events gesture towards a traditional cosmopolitanism, both in presenting the local plight of Katrina to a world audience as an indictment of America and in exposing certain globalizing markets (of water) to a population of general human concern. The response to such demonstrations of political mapping would be some form of cosmopolitical activism: such concerns would—as in twenty-first climate change rhetoric more generally—be those of viability, sustainability and the maintenance of humanity. How will we live on, into the future, if this most basic of elements becomes politicized, becomes a weapon or resource that is subject to plays of power among humans? Another politics of water is also possible, one that would be musical in Deleuze and Guattari's sense (if music refers to the relations established among expressive qualities and their capacity to create forms, territories, identities *and* to open to the cosmos). We can begin by thinking about water's elemental or musical qualities (its semi-autonomous power to enter into relations beyond human polities) through Roman Polanski's *Chinatown* of 1974. Ostensibly a detective drama about the theft and re-channeling of water that is political in the most traditional of senses—to do with local contests and human interests—the film also allows water to become a visual quality. This is not when water is *seen or made visible* but when its absence or inhuman power takes over the screen: set in a heat-wave, the drama is shot through a heat haze in which the flows of human perspiration are matched with a barely discernible visual fluidity that takes the form of a slightly out of focus point of view. It is as though beyond the political plays of power something of the cosmic force of water—its resistance to human manipulation, its brutal and inhuman potentiality—threatens the person-to-person drama of the plot. *Chinatown* is at once about a cosmopolitics of water—about the ways in which corporate powers can take over local management and resources—at the same time as it is counter-political in its presentation of water as expressive or sensuous matter; water is not just represented as a human commodity but also takes over the formal elements of the screen, becoming an element from which the visual field is composed. A more specifically musical mode of cosmic deterritorialization occurs in the American composer Sebastian Currier's *Next Atlantis* string quartet (Currier 2008).[4] Here, sounds of water (which have been electronically synthesized, becoming almost melodic) are interspersed with sounds from the string quartet, which take on the quality of 'becoming-water.' At once the most formed and mannered of genres, the string quartet enters into relation *not* with the forces of the earth as territory (where water, say, is a humanized, nationalized quality) but with the cosmic force of water—its capacity to enter into variation and bear a sonic power beyond that of the polity. One might refer to such uses of the sounds of the cosmos as deterritorializing in a higher sense: the form of the work—its relations of varying sounds in dialogue—is also its matter, the work *is* the synthesis and forming—deforming of the elemental sound of water.

Why would such an opening to the cosmos be worth anything today? Is not the urgency of twenty-first century climate change a condition of such intensity that one must manage, now, as efficiently and bureaucratically as possible the sustainability of human life? Perhaps climate change calls for the most cosmopolitical of responses: the taking hold of the world's resources away from nation states and local polities for the sake of the viability of ongoing life. Such an imperative would, though, be in the name of the sustaining of human life, and of human life as it is already formed, already politicized and already organized. If we were to think otherwise, and if the crises of the twenty-first century were to prompt us to think at all it may be in a cosmic and inhuman mode, asking—at least beginning to ask—what the elements of this earth are, what force they bear, how we are composed in relation to those forces. If climate change politics has taught us anything to date—*if* it has, and *if* there is an 'us' or 'we' who might learn from, or be destroyed by, such events—it is that information and data directed to the maintenance of the polity has not yielded any affective response. Climate change skepticism is increasing, and this possibly because the cosmic force of destruction is now pushing beyond the *political* imagination, beyond our capacity to imagine ourselves and others like us in a future that will not be an extension of the present. Perhaps something other than a discursive politics among communicating individuals needs to open up to forces that are not our own, to consider the elemental and inhuman, so that it might be possible to think what life may be worthy of living on. Such an approach would require a thought of the cosmos—of life and its durations—that would be destructive of the polity, that would not return all elements and forces into what they mean for 'us.'

Notes

1.   Brennan (2001) argues that globalism is the economic ground upon which cosmopolitanism as a cultural and (putatively) critical phenomenon is based. He criticizes writers such as Mignolo (2000) who argue for a disjunction between a managerial cosmopolitanism that retraces market forces and an emancipatory cosmopolitanism that would be liberated from economic imperatives.

2.   Hardt and Negri (2000) argue that the economic conditions of immaterial labour in globalism allow for the creation of a commonwealth irreducible to any modes of connectivity and affect other than those of humanity's own self-constituting striving.

3.   On the nature of intensive versus extensive differences see De Landa 2002.

4.   http://www.boosey.com/cr/music/Next-Atlantis/54870

Chapter 6

Time And Autopoiesis: The Organism has No Future

There was a critical scene that was narrated frequently in the theory-frenzied years of the 1980s, operating as an often-invoked tableau that would awaken us from our literalist slumbers. The child faces the mirror, jubilantly rejoicing in the image of his unity :

> The jubilant assumption of his secular image by the kind of being—still trapped in his motor impotence and nursling dependence—the little man is at the *infans* stage thus seems to me to manifest in an exemplary situation the symbolic matrix in which the *I* is precipitated in a primordial form, prior to being identified in the dialectic of identification with the other, and before language restores to it, in the universal, its function as subject. (Lacan 1977, 76)

This scene captured the predicament of misrecognition: the self is not the naturally bounded organism (a thing within the world), but a site of desires, relations, drives, fantasies and projections that cannot possess the coherence of a body. There is a radical disjunction between the subject, who is nothing more than an effect of its relation to an other whom it cannot read, and the self, ego or individual that we imagine ourselves to be. It is the body as bounded organism, centerd on a looking face whose gaze can be returned by the mirror, that not only represses the chaotically dispersed and relational manner of our existence; it also operates as a figure of reading. We read other bodies as though they harboured a sense or interior meaning that might be disclosed through communication, and we read texts as though they operated like bodies—as well-formed wholes possessing a systemic logic, the sense of which might become apparent (Felman 1987). In this respect the Lacanian notion of Imaginary *meconnaissance*—where we live the decenterd and dispersed incoherence of the symbolic order as some illusory whole—repeats a criticism of the organism that goes back as far (at least) as Husserlian phenomenology. For Husserl it was quite natural to regard oneself as a thing among things, but that 'natural attitude' concealed the true nature of the subject: a subject who is not a thing but the condition through which things are given (Husserl 1965). Husserl, here, radicalized Kant's distinction between subject and body. For Kant, I know and experience myself as a body within the world, but I can only do so only because of the transcendental subjectivity that is not itself spatial or temporal. Kantian ethics, and the liberal tradition that follows from it, relies on this distinction between the natural self, that may be an object of calculation and science, and the subject that can neither be known nor predicated. In the absence of any knowledge or experience of the subject, selves can be given only through the procedures and decisions that they inaugurate. For Husserl, Kant did not go far enough in his distinction between subject and body, for it is not only the case that the subject in itself cannot be known or experienced as a thing within this world; the subject is the very origin of the world (Fink 1970). There can be no sense, givenness, time or being outside the event of transcendental synthesis. Although Heidegger would place more emphasis on Being's disclosure, regarding the subject as a clearing for the event of revealing, he also was highly critical of mistaking *Dasein* (a disclosing relation) for *das Man* (a psycho-physical body) (Heidegger 1996). This, indeed, was Heidegger's criticism of humanism. In a typically Heideggerian manner, Heidegger locates a moment of philosophical opacity and forgetting in a transition from Greek to Latin, from *legein* and *logos* or 'speaking about' to *logic,* or some preceding system through which the world would be ordered. Since the Roman understanding of *humanitas,* man has been understood as an organism with an additional capacity of reason (Heidegger 1998). The problem with humanism, for Heidegger, is not that it defines 'man' as a special or privileged being, but that it still defines man as a being. Man is not a being or thing, and he is certainly not a foundational being that would enable us to explain all other beings. A phenomenology of 'social construction' would, from a Heidegerian point of view at least, not be phenomenology at all; for it would merely have placed one more being—man—as the ground of all other beings, without asking how man himself appears. Taking up phenomenology in France, Sartre insisted on the radical transcendence of the ego: there is being on the one hand, which simply is 'in itself,' and then the relation of difference to that being which can never (authentically) be experienced or lived other than as nothingness, as the negation of what simply *is* (Sartre 1957). Bergson, despite his difference from phenomenology, also criticized the ways in which the efficient intellect would reduce all its complex experiences into stable objects; this reifying process was perfectly appropriate for non-living beings but a disaster when turned back upon the human knower himself who then experienced himself as just one more thing among things (Bergson 1931).

Whereas Husserl, Bergson, Sartre and Heidegger lamented (and aimed to correct) a history of philosophy that had mistaken the subject who was *not a thing* for the human body, psychoanalysis acknowledged that the condition of misrecognition is irreducible. There is a tendency towards 'organic thinking' captured in Lacan's notion of the Imaginary; we are Oedipal insofar as we consider ourselves as self-bounded bodies lamentably subjected to condition of difference. We imagine a form of bodily integrity that has been subjected to some prohibiting system or law; what we fail to recognize is that the bounded unity of the body is a figural lure that precludes us from recognizing that we are nothing more than an ongoing, dispersed and ex-centric condition of speaking being that can neither be localized nor experienced beyond law and language. (Deleuze and Guattari will not challenge Lacan's reading of the tendency of the human organism towards privatization, or to regarding the world of difference and relations as a nightmarish beyond. They will however write a genealogy of that lure of the bounded body, arguing that what Lacan deems to be transcendental is a historically specific condition of the modern speaking 'subject.') For Lacan, the yearning to retrieve the lost child who was once complete (before its submission to unreadable relations) follows from our organic dependence. The child appears to himself, in the mirror, as a unified whole—an identity. What that delightful recognition of one's bodily integrity covers over is the condition of subjection: that we speak and are, not through being our own self, but as always situated within a system of symbolic relations of which we are only ever effects. These effects are never given as such, but always relayed through relations of enigma, misrecognition, anticipation, projection and unattainable desire (Butler 1997; Butler 2004; Butler 2005; Laplanche 1999; Mitchell 1975; Wright 1984). In the beginning is the bodily image as lure or alibi that covers over temporal dispersion; from that initial imaginary unity we imagine that there must have been some other who robbed us of our pure plenitude, unboundedness and connectedness; we *read* this other as holding the key or power to our enjoyment.

This notion of the subject as formed through relation to an unreadable other has been reinforced recently by Judith Butler who has placed less emphasis on her earlier notion of the self as effected through performance of social norms, and has turned instead towards Laplanche and his insistence that our ex-trinsic condition of existence is one in which we are always placed in a relation of reading an other who is essentially unreadable (Butler 2005). The reasons for returning to, while adapting, Lacan are manifold. The Lacanian ego is at once formed through body image, even though the imagined body does not exhaust the subject's being; subjectivity is always other than itself, always split between the speaking/seeing self and the self spoken and viewed. Perhaps the most difficult aspect of this intertwining of subject and ego was the emphasis Lacan placed on the phallus, the body part that is not a body part. For Lacan it is the condition of subjection, prohibition and loss (the condition of speaking through a system that is not one's own) that creates the fantasy that there must once have been, or will be, mastery. There must be a phallic power of possession, even if it is one that I as a speaking (subjected) being do not have. Laplanche was explicitly critical of Lacan's centering of the Oedipal predicament on the phallus: yes, we are all constituted through a reading of the other, but we do not read that other as the one or other who possesses the phallic law, the power of castration. This liberation of the imaginary from the phallus would, at first glance, be an improvement: why should a body part be privileged when we think about the ways in which we fantasize our existence? For Laplanche there is a structural truth to the Oedipal complex, for every child lives its own world and history as if there had once been an integral unity that was then displaced by submission to an other, as though we were once perfectly bounded organisms who underwent subjection to an alien order. Whereas Lacan figured alienation in linguistic-phallic terms, with the imposition of speech being fantasized as submission to the law of the father who holds the phallus, Laplanche's 'enigmatic signifier' was not language in the symbolic sense but the look or gesture of the other who forces us to read their desire.

Now it might seem, today, that it is Laplanche's emphasis on the look of the other and each specific body's relation to the law that might be a more fruitful understanding of our body's relation to language *and* that this would accord, too, with Deleuze and Guattari's criticism of the tyranny of Oedipus and the 'despotism' of the signifier. But this is not so: for Deleuze and Guattari write a genealogy and diagnosis of the Oedipus complex and the privileging of the phallus. The virtue of the Lacanian critique is its ideality and inhumanity: before there is a human-human look or relation, something like the human organism has to be formed as an image. The body and its organs are historical and political phenomena. The modern man of capital does indeed live the relation among his body parts as Oedipalized: he is the man of speech who must articulate his desires through language as a symbolic order, and who will also live in fear of the loss of that order. In *Anti-Oedipus* Deleuze and Guattari maintain the importance of the virtual body part (Deleuze and Guattari 1977). The body has been increasingly 'privatized:' no longer living its forces collectively or intensively. Instead of the phallus being a collective totem, capable of generating the powerful spectacle of a tribal body moving in rhythmic pulsations, ears all responding to the beating tempo, eyes all feeling the intensity of the common spectacle, flinching as knife meets skin in rituals of castration, the body has become folded in on itself. Modern man is a speaking animal, subject to no law other than that of articulating his desires in speech. The organs are now private: the eyes that look out on a world as so much calculable matter to be mastered by the hand that will labour to transform the world into exchangeable commodities. This privatization of the organs means that desire can only be experienced as secret and personal, lost in its passage through collective speech, and never capable of reaching that full masterful voice of the phallic master.

Thinking about Deleuze's philosophy in relation to the body requires stepping back from a too easy dismissal of Lacan and the virtual body part. A social machine occurs when flows of desire are given relative stability: all the dancing bodies of the tribe gazing wondrously on the phallic symbol that allows for the creation of a territory. Body parts are always virtual before they are actual; the organized organism—where the eyes sees the same world heard by the ear and narrated by the voice—is the result of a history of co-ordinations and stabilized relations. Lacan was aware that the gaze of the infant was never a virgin glance: to look at a world of speaking subjects was to take on the history of the organism. For Deleuze and Guattari politics could only begin with this organized and Oedipal body, a body centered on the speaking voice submitted to the law of the signifier, always articulating a desire for a mastery and phallic dominance that is possessed by no-one.

Only if one acknowledges the crucial role of the body in politics can one begin to think the body without organs. In this respect if one thinks of the body as, say, gendered, then one buys into the phallic order. If we see bodies as receiving their identity through the imposition of social norms, then we assume a body as a whole that is then given identity and selfhood through normativity. Deleuze and Guattari take up the Lacanian challenge and ask how this dispersed collection of organs—the eye, ear, voice, brain, skin—comes to be organized as a speaking animal. Should we not ask how bodies that once existed through collectively intense organs—all eyes gazing on the cut into flesh, all ears feeling the stamping of feet, all voices screaming with the cry of a totem animal—became this point in space submitted to the laws of normativity? This means stepping back from *the* body to think the composition of organic powers, powers of organs rather than parts of the organism. Is not this what philosophy aims to do: to free the brain from the sensory motor apparatus of survival (Deleuze and Guattari 1994)? And is this not what visual arts aim to do: freeing the eye from reading, coding and recognition (Deleuze 2004)?

Let us pause, then, and look back to the theorizations of 'the body' that reinforce our sense, today, that we have overcome 80s textualism and theory and no longer assume the primacy of language. Judith Butler's *Bodies That Matter* of 1993, Elizabeth Grosz's *Volatile Bodies* in 1994 and then a series of 'body' readers and critical guides were not simple returns to the organism before language, so much as a recognition that the linguistic paradigm itself entailed at least some minimal image of embodiment. To say that the 'I' is an effect of language, an effect of the act or performance of speech, implies that one will at least imagine or construct some image or figure of the speaking body. Even if the subject is deemed to be effected through language, language can still create a body as constructed through a series of norms and figures. It was the status of the body *as image* that perhaps allowed for a confidence that one was no longer dealing with a literal pre-critical body; one could write about embodiment without appearing to be a vulgar materialist. Both in feminist criticism, and beyond, the body was primarily a literary and rhetorical problem. Although a great deal of literary and cultural criticism turned to 'the body,' this was always a consideration of how the body had been written, figured, problematized or constructed through various discourses (Kirby 1997; Wilson 1998). Even fiction (such as Jeanette Winterson's *Written on the Body* of 1993) responded to this trend of coupling writing and the body: to write or speak is to imagine oneself as a subject, but that imagined subject is always embodied, and the body is always constituted through tropes. (This idea of the body as being a 'lived schema' through which the world is mediated is sustained today across a range of disciplines including neuropsychology, linguistics and political theory [Gallagher 2005; Gibbs 2006]).

However, it was just this sophisticated post-Butler attitude of thinking of the body as *other than representation and yet constituted through representation* that precluded one from really thinking what the body might do. Butler published *Bodies That Matter* at least partly in response to the putative linguisticism of *Gender Trouble*. If we accept the argument of the massively influential *Gender Trouble* that the 'sex' that would supposedly be represented, mediated or imagined *through* cultural figures of gender is actually always figured as *other than* gender, then we also acknowledge that any appeal to 'the' body is a negative critical manoeuvre against received images and figures but is enabled only in its distance and difference from those figures. The body that matters, then, is not some brute 'in itself' that would precede cultural imagination, with cultural imagination in turn being some system that adds itself to a passive matter; for matter is just that which appears in the splitting of a seemingly prior 'before' from a no less illusory after:

> To 'concede' the undeniability of 'sex' or its 'materiality' is always to concede some version of 'sex,' some formation of 'materiality.' Is the discourse in and through which that concession occurs—and, yes, that concession invariably does occur—not itself formative of the very phenomenon that it concedes?
>
> [...] to refer naively or directly to such an extra-discursive object will always require the prior delimitation of the extra-discursive. (Butler 1993, 10-11)

There 'is' no matter as such, no body as such, only a body that matters—a body known only insofar as it is recognized—and only a matter that is given as there for this body in its potentiality. Matter is given only as lost, as having been there for the work of culture and speech. Temporality is at once that which gives matter; for matter is that which *must have been*. At the same time, temporality is that which is the other of matter: we live and endure as the same bodies through time only in the re-iteration of an identity; this iteration that produces the subject as the same through time is also that which, through failure, can disturb and disrupt identity. There is always, in the subjection to identity, that which remains other than the normative matrix that recognizes identity. Matter in itself would be imagined, mourned or figured as that strange non-identity beyond all relations of inside and outside, before and after.

Grosz's *Volatile Bodies* was avowedly less linguistically or—if we are not to have a narrow view of language—less performatively oriented. Butler took up the notion of the performative as the linguistic *act* that constitutes its referent. But this is an act that is not grounded upon a static body: quoting Nietzsche, Butler insists that there is 'no doer behind the deed.' One should not imagine that there are speaking subjects who then come to make statements about material bodies. On the contrary, there is the act or event of speaking from which one is effected as a subject who speaks. The performative is an act that relies on and maintains relations among bodies, granting and sustaining each body in its force. I can be a body that matters, a body who matters, only if 'I' act in such a way that something like an 'I' can be recognized. For Grosz, in contrast with Butler and a series of other approaches to embodiment that were even more constructivist than Butler's careful negotiation of performance, the body was not achieved through the act of performance, even if that act was taken to be that which effected the 'I,' rather than being the act *of* some 'I.' Nor was Grosz simply turning back to the motility of the phenomenological 'lived' body. (Recently there has been a widespread return and resurgence of interest in the lived body of phenomenology against the theories of language and cognition that paid too little attention to the organism's relation to the world. Such a return is premised upon correcting a supposedly disembodied subject that underpins Western reason and cognition [Thompson 2007]. Grosz's corporeality is neither the lived nor the constructed body; in fact, her body is closer to something like an inhuman embodiment that gives itself through humans, but is also expressed in animal bodies, and the bodies of things.) Recognizing that the very notion of the act, force, performance or utterance would require some minimal relation, Grosz's *volatile* bodies were poised membranes or borders, ongoing productions of an interior in relation to an exterior. Drawing on (but also surpassing) the lived body of phenomenology—insisting that one could only act or orient oneself in a world if there were some space that would always be the space for this body with its potentialities—Grosz also noted that this underlying lived body that enabled spatiality would in turn have its prior and not necessarily bodily (and certainly not organic) conditions. These conditions were explained by Grosz through the frequently used example of a moebius band: the relation between interior and exterior, the establishment of a bounded body from which potentiality and motility might be thought, could not be taken for granted and was itself effected from a whole series of relations.

The most important relation, both for Grosz at this stage and for many writers working on embodiment, was the image. It is with the look towards another bounded body, taken as the sign of an impossible interior, that I might also live my own skin and physique as similarly blessed with its interiority. To live my physical being and its potentialities both as *mine,* and as the ongoing subject of action, requires the experience of interior and exterior, the production of a bordered limit that would also be vulnerable to infraction and traumatic intrusion. What it means to be a self has therefore always been intertwined with what it means to be a body, and both these terms—self and body—have, in turn, been defined through a capacity of trauma, where trauma is imagined as the rupture of a border. What I want to do in the pages that follow is consider a series of possibilities: is it possible to think beyond that image of the bounded body? Such a possibility would be salutary today precisely because all those seeming gains in theoretical maturity that were won by posing the question of the body after the linguistic turn appear to be threatened, and threatened precisely because we can only imagine threat, trauma and non-life as *other than* the bounded body. That is, once it was accepted that bodies were not passive matters to be inscribed by culture, it was also acknowledged that the body's borders were the result of relations, encounters and—as Grosz so aptly demonstrated—morphologies: one can be a bounded body only with a sense, figure or image of one's limits. But this raises a problem: is life necessarily bounded and embodied life, a body of inside and outside? If we accept systems theory, body theory and the once-dominant idea of the self as constituted in relation to an other, then the answer is 'yes.'

There are, though, other forms of life beyond that of the organism, and beyond that of the autonomous living being. (Such a consideration can be read in Grosz's more recent work on Darwin concerning itself with a force of sexual selection that cannot be grounded in a body's or gene's survival: although sexual selection has a visual field and power as its milieu, it is no longer a visuality of the bounded image of recognition [Grosz 2011].) The departure from the lived body would need to be at least twofold, considering life beyond bodies and bodies beyond life. First, one might question the decision to consider viruses as other than life, a decision that is based on the virus as parasitic and non-self-maintaining (Ansell-Pearson 1997). Second, one might question the exclusion of techne from life: if one were to distinguish between life and techne, then a living organism would be bounded and self-maintaining and distinct from various inorganic or created supplements. But life presents us with a series of movements and mutations, such as computer viruses, technical evolutionary imperatives and the ways in which organs develop in response to machines that behove us to consider the imbrication of bodies and technology. Third, one might ask whether it is fruitful at this point in human history to consider life primarily from the point of view of the organism: are we not being forced to encounter the ruptures of organic timelines as we become aware of the depletion of the cosmos and the decay of our milieu, even if such erosions are never experienced or lived as localisable events?

Before moving on I would like to look back at the classic meditation on the image of the bounded body, Freud's *Beyond the Pleasure Principle*, where Freud posits that pleasure—the maintenance of a constant energy or equilibrium—may have some 'beyond' that would take the form of a dissipation of all energy (Freud 1975). The first principle of equilibrium and pleasure is still recognisable today in a series of post-Freudian observations regarding an organism's relation to life. A completely closed body that had no world would be deprived of the means of ongoing life; an absolutely open body without borders would not be a body at all, would have no ongoing identity. What is required then is a border or membrane that enables communion with an outside, but an outside that is always an outside *for* this bounded body, and that is managed so as to produce only the alteration or perturbation required for ongoing self-maintenance. The now widely cited and philosophically consecrated systems theory of Maturana and Varela (1987) deploys a series of terms to describe this necessity: *coupling* (where a body's autonomous or self-maintaining movements are established in relation to outside variables); *autopoeisis* (where the body does not interact mechanically with its outside but does so in a way to maintain its own balance and sameness); *relative closure* (so that a body at once maintains itself but also adapts to changing external perturbations); and *meaning* (for the outside of a body is always *its own outside or world,* experienced or lived in terms of a range of possible responses rather than an objective representation).

The ideal body must therefore balance two contrary requirements: completeness and self-sufficiency. A body detached from all that was other than itself would be hopelessly incomplete, divorced from the means of its own sustainability. A body must complete itself in order to maintain itself; it must not remain as some detached fragment but must be united or coupled with a world, open to what is not merely itself. (This requirement, as described by Freud, exposed the organism to contingency and the risk of loss and could lead to a destructive attack on the desired object to which the organism is subjected [Freud 1961]. The erotic drive to connection and completion, depicted by Freud's as two halves of a body seeking to be re-united, harboured an aggressive potential [Freud 1975]. The organism desires a plenitude or non-separation that requires it to go beyond itself, abandoning its original and mythic self-enclosure of primary narcissism; but it is just this overcoming of the violent self-containment of original closure that may in turn lead to a destructive drive to destroy the object that lures the organism from its quiescence. That destruction could even be turned back upon the self, after losing the object, if mourning is not completed in a life-serving manner).

Many writing after Freud have not regarded the organism's condition of coupling as anything other than benign, insisting on the originally world-oriented, meaning-making and other-directed dynamics of bodily life. The very logic of today's insistence on the 'embodied mind,' the 'extended mind,' the 'synaptic self,' the 'global brain' and even the 'mind in life' blithely sail over the deep and essential contradiction of the living body (Varela, Thompson and Rosch 1991; LeDoux 2002; Bloom 2000; Clark 2008). All the criticisms of the detached and disembodied Cartesian subject that insist upon the self's primary and dynamic connectedness ignore what Freud and Lacan recognized as the imaginary lure of the body: for all the self's world-orientation and openness there is also a primary blindness and enclosure that is necessary for the very experience of oneself as embodied, bounded and located in a milieu. As *alive* the body must be oriented or related to what is not itself, must desire a completion. However, because such completion is always sought on the organism's own terms, always for the sake of the organism, a body is necessarily blind to those forces that lie beyond its range. The very desire for completeness that drives the organism to couple with its world will also preclude it from seeing the world in any terms other than its own.

Whereas philosophers have happily celebrated this necessity of the world always being meaningful, or the world always being a world *for me*, we might suggest that such blissful enclosure in *meaning* precludes the very striving for completeness it is supposed to serve. The desire for completeness comes into conflict with self-sufficiency or the desire not to be exposed to contingency, risk or an influx of otherness so great that it would destroy all border and limit (and this would count as trauma).

One might say then that pleasure—today's celebrated processes of equilibrium, homeostasis and autopoeisis, or processes deemed to be synonymous with the life of the organism—are necessarily destructive of life that cannot be experienced in terms of the bounded body. Freud's second principle of a 'beyond' to pleasure or self-maintenance would not be in opposition to life; it would not simply be the death of the organism. Nor would it be a force regarded as traumatic, as that which is initially unassimilable but that could, through working and representation, be brought to coherence and sense. A genuine *beyond* of pleasure and a genuine beyond of the organism and its closed world of meaning would also be beyond trauma, for it could not be regarded as an infraction of the body from outside. This is precisely why Deleuze and Guattari suggest that one moves beyond death as a model—death as defined in relation to the bounded organism—to the *experience* of death.

> The experience of death is the most common of occurrences in the unconscious, precisely because it occurs in life and for life, in every passage or becoming, in every intensity as passage or becoming. It is in the very nature of every intensity to invest within itself the zero intensity starting from which it is produced, in one moment, as that which grows or diminishes according to an infinity of degrees … insofar as death is what is felt in every feeling, what never ceases and never finishes happening in every becoming—in the becoming-another-sex, the becoming-god, the becoming-a-race, etc., forming zones of intensity on the body without organs. Every intensity controls within its own life the experience of death and envelops it. (Deleuze and Guattari 1977, 330)

Such an experience would shatter the bounded body, and occur not as the body's other or limit but as a pure predicate, potentiality or intensity taken away from the coordinates of the organism. If we do not begin the question of life from the point of view of the bounded organism and its world, then we are compelled to think life beyond the opposition between pleasure and trauma, between boundary and infraction. Instead, one would note a necessarily self-destroying or suicidal trajectory immanent in life. Is this not what timelines of the inhuman now compel us to note, if not comprehend? A species can only survive by mutation and by *not* being itself; any species also—through that very survival—takes a toll on its milieu that might lead (as in the case of man) to the destruction of life in general. How could one define this dissolution as tragic or traumatic or, more simply, undesirable if one were not to assume already the primacy of bounded self-maintaining life?

This raises two questions for the future of this body we recognize as human, a body that is facing—today—two possible traumas. Has this body so oriented itself to its own sustainability—seeing the world clearly only in terms of its own perturbation—that it has no sense of the distinct perceptions and souls that are destroying it from within, and no perception of the folds and series that are traumatizing the milieu itself? Is it possible to speak of, or object to, the dissolution of the organism that we know as human?

How might we use these two notions of life—one that is bounded, embodied and open to trauma, and another that is post-traumatic—to assess what we mean by theory and thinking today? I would suggest that a certain notion of the theoretical, where theory is the look that we direct to our own acts of perception, has always been intertwined with a vital and normative account of life, and that it would be worthwhile to consider a theory that might entertain a thought of viral or radically malevolent life. In order to pursue this counter-possibility of a life that is not defined in relation to trauma, I want to conclude by looking at the ways in which a certain image of the body has underpinned theory and its temporality.

Consider a certain diagnosis of disembodied life that is dominant, possibly necessary, in contemporary thought. In a series of disciplines, ranging from neuroscience, cognitive science, philosophy, evolutionary psychology, sociology, future studies and cultural studies, it is now common to begin with the criticism of the Cartesian intellect. (The historical thesis is that there was, once upon a time, a unified human existence, where the self was defined socially and collectively, and where nature was not yet disenchanted or seen to be brute matter opposed to mind.) Various disciplines have taken up distinct criticisms of the Cartesian concept of 'mind.' I will take these criticisms in turn, and look at the ways in which a certain idea and ideal of the body-as-organism is posited as the remedy for the fall into the abstractions of Cartesian intellectualism. In contrast with a disembodied mind, and a matter deemed to be passive, mindless, inert and without relation, theories of living systems have sought to see any supposedly distinct beings as emerging from relations. The words 'autopoiesis,' along with 'homeostasis' and 'equilibrium,' operate across all these disciplines with their inter-related diagnoses of the present inertia of thinking life.

First, neuroscience: this mode of enquiry has benefited greatly from the decade of the brain declared by President Bush in 1990, and from the accompanying technological developments enabling new means of imaging. Although neuroscience is a diverse field, its very potentiality is marked by a single critical shift; the neuroscientist is not concerned with finding the 'bit' of the brain responsible for a certain thought or idea, but can now look at systems of relations. A perception does not occur in some simple one-to-one correspondence between object in the world and picture in the brain, but through complex and distributed patterns of relation. We respond to the world, not as blank slates being imprinted with data, but as dynamic and self-regulating systems. Life strives to maintain itself, and does so not by 'picturing' an outside world, but through an ongoing, interactive, and non-linear system of responses and adjustments. The non-linearity is crucial, even in the most simple of perceptions. There is not a self who captures the image of an object, but a body orienting itself toward (and anticipating) the world that is always given in a certain way. This dynamic engagement will enable the synthesis and relation to data, which in turn produces certain bodily relations, and these in turn allow further interaction with the world. If we want to understand thinking, according to Antonio Damasio, then we should not begin with cognition or representation—some mind housed in a body— but begin with the body as a self-regulating system, a system that does all it can to maintain its own state of equilibrium, and that will ultimately experience any bodily emotions or ongoing adjustments as 'the feeling of what happens.' More importantly, that process of interaction can only be between organism and world if there is some boundary that distinguishes between surviving life and milieu:

> the urge to stay alive is not a modern development. It is not
> a property of humans alone. In some fashion or other, from

simple to complex, most living organisms exhibit it. What does vary is the degree to which organisms *know* about that urge. Few do. But the urge is still there whether organisms know of it or not. Thanks to consciousness, humans are keenly aware of it.

> Life is carried out inside a boundary that defines a body. Life and the life urge exist inside a boundary, the selectively permeable wall that separates the internal environment from the external environment. The idea of the organism revolves around the existence of that boundary. (Damasio 137)

What we must remove is 'Descartes's error,' or the idea of mind as something distinct from life, for life just is an ongoing dynamic process of response, interaction, adjustment, orientation and—most importantly—*sense.* There is no possibility of a brute event, a body encountering a force that is not always already *meaningful.*

This insistence on meaning need not be an anthropomorphic notion. And to see this we can turn to the broader and highly influential theory of life as necessarily autopoetic, particularly as adopted by the cognitive science of Maturana and Varela. One of the crucial features of Maturana and Varela's work is their definition of life that requires some form of boundary or membrane. Their definition allows, then, for autopoesis and meaning. Life is autopoetic because a living being maintains its own internal relations; a living system must be able—through interaction with its milieu—to sustain itself. Living systems are coupled to environments that are always defined as being what they are *for* that specific system; and this is how autopoiesis is tied to meaning. The environment of an organism is constituted in terms of that body's possible responses:

> This basic uniformity of organization can best be expressed by saying: all that is accessible to the nervous system at any point are states of relative activity holding between nerve cells, and all that to which any given state of relative activity can give rise are further states of relative activity in other nerve cells by forming those states of relative activity to which they respond. (Maturana and Varela 1980, 22)

Further, life—unlike other living systems—has a certain self-productivity that is crucially defined in relation to that system's border. If a cell can live on, and even reproduce, simply by existing in its milieu then we can call that cell a living system. Its living-on requires no intervention of any process or force other than relation to milieu. A clear contrast, of course, would be a machine or mechanism; a typewriter can produce text if connected to a human body, an ink ribbon and paper, but a typewriter placed in its milieu—sitting on a desk among papers—does nothing more than decay through time (even if that decay is considerably slow). Maturana and Varela, tellingly, draw upon the philosophical tradition of phenomenology and its criticism of Cartesian notions of disengaged mind. As long as we define mind as a closed being that may or may not encounter some external world, and as long as we see that world as being encountered through knowledge, or perception as a mode of 'picturing,' then we will never understand the life of thought.

This brings us to the next discipline that draws on notions of distributed and embodied cognition, linear systems and self-production: artificial intelligence. There had been a criticism, early in the rapprochement between philosophy and artificial intelligence, that had insisted that—following Heidegger—it was the very embodied, active, worldly and practical nature of thinking life that precluded anything like an 'intelligence' that might be replicated in a computer (Dreyfus, Dreyfus and Athanasiou 1986). But those very Heideggerian insights regarding the necessarily embodied and temporally complex nature of thinking have now enabled new developments in artificial intelligence. If we want to create thinking we should abandon the Cartesian model of an information center that would direct parts of a body-machine; instead we should begin with the response. In the beginning is the action in relation to an environment, and this action always occurs in an ongoing process of adjustments and responses. Creating a robot could be successful, not by building an information-loaded brain-like center, but by creating parts that were capable of adjusting and allowing feedback responses with an encountered environment. At the simplest level, for example, we would have more success in creating a walking machine if we were to begin with leg-like parts that could roll and re-balance in response to surfaces. This in turn might tell us something about human embodied cognition; we are not computing or representing minds who happen to be placed in bodies that then have to encounter some world. On the contrary, we are originally responsive and action-oriented and also—more importantly—naturally prosthetic, taking whatever we can from the world as an *extension* of our already world-oriented and can-do openness to life:

> The old puzzle, the mind-body problem, really involves a hidden third party. It is the mind-body-*scaffolding* problem. It is the problem of understanding how human thought and reason is born out of looping interactions with material brains, material bodies and complex cultural and technological environments. We create these supportive environments but they create us too. We exist as the thinking beings we are, only thanks to a baffling dance of brains, bodies, and cultural and technological scaffolding (Clark 2003, 10)

We therefore need to rid ourselves of the idea of a mind that would be pure and would *then* use its body or supplement its body with alien materials. For matter, like the body, is always already familiar, already potentially available for the extension of our being as we make our way through life. In the ongoing striving to maintain ourselves all that we encounter may be incorporated, taken up as part of our ever-extending and constantly relational being:

> Autopoiesis in the physical space is necessary and sufficient to characterize a system as a living system. Reproduction and evolution as they occur in the known living systems, and all the phenomena derived from them, arise as secondary processes subordinated to heir existence and operation as autopoietic unities. Hence, the biological phenomenology is the phenomenology of autopoietic systems in the physical space, and a phenomenon is a biological phenomenon only to the extent that it depends in one way or another on the autopoiesis of one or more physical autopoietic unities. (Maturana and Varela 1980, 113)

Evolutionary psychology has also, in a number of different projects, taken its inquiry into the emergence of mind away from attention to cognition, grammar and formal systems, and instead considered bodies in relations that are always already affective, sensually attuned, emotionally responsive and autopoetic or homeostatic (on an individual and on a 'social' level). Steven Mithen has argued that before we have language as some system for conveying information, or before we have a grammar that would synthesize and organize a perceived world, there is an originally and communally-affective enjoyment of sound, that both gives each body a sense of its self in relation, and produces the social system of constitutive relations (Mithen 2006). Robin Dunbar has argued for the originality of gossip (Dunbar 1996). Against the idea that language begins as one body relaying content to another, Dunbar suggests that sound begins as a purely relational and communal phenomenon, allowing bodies to exist in community, through the feeling of sound and responsiveness.

These developments in the sciences and social sciences have led to the emergence of a narrative regarding theory and the time of theory. There was a time when, suffering from the disease of intellectualism or mind-centered (or simply centered) approaches, we examined social systems in terms of conscious agents. In so doing we adopted linear notions of causality, rather than looking at the complex, dynamic, interactive and materially distributed systems that contribute to any event (De Landa 2006). We also, no less disastrously, suffered from the linguistic paradigm, where 'a' system was seen as the ground through which we might interpret the world, when in fact the world is a dynamic network of interacting, affectively-attuned, responsive and self-maintaining bodies. Often this diagnosis of our misguided commitment to Cartesian notions of disembodied mind has been coupled with a moral program for cultural reinvention. Recent work in philosophy has suggested that if we turn to non-Western understandings of 'mindfulness,' where selves are not command centers but *properly* attuned to the world, existing as nothing more than a series of ongoing adjustments and mutual encounters, then we will be able to think more ecologically, less instrumentally and—most importantly— with far greater managerial success (Flanagan 2007).

The three concepts of autopoeisis, equilibrium and homeostasis function in all these domains, of neuroscience, cognitive science, philosophy of mind, social theory and future studies. These concepts all presuppose a certain understanding of time, and indicate that the organism has no future. The world of the organism is always the organism's own, unfolded from its own responses and potentialities; any properly futural future would be a break with the self-constitution of the organism's always immanent time, and yet all theories of relational organic life posit that without some departure from its sphere of ownnness the organism would have no life. In itself, or if it remains in itself, the organism has no future. There can only be a time to come if we open out from our embodied, relational, world-attuned being. The world within which we are situated—if we accept that 'we' are nothing other than the situated and responsive beings that we are—is always a world encountered in terms of possible responses. We exist in meaningful milieus. Our condition as embodied, as relating to the world *as* the beings that we are, is that the world is given *as* this world for us. To a certain extent, then, we are proto-ecological, originally attuned to our milieu. If we have a future, so it is argued, it cannot be one of calculation, instrumental reason and the mere continuance or ourselves in isolation. Our future could occur only if we remind ourselves of embodiment, if we recall what we really are and once again live our attunement to our milieu not as accidental but as intrinsic to our very being.

But there is another sense in which the organism has no future, and it is here that I want to turn back to the exclusion of non-bounded life from the definition of life in general. As long as we think of life as auto-poietic, as that which strives to maintain itself, and as that which is necessarily attuned to a milieu, we will regard disembodied life as that which ought not to have occurred, or as a simple error: a certain living being—man—mistook himself for mind, but can always correct that error and recognize himself as properly embodied. In defining Cartesian 'mind' as nothing more than a falsehood we will fail to account for its force, its persistence and the possible futures it presents to the organism that can only have a world of its own. Consider what needs to be excluded as long as we insist on life as that which is defined by self-maintenance: the virus, malevolent thinking, and inhuman futures. I want to conclude by placing these three excluded lives in contrast with three too-frequently cited normative bodies: the child, the Buddhist and the animal. In the current literature the Cartesian horror of the disembodied intellect—that is, the power of thinking that would not already be attuned to the world, that would not be affectively-oriented via a permeable border—is frequently cured by reference to animal, infant or non-Western life. The animal is nothing more than orientation or potential action for the sake of ongoing life, not yet burdened by the life-stultifying questions of the intellect. Animals also provide the norm for an originally affective and praxis-oriented language; birds and monkeys use sounds as ways of creating bonds or affective relations, not as the representation of some idea in general. The same applies to infants, whose perceptions are originally less cognitive than affective—seeing the world in terms of what enhances or harms the self, and experiencing sound as a sonorous caress (not as the vehicle of information). Finally, the Buddhist: if we suffer in the West from centered, disembodied, linear and instrumental notions of mind, then we would do well to pay attention to the eastern tradition of mindfulness. Stephen Mithen has appealed to both infants and animals as indicating an origin of speech in non-semantic but embodied-relational modes of sound, while a series of texts on mindfulness, including the work of Owen Flanagan, has criticized Western instrumental consciousness and appealed to the more attuned modes of Buddhist awareness (Mithen 2006; Flanagan 2007).

As I have already suggested, these ideals of a body that is at once identifiable through time yet also nothing other than its ongoing attuned responses must exclude other lines of life and time that are defined less through the maintenance of a border in relation, and more in a form of rampant and unbounded mutation. A virus cannot be defined as a form of life on the Maturana and Varela model; its lack of a border or membrane means that it cannot be considered in relation to *its* milieu. It does not maintain itself, and is not a living system precisely because it *is* only in its parasitic capacity to open other life forms to variations that would not be definitive of an autopoetic relation. What might the future or temporality of viral life be? It could not suffer trauma, could not be subject to an excess of influx that would destroy its living balance precisely because a virus is nothing other than a process of invasion, influx and (to a great extent) *non*-relation. A virus does not have a world: it is not defined according to its potential responses that would enable its ongoing being. In one respect then, it is only viral life that has a future: both in the sense of being able to live on (or more accurately mutate beyond itself) without its own world, and in the sense that 'our' future, our world in all its bounded and delicate attunement, is not really a future so much as the maintenance of the same through the constant warding off of a future that would be other than our own.

This brings me to the next non-bounded life, malevolence. If we are autopoeietic, embodied, attuned, responsive, dynamic and system-dependent beings, how is it that we have acted in such a way that we have created a future that will no longer be a milieu for the organisms that we are? If humans are so organically attached to a world that is itself a living self-maintaining and organic whole, how did the destruction of this symbiotic domain of life take hold? Can we say that the Cartesian figure of disembodied life as really a mistake, or is it not a more accurate picture of 'man' in the anthropocene era? This, I think, suggests that we need to consider the future that this non-organic, non-relational, rigidly disembodied life has allowed to occur. If life in its bounded form is relational, mindful, attuned, responsive and dynamic (and if this life has no future that is not always already its own) then what of the life that did not act to maintain itself, that did not respond to its milieu, that did not live with the sense of its trauma-sensitive membrane? As long as we fail to consider this life we fail to address the future. In recent attempts to deal with our future, and the malevolent damage or willful destruction we have enacted upon ourselves, it is often implied that once we recognize our truly relational and embodied condition we will indeed have a future. If we could only see that we are not Cartesian minds contingently placed in a world that is of no concern to us, then we will recognize our originally ecological condition and once again live with a sense of the world (where sense is mindful orientation).

One concrete example of an ethic of the future, based on a recognition of our proper embodiment, is the turn to mindfulness. From philosophy to business management, it is argued that if we recall to ourselves our intrinsically embodied and in-the-world being, then we will act with respect and care (rather than destructive dominance) to what is not the self (but yet is always already constitutive of the self). Do we not, with this faith in the malleability, adaptability and possible future of this human body that could overcome its Western violence and rigidity, simply repress and belie that other viral tendency in life? That other tendency would not be self-maintaining and autopoetically relational, but blindly active and mutational. What any ethic of mindful responsiveness must do is dismiss as non-existent, or non-living, those forces of viral malevolence which have, until now, quite happily proceeded to make their way through the world without a thought of sustainability, and without a sense of the human as necessarily relational, embodied and affectively sensitive. How might we act if we acknowledged or even entertained the possibility of this viral and malevolent life, and if we considered the human not as a body coupled to a milieu, but as a series of potentialities that could branch out into territories beyond its own self-maintenance. How would we act if we recognized that insofar as the organism's future is always the *organism's own* then the organism has no future? Its time will always be determined in advance as the time of its own relations; and without the recognition of that other life that destroys such relations the organism's time will come to an end.

A molecular or viral politics that did not assume the benevolence or trauma-resisting membranes of a self-defining body would have the following features. First, an attention to mindlessness: how do unbounded, non-self-maintaining processes—processes with no sense of relation— create a *political territory* that is not that of the polis or mutually recognizing bodies? And how do those bodies that we are, with only a sense of processes in relation to our own living systems—resist all recognition and interaction with the mindless? Why do we not have the strength or force to think of a world that is not our milieu? Second, a politics of viral futures: if we accept life-potentials that are not self-maintaining but that operate as nothing more than mutant encounters, then we move beyond *a politics of negotiation among bodies to a politics devoid of survival*. Perhaps it is only in our abandonment of ownness, meaning, mindfulness and *the world of the body* that life, for whatever it is worth, has a chance. This, indeed, is the direction offered by Deleuze and Deleuze and Guattari's thought: a capacity to take intuition beyond the organism's own duration to imagine qualities as such, a desire to overcome the brain of the organized body and approach thought *as such* opening to the eternal, and a relation between art and philosophy that does not assimilate sensation (the sensible) to what can be thought (the sensed) but approaches their warring disjunction (Deleuze and Guattari 1994). Finally, the move beyond 'man' as isolated thinker will not be back towards the body, but forward to the 'superman'—to the inorganic potentialities that exist now only in confused and all too human composites (Deleuze 1988B).

Chapter 7

Face Race

Defacing and Facing Humanity

The human race is facing extinction. One might even say that there is a race towards extinction, precisely because humanity has constituted itself *as a race*. The idea of a single species, manifestly different but ultimately grounded on a single human race of right and reason, has enabled human exceptionalism, and this (in turn) has precluded any questioning of humanity's right to life. In *actuality* humanity is not a race; it becomes a racial unity only via the virtual, or what Deleuze and Guattari describe as a process of territorialization, deterritorialization and reterritorialization. In the beginning is what Deleuze and Guattari refer to as the 'intense germinal influx,' *from which* individuated bodies (both organic and social) emerge. Race or racism are not the results of discrimination; on the contrary, it is only by repressing the highly complex differential forces and fields that compose *any* being that something like the notion of 'a' race can occur. This is why Deleuze and Guattari argue for a highly intimate relation between sex and race: all life is sexual, for living bodies are composed of relations among differential powers that produce new events; encounters of potentialities intertwine to form stabilities. Such encounters are desiring or sexual because they occur among different forces that create new and dissimilar outcomes. If sex and desire refer to the relations among different quantities of force, race and races occur when those productions of differences are taken to be differences *of* some relative sameness. In the beginning is sex-race or race-sex: the encounter of different potentials to form new emergent (relative) identities. Race and racism occur through such intersections of desire, whereby bodies assemble to form territories. All bodies and identities are the result of territorialization: so that race (or kinds) unfold from sex, at the same time that sexes (male or female) unfold from encounters of genetic differences. All couplings are of mixed race.

It is through the formation of a relatively stable set of relations that bodies are effected in common. A body becomes an individual through gathering or assembling (enabling the formation of a territory). A social body, tribe or collective begins with the formation of a common space or territory but is *de*territorialized when the group is individuated by an external body—when a chieftain appears as the law or eminent individual whose divine power comes from 'on high.' This marks the socius *as* this or that specified group. *Race* occurs through *re*territorialization, when the social body is not organized from without (or via some transcendent, external term) but appears to be the expression of the ground; the people are an expression of a common ground or *Volk*. The most racially determined group of all is that of 'man' for no other body affirms its unity with such shrill insistence. 'Humanity' presents itself as a natural unified species, with man as biological ground from which *racism* might then be seen as a differentiation.

The problem with racism is neither that it discriminates, nor that it takes one natural humanity and then perverts it into separate groups. On the contrary, racism does not discriminate enough; it does not recognize that 'humanity,' 'Caucasian,' or 'Asian' are insufficiently distinguished. Humanity is a generality or the creation of a majority of a monstrous and racial sort. One body—the white man of reason—is taken as the figure for life in general. A production of desire—the image of 'man' that was the *effect* of history and social groupings—is now seen as the ground of desire. Ultimately, a metalepsis takes place: despite surface differences it is imagined that deep down we are all the same. And because of this generalizing production of 'man in general' who is then placed *before* difference as the unified human ground from which different races appear, a trajectory of extinction appears to be relentless. Man imagines himself as exemplary of life, so much so that when he aims to think in a posthuman manner he grants rights, lifeworlds, language and emotions to nonhumans. (And when 'man' imagines animal art or language he does so from the perspective of its development into human art and language; what he does not do is animalize human art, seeing art not as an expressive extension of the body, but as an expressive matter in its own right.) Man's self-evident unity, along with the belief in a historical unfolding that occurs as a greater and greater recognition of identity (the supposed overcoming of tribalism towards the recognition of one giant body of human reason) precludes any question of humanity's composition, its emergence from difference and any further possibility of its un-becoming. Humanity has been fabricated as the proper ground of all life—so much so that threats to all life on earth are being dealt with today by focusing on how *man* may adapt, mitigate and survive. Humanity has become so enamored of the image it has painted of its illusory beautiful life that it has not only come close to vanquishing all other life forms, and has not only imagined itself as a single and self-evidently valuable being with a right to life, it can also only a imagine a future of *living on* rather than face the threat of living otherwise. Part of the problem of humanity as a race lies in the ambivalent status of art, for art is the figure that separates white man *par excellence*: humanity has no essence other than that of free self-creation, all seemingly different peoples or others must come to recognize their differences as merely cultural, as the effect of one great history of self-distinction. However, if art were to be placed outside the human, as the persistence of sensations and matters that cannot be reduced to human intentionality, then 'we' might begin to discern the pulsation of differences in a time other than that of self-defining humanity. Art would not be an extension of the human, a way in which man lives on and creates himself through time. Art would be bound up with extinction, signaling the capacity of matters to insist and persist beyond any animating intent.

Far from extinction or human annihilation being solely a twenty-first century event (although it is that too), *art* is tied essentially to the non-existence of man. Art has often quite explicitly considered the relation between humanity and extinction. For it is the nature of the art object to exist beyond its originating intention, both intimating a people not yet present (Deleuze and Guattari 1994, 180), and yet also often presupposing a unified humanity or common 'lived.' Wordsworth—yes, Wordsworth!—was at once aware that the *sense* of a poem or work could not be reduced to its material support, for humanity is always more than any of the signs it uses to preserve its existence:

Oh! why hath not the Mind
Some element to stamp her image on
In nature somewhat nearer to her own?
Why, gifted with such powers to send abroad
Her spirit, must it lodge in shrines so frail?
(Wordsworth 1991; *The Prelude* V 45-49).

If the archive were to be destroyed, would anything of 'man' remain? Art gives man the ability to imagine himself as eternally present, beyond any particular epoch or text, and yet also places this eternity in the fragile tomb of a material object: 'Even if the material lasts only for a few seconds it will give sensation the power to exist and be preserved in itself *in the eternity that coexists with this short duration*' (Deleuze and Guattari 1994, 166). 'Man' as a race (as a unified body imagining himself as a natural kind) is essentially tied to extinction: for man is at once an ex post facto or metaleptic positing of that which must have been there all along, awaiting eternal expression. At the same time 'man' is also that being who hastens extinction in general by imagining himself as a single tradition solely worthy of eternal life, stamping the world with his own image. This unified humanity that has become intoxicated with its sense of self-positing privilege can only exist through the delirium of Race, through the imagination of itself as a unified and eternal natural body:

> All delirium is racial, which does not necessarily mean racist. It is not a matter of the regions of the body without organs 'representing' races and cultures. The full body does not represent anything at all. On the contrary, the races and cultures designate regions on this body—that is, zones of intensities, fields of potentials. Phenomena of individualization and sexualization are produced within these fields. We pass from one field to another by crossing thresholds: we never stop migrating, we become other individuals as well as other sexes, and departing becomes as easy as being born or dying. Along the way we struggle against other races, we destroy civilizations, in the manner of the great migrants in whose wake nothing is left standing once they have passed through. (Deleuze and Guattari 2004a, 94)

Racial delirium is not only a passage through differential flux from which identity emerges; it also entails that 'we destroy civilizations'— affirming the potentiality of reducing any produced culture or tradition to ruins. Man exists above and beyond any particularity; as one grand racial unity, he is that through which cultural distinction emerges. If racial delirium occurs as an affirmation of the possibility of anything becoming extinct, racism is a neurotic grip on survival. Racism—including, and especially, the affirmation of 'man'—is a repression of racial delirium; racial delirium would open up to all the differences and intensities beyond any unified or generic 'man.' By contrast, racism affirms one great unity—the properly human—in which various kinds might be seen to differ by degree, being more or less human. Humanity is always a virtual production or fabrication that posits itself as ultimate actuality, occluding the differentials from which it emerges.

The fabrication of man as a race that at once enables the lure of essential unity, and yet places that unity in the fragile monuments of art today (in the twenty-first century) faces the actual threat of extinction. Given that threat, how might art adjust to a milieu of imminent, probably certain, disappearance? How might this race that has for so long surrounded itself with art, and mirrored itself in art, open out to the world upon which it depends but which it has nevertheless almost annihilated? How does the human race turn from mirroring itself, enclosing itself in the cave of its own images, to thinking its inextricable intertwining with fragile life?

These questions are not new. All art has the problem of extinction and race at its core.

Any sentence that begins with 'All art…' needs to be treated with extreme suspicion. The logic of racism, after all, has always defined the properly human from a single moment—deep down they are all (or should be) just like 'us.' And, as already mentioned, the figure of art is crucial to this unifying lure: deep down we are all human, all the same, and express ourselves differently in the grand tradition of human art. Such claims are less often made by art historians than they are by philosophers, who are fond of speaking of art as such, or art in general, or the essence of art, and who usually deploy such concepts to smuggle in normative concepts of humanity. When a philosopher defines what art *is* he is usually making a moral claim about life, and this is especially so

when philosophy seemingly detaches itself from the assumptions of normativity, when philosophy speaks for man in general. Kant's insistence
on aesthetic judgment as reflective, presupposes Western art practices of
framed and detached art objects: man realizes that he is not just a physical body, but a subject who can feel himself as a creative being responsible for the reason of the world. When Jacques Derrida affirms that 'literature is democracy' (Thomson 2005, 33; Kronick 1999, 166) he includes
all literary practice under a high modernist norm of framed voice (art is
not *what* is said, but a presentation *that* there is 'saying'); when Theodor
Adorno (2004), more explicitly, shows the aesthetic as properly disclosed in modernist formalism he allows art in general to be oriented
towards the disjunction between concept and reality; various Marxisms
or historicisms will begin an account of art in general from this or that
exemplary object (the social novel, Greek tragedy, postmodern reflexiv-
ity). Deleuze and Guattari seem both to fall into this (possibly unavoidable) universalizing tendency with their distinction between an art of
affects and percepts and a philosophy of concepts. And yet their insistence that art emerges from a pre- or counter-human animality and that
this 'art' lies in the capacity of sensations to persist in themselves, opens
the thought of an inhuman time, and an eternity outside man (Deleuze
and Guattari 1994, 182). This is why, also, they pay so much attention to
the twinned concepts of race and face: for it is art that at once forms the
figure of a common humanity (man as *homo faber*), at the same time as
the resistance and decay of art objects opens life and creation to temporalities beyond those of a self-legislating humanity.

It is most often philosophers, determined to secure a domain of life
that is not yet submitted to convention, instrumentality, recognition,
opinion, or assumptions of human nature, who will find in art *as such*
that which precedes, exceeds or disturbs given systems. Art either offers
us the capacity to reflect upon the worlds 'we' have formed (Habermas
1987), or, art brings 'us' back once again to humanity's eternal capacity
to be nothing other than the image it creates from itself (Agamben 1999,
68). But there are two ways this eternity might be thought: as humanity's
destiny—man as the capacity to create the thought of the universal—*or*
as humanity's annihilation: for perhaps it is not man (or man alone) that
witnesses or evidences a temporality outside organic specified life. If art

is necessarily always concerned with annihilation and specification (or the production of species, and the persistence of sensations beyond the life of the creator) then any claim that art is essentially or eternally of a certain mode belies art's distinct fragility. That is, the claim to something like *art in general* reinforces the sense of man or humanity in general, and occludes what Deleuze and Guattari have presented as the animality of art, its existence in pure matters of sensation.

When Deleuze and Guattari [1994, 165] argue for art as the preservation of sensations that exist before man—sensations that persist in themselves—they go a long way to destroying the race of man.

> [P]henomenology must become the phenomenology of art because the immanence of the lived to a transcendental subject must be expressed in transcendent functions that not only determine experience in general but traverse the lived here and now, and are embodied in it by constituting living sensations. (Deleuze and Guattari 1994, 178)

Art is not the expression of humanity, in general, but the destruction of any such generality through the preservation and temporality of the 'nonorganic life of things' (Deleuze and Guattari 1994, 180). Art, traditionally conceived, has been racial in a double sense: it offers figures of man in general (always—in Western art—the white face of the subject); and is then archived as the expression of a humanity that comes to know and feel itself through the creation of its own pure images.

Art, Face, Race

Art is always the preserving of a sensation that is of its time, but that is submitted to existence for all time. If art is to figure something like 'the human'—and if the human is, philosophically, an openness to world that is given best in the face—then it must always do so through the material figure of some specified head. Emmanuel Levinas's argument that the face is singular, and that the singular relation to any face disrupts a logic of calculation and specification, is an extreme philosophic argument; it takes up the premise of philosophy—of a radical transcendence that is

Figure 1: Joanna Kane, William Blake deathmask, from *The Somnambulists*,
2008. Dewi Lewis Publishing 2008. Photo courtesy of Joanna Kane.

not of this world of beings—and yet returns that transcendence to the
privileged body of man:

> The same and the other can not enter into a cognition that
> would encompass them; the relations that the separated being
> maintains with what transcends it are not produced on the
> ground of totality, do not crystallize into a system. Yet do we
> not name them together? The *formal* synthesis of the word
> that names them together is already part of a discourse, that is,
> of a conjuncture of transcendence, breaking the totality. The
> conjuncture of the same and the other, in which even their
> verbal proximity is maintained, is the *direct* and *full face* wel-
> come of the other by me. This conjuncture is irreducible to
> totality; the 'face to face' position is not a modification of the
> 'along side of ...' Even when I have linked the Other to myself

with the conjunction 'and' the Other continues to face me, to reveal his face. (Levinas 1979, 80-81)

Levinas's elevation of the face relies on an experience of a singularity that would be liberated from all generality, that would not be a specification of this or that universal type. Levinas's appeal to the face is at once non-semantic, for the face disrupts generality and communication or shared notions of what counts in advance as human; the face appears in its singularity as this face, before me, here and now. If, however, such a face were to be figured in art it would need to take on some specification, where specification is always *of the species* or race. A face 'as such' without species might be *thought* but it could only be figured through this or that concrete head. Even when it does not figure human bodies, persons or faces, art is always about face and always about the extinction of species. It is always a presentation of this earth of 'ours' witnessed from our race: 'All faces envelop an unknown, unexplored landscape; all landscapes are populated by a loved or dreamed-of face, develop a face to come or already past' (Deleuze and Guattari 2004b, 191). So there are two twinned (yet necessary) impossibilities. First, a work of art can live on, as eternal and monumental, only if it takes on a material support: my thoughts can be read after my life only if I inscribe them in matter. And yet, second, that matter is also essentially fragile, corruptible and subject to decay. A face—or the witnessing of the subject in general—can only occur through some racialized head: I can only imagine humanity in general, as spirit, through the species. The eternal—the sense of art, the subject of the face—is always constituted through this object, this head. The logic that intertwines face, race and art is the logic of life: a unified body or species can only occur through persisting beyond individual bodies— a race is like an artwork or monument, surviving beyond individual life—and yet, such persisting unities also only survive through variation. A race or species varies and opens to other differences in order to live on, just as the individual human subject can persist through time, beyond himself, only by supplementing himself through the matters of art.

A work of art is only a work if it has taken on some separable and repeatable form, but it is just that taking on of a body (or incarnation) that also suffers a process of decay. That is, just as the art object is possible because of a selection of matters that will both resist dissolution (in the short

term) and be exposed to inevitable decay, so the bounds of a race are possible only because of a specification that requires an ultimately annihilating variability; a race or species is possible only because of something like
an art in life, a variability that both enables the formation of living borders
but that also entails the annihilation of bounds. A race is at once the gathering of sameness, a certain genetic continuity, and an openness to difference—for a race continues through time via sexual variation.

In the remaining sections of this chapter I want to explore two ideas
about extinction and race in relation to art works that will allow us to look
at the ways in which all life is oriented to an oscillation between extinction and specification (or 'raciation'), and that this leads to an impure
border between the faces of philosophy—or the idea of a humanity as
such—and the heads of art, or the material figures through which that
humanity is given.

As a preliminary opening to these two ideas of race and extinction I
want to consider three visual images, the first of which is the smiley face
that came to stand for acid house culture, while the second is William
Blake's death mask refigured first by Francis Bacon's 1955 'Study for
Portrait II (after the Life Mask of William Blake),' and second by the
contemporary Edinburgh photographer Joanna Kane (Kane 2008).
All of these images, in different ways, problematize the distinctions
between the face and the head, between philosophy and art, or between
species-survival and extinction. If we want to consider something like a
pure form of the face (theorized philosophically) then we could turn to
Levinas's detachment of the face from all generality, calculation, mediation and specification: for Levinas a face is not a head. The latter is a body
part, and might also figure something like the biological human species
to which 'we' would owe certain allegiances and contracts. On a bodily,
psycho-physical or (for Levinas) non-ethical level, it is because others
have bodies like mine that I enter into certain sympathies, and this would
allow 'us' to maintain ourselves in relation to external threats and a milieu
of risk (so the head would also signal something like Bergson's 'morality,'
which is a bonding formed through relative likeness [Bergson 1935]).
For Levinas, all philosophy that has been grounded on being, or that has
tried to determine some ideal of justice, humanity and order *in advance*
emanating from a general physical humanity, annihilates the radical

singularity of the face. It is the encounter with *this* face, here and now, that disrupts convention, sign systems, repeatability and doxa; it is this singular face that prevents the reduction of otherness to an event within the world. The face enables us to pass from (or through) the heads that we recognize as part of a common species, to the other whom we can encounter but never know. Or, in Bergson's terms: from something like a common morality of humanity premised on a specified kind, one would pass to the thought of a virtual, not yet present and singular other.

The face would give us something like pure life: not the form or matter that one recognizes as the same through time and that is subject to decay and exposure to risk, but the animating spirit of which matter is a sign. The face for Levinas is, after all, not a sign or mediation of humanity so much as an experience or rupture with all mediation and sense. (The same applies for those who invoke his work today, amid conflicts among peoples [Butler 2006, 133].) Life, however, is never pure and its processes of variation and creativity are known only through the relative stability of bounded forms. These forms and bounded beings are perceived as the beings that they are only by reducing the intense fluctuations and differences into ongoing and recognizable figures. At the other end of the spectrum from the pure life of a perception that is not yet frozen or determined into any relatively inert figure is the mere head. If the head for Deleuze and Guattari occurs with a pre-modern tribal individuation that is not yet that of humanity, it is possible to see this head again today in the post- or counter-human head of the smiley face. So lacking in distinction that it has neither race, nor humanity, nor artfulness, the smiley face signals loss of life (having become a punctuation mark in emails and text messages: ':)'). It is the retreat from specification and the removal of any definitive body—anything that would allow for engaged sympathy—that makes the smiley face at once the most vulgar of heads, as though even the primitive animal totem heads (or portraits commissioned through patronage) were still too singular to really enable the joys of a loss of face.

In two recent books the neuroscientist Susan Greenfield has commented on the contemporary problem of meaning, sensation and identity. Drugs that work to overcome depression may operate by relieving the brain of its syntactic work, allowing the body to experience *sensation as such* without laboring to tie it into significance. A depressed person cannot, Greenfield argues, simply enjoy a sip of espresso, the feel of sunshine on the skin or the sound of a flowing stream (Greenfield 2000). The depressive is focused on meaning or connection, tying sensations into a resonant whole, and cannot therefore experience the senseless ecstasy of sensation as such. An experience is meaningful if it is placed in the context of past encounters and future projects, but a certain joy is possible only if that neural network of sense is also open to sensation. One must be a self—having a certain face and singularity that defines one as who one is in terms of one's projects—but one must sometimes also be just a head: a capacity to feel or be affected without asking why, or without placing that sense in relation to one's own being and its ends. Greenfield's more recent book, *ID*, has—despite her earlier recognition that we sometimes need to let go of identity and meaning—lamented what she sees to be an attrition of our neural architecture (Greenfield 2008). While the current drug and computer-fuelled retreat from syntax and recognition—and its accompanying sense of self—has its place, contemporary culture's focus on flashing screens, disconnected sensations and immediate intensities is hurtling in an alarming manner to a total loss of face. There is a widespread loss of being *someone,* and a disturbing tendency towards being 'anyone.'

That such a process of neural extinction accompanies species extinction is not a mere coincidence, and that such a movement towards *not* being someone is symbolized by the smiling head of ecstasy use should give us pause for thought. As the species comes closer to the extinction that marked its very possibility *as species,* it has retreated more and more into its own self-identity, becoming more and more convinced of the unity of race (the humanity of man in general). One could only become this or that marked race—especially the race of man—by closing off absolute difference and englobing oneself into a determined and self-recognizing kind: 'When the faciality machine translates formed contents of whatever kind into a single substance of expression, it already subjugates them to the exclusive form of signifying and subjective expression' (Deleuze and Guattari 2004b, 199). Is it any surprise that today, confronted with actual species extinction, 'man' ingests drugs that relieve him of meaning, buys screens that divert his gaze away from others, and consumes media that pacify him with figures of a general and anodyne 'we'? Is this loss of face something that is accidentally destructive, or could we not say that the face of man emerges from such self-enclosure? Is not the grand scene of Levinas's ethics—one face to another without intrusion of a third or any other world—not *the* mode of coupling that has led to the earth's deface-ment? Today's culture of self-annihilation—an overcoming of face, sense and bounded recognition—may not be as lamentable as Greenfield and others suggest. It may be a perfectly inhuman (and therefore wonder-ful) response to a world in which the value and art of one's species is no longer unquestionable. Is face, human face in its radical distinction and immateriality, really what one wants to save?

Acid house visual and aural culture, apart from being signaled by the smiley face, rely on an elimination of a time of development and figura-tion in favor of a time of pulsation. Music of this style, along with trance and later forms of dubstep and brostep, destroy the man of speech and reason for the sake of sensations liberated from humanity. Not only do the drugs that accompany trance and house music allow for the experi-ence of sensation without a framing of sense, the music is character-ized by instrumental—usually digitally synthesized—repeated chord sequences, with infrequent and non-complex modulations, pulsing rhythms and uses of language that are sonorous rather than semantic. Visuals that accompany this music are not so much abstract as minimal, not geometric forms and figures but intensities of light and color. That this movement of acid house is part of a broader tendency towards loss of face is signaled by the smiley head it takes as its totem, by the general cul-ture of counter-syntax described by Greenfield, and by the strange neural tie between the face and specification. What such late capitalist events disclose is what Deleuze and Guattari refer to as a 'higher deterritorialis-tion;' there is not a movement back to the one single ground of humanity, but a creative release that opens out towards a cosmos of forces beyond humanity. More specifically one might note, then, that it is not by inclu-sion or *extension* of the categories of rights and humanity that one might overcome the intrinsic racism (which is also a species-ism) that regulates the concept of man. Rather, it is by intensifying sensations that one is lib-erated from the face of the signifying subject, opening forces to the inhu-manity of the cosmos:

The face is not animal, but neither is it human in general; there is even something absolutely inhuman about the face. To the point that if human beings have a destiny, it is rather to escape the face, to dismantle the face and facializations, to become imperceptible, to become clandestine, not by returning to animality, nor even by returning to the head, but by quite spiritual and special becomings-animal, by strange true becomings that get past the wall and get out of the black holes, that make *faciality traits* themselves finally elude the organization of the face…. (Deleuze and Guattari 2004b, 189)

One of the most commonly cited neural disorders in much of the current popular literature regarding the brain is Capgras syndrome, where a patient without any delusion or loss of *cognitive* function, sees a close relative but then claims that this relative is an alien or imposter (Feinberg and Keenan 2005, 93). (This would be the opposite tendency of ecstasy culture where every stranger appears as a beloved.) What is missing is not any visual or cognitive input but affective response: if the emotional intensity or affect is not experienced then I claim—despite all evidence to the contrary—that this is not my mother, or child or partner. This syndrome has been widely cited in order to claim that we are not solely or primarily cognitive beings, and that our relation to others requires an affective response to their visual singularity—not simply the knowledge or recognition of who they are. This might seem both to support and refute the Levinasian face. On the one hand it seems that—despite Levinas's claims that *the* face of *the* other makes an impelling claim on me—it is really only certain faces with a specific visceral genealogy pertinent to our own being that are truly experienced as faces; everyone else is a mere head. On the other hand, it also appears that the face is not one object in the world among others, not reducible to a knowable and identikit type, for faces are radically singular. Faces engage affective registers that cannot be overridden by cognitive or simply visual inputs. A face at once has no race, for if I see this other as a face then I am devoted to an affective response that has nothing to do with general (or genetic) specifications. On the other hand, the face is absolutely racial, for there is no such thing as the face of humanity in general, or a global fellow feeling; the face that engages me, disturbs me and transcends cognition is the face that is bound up with my own organic and specified becoming. The face is at once that which is radically exposed to extinction, given that I experience *as face* only those heads bound up with my world, time and life. At the same time, the face appears to be quite distinct from organic survival; the body of the other person is before me, and yet something is missing. The affect, which is not a part of their body but is bound up with their capacity to be perceived in a certain manner, is what marks their singularity:

> The human head implies a deterritorialization in relation to the animal and has as its correlate the organization of a world, in other words, a milieu that has itself been deterritorialized (the steppe is the first 'world,' in contrast to the forest milieu). But the face represents a far more intense, if slower, deterritorialization. We could say that it is an *absolute* deterritorialization: it is no longer relative because it removes the head from the stratum of the organism, human or animal, and connects it to other strata, such as significance and subjectification. (Deleuze and Guattari 2004, 191)

One response to the border of the face—to this strange body part that is at once an organic head and also a marked out, fragile and exposed singularity—is a form of willed extinction. If there has been a tradition of art dominated by portraits, signatures, leitmotifs and claims to radical distinction and living on, there is also a counter-tradition of the head rather than the face, concerned with annihilation, indistinction and becoming no one. Faced with the all too fragile bounds of one's specified being one could either cling more and more desperately to one's englobed humanity—asserting something like Levinas's pure face as such—or one could confront the head head-on.

Both Francis Bacon's portrait of Blake and the contemporary Scottish photographer Joanna Kane's photograph are taken from William Blake's death-mask. Blake, perhaps more than any other artist, exposed the impure logics of extinction, specification and art. Resisting an increasing culture of commodification and the annihilation of the artist's hand, Blake would not submit his poetry to the printing press, nor subject his images to the usual methods of reproduction. Determined not to lose

himself in the morass of markets, mass production and already given systems, Blake engraved every word of his poetry on hand-crafted plates,
colored every page with his own hand, invented his own mythic lexicon
and gave each aspect of every one of his 'characters' a distinct embodied
form. As a consequence of seizing the act of production from the death
of general systems, and directly following the assertion of his own singularity against any general humanism, Blake's work is more subject to
decay, extinction and annihilation than any other corpus. Because Blake
resisted the formal and repeatable modes of typeface, and because he
took in hand his own creation of pigments and techniques of illuminated printing, it is not possible to detach the pure sense or signature of
Blake's work from its technical medium. The more Blake took command
of technicity or matter—the more he rendered all aspects of the work artful—the more exposed his work was to the possibility of annihilation.
It was because Blake's work was so specific, so distinct, so committed to
the living on and survival of the singular, that it was also doomed to a
faster rate of extinction. (Blake's work can never be fully reproduced or
anthologized.)

Similarly, one can note that it is because it was so masterful at survival,
at securing the sense of itself and its worth as a species, that humanity as a
race faces accelerated destruction.

Both Bacon and Kane depict Blake not through the surviving portrait,
but through the death-mask. If the *portrait* is one of the ways in which the
head is framed, signed, attributed and placed within a narrative of artist as
author, creator and subject of a world of intentionality that can be entered
by reading and intuition, this is because the face of the portrait is tied to
an aesthetics of empathy, in which the hand of the artist is led by the idea
of a world that is not materially presented but that can be indicated or
thought through matter. In this respect the portrait can be aligned with
what Deleuze refers to as a history of digital aesthetics, in which the hand
becomes a series of 'digits' that in turn allows the world to be visualized,
not as recalcitrant matter, but as a quantifiable mass in accord with the
eye's expectations (Deleuze 2005, 79). The digital—as universalizing and
generalizing of the world—therefore presupposed what Derrida referred
to as a Western assumption of a pre-personal 'we'—the humanity in general that *would be able* to view and intuit the sense that is before me now

(Derrida 1989, 84). For all its supposed resistance to mediation, representation and a history of Western being that has reduced the event of encounter to a general 'being,' Levinas's 'face' is insistent on an immediate relation to otherness that is not diverted, corrupted or rendered opaque by the decay-prone flesh of the head. What sets the aesthetics of empathy, which would discern a spirit in the bodily figure, apart from the aesthetics of abstraction is just this positing of an immateriality that transcends matter. It is the other, given through the face, whose presence is not arrived at by way of analogy or concepts. This is possible only if all those matters that tie a subject to specification and therefore certain extinction are deemed to be transparent or external to some pure otherness as such, to some pure face that is not corrupted by the head.

The portraits of Blake, like the sense of Blake's work in general, do indeed survive and circulate beyond the author's living body. Even so, that face of Blake and the sense of the work that survives beyond decaying matter are possible and released into the world only through a matter that is intrinsically self-annihilating. An aesthetics of abstraction, in contrast with empathy, is possible through a production, from matter, of pure forms; abstraction constitutes formal relations distinct from the singular, localized and subjective experiences of living organisms. One might therefore say that it is only through racial delirium—passing through and annihilating all the species of man—that one finds something other than racism, or man as he properly is. This might effect an 'about-face.' Blake's work already confronted this relation between, on the one hand, discerning the world as possessed of spirit (a world of innocence in accord with an ultimately human face), and, on the other hand, a world of matter devoid of any life other than its reduction to pure forms of digits (the world of 'single vision and Newton's sleep,' where experience knows in advance all that it will encounter). In his illuminated printing and engraving techniques Blake's works confronted the resistance of the hand in relation to a matter that was neither pure form, nor living spirit, but yielded something like an analogical aesthetics—the genesis of forms and life from the chaos of materiality. One could refer to this as a radically haptic aesthetic in which the eye can see the resistance of form emerging from matter, feeling the resistance of (in Blake's case) the hand, and in the case of the deathmask the curvature of the head (Colebrook 2012A).

Bacon's paint adds its own flesh of color to the form of the mask, while Kane's highly finished photography renders the material object spiritual, not by gesturing to the face but by granting the matter itself its own luminosity. The visual surface of the photgraph, rather than the gazing face of the portrait, seems to posses at once its own spirit and its own temporality, specification and line of duration. It is matter itself, and not the living form it figures, that seems to endure opening its own line of survival, extinction and specification. Kane's faces-heads are higher deterritorializations in two senses. The face that enables empathy and alterity becomes a head again, but not a head of the living organism so much as a material artifact of matters that are themselves expressive. The art object that would seem to signal the human organism's potentiality to free itself from mere biological life, to create that which endures beyond its own being, itself shows all the signs of material fragility, exposure and annihilation. Philosophy finds faces in art; art is that creation of a signification of a sense beyond any body, of an endurance liberated from the instrumentality of the human organism. But there is always something of the crumbling, decaying, unspecified head in the faces of art.

Chapter 8

Posthuman Humanities

Suddenly a local object, nature, on which a merely partial subject could act, becomes a global objective, Planet Earth, on which a new, total subject, humanity, is toiling away (Serres 1995, 5).

There was something odd about Stanley Fish's speedy intervention in the 'debate' about the closure of certain humanities departments:

> But keeping something you value alive by artificial, and even coercive, means (and distribution requirements are a form of coercion) is better than allowing them to die, if only because you may now die (get fired) with them, a fate that some vision-ary faculty members may now be suffering. I have always had trouble believing in the high-minded case for a core curricu-lum—that it preserves and transmits the best that has been thought and said—but I believe fully in the core curriculum as a device of employment for me and my fellow humanists. But the point seems to be moot. It's too late to turn back the clock. (Fish 2010)

In the general milieu of non-debate that pitched economic rationalism against an unquestioning right for the humanities to continue existing in its current form, Fish admitted that certain nineteenth-century 'pieties' would, today, not be believed. Fish himself did not disclose whether he believed these pieties or whether they ought to be believed; he went on to admit that keeping the valued humanities alive would require possibly coercive means. These means would not be a justification of the humani-ties but 'aggressive explanation' of the 'core enterprise.' Along the way Fish laments that it would be *French* departments—*French, the once hot-bed of real ideas*—that seem to be expendable in the way that Spanish is not. Now, such a paean is odd given that one might have thought that if one really valued and wanted to sustain what 'we' learned from the French in their high theory heyday it might have been that education as a 'core enterprise' might be worth questioning (both for reasons of politics in Foucault's sense, or the way disciplines constitute illusions of 'the' polity, and for reasons of good thinking, such that 'keeping something you value alive' might best be achieved *not* by clinging to survival but by a joyously destructive and active nihilism). Fish already suggests in his title—'The Crisis of the Humanities *Officially* Arrives'—that the crisis was implicit up until now. Indeed the humanities have been in crisis, and for good reason. If, as Husserl already noted very early in the last century, the 'sciences' were in crisis because of a certain notion of 'man' as a natural animal blessed with technical reasoning capacities, then such a crisis could not but affect the humanities. Even Husserl accepted the impossibility of grounding any new knowledge or future-oriented discipline on man as he actually is and suggested that dealing with the crisis would entail opening a new line of thought beyond natural 'man.'

Today, in a century that can begin to sense, if not articulate, humanity's capacity to destroy its own species-being, along with the milieu that it has constitutively polluted to the point of annihilation, what sort of defense might one make for the future of humanities disciplines? Should one not, rather, say 'no' to everything that has defended and saved man and *his* future, especially to the concept of life and potentiality of which man would be the utmost expression? Do we not require a new discipline? This would need to take the form *not* of the humanities, especially if the humanities were to take on a certain motif of the posthuman. That is, if the humanities were to live on by consuming, appropriating and claiming as its own the life of animals, digital technologies, inter-disciplinarity (or the rendering of science as human) then there would merely be a continuation of a reactive nihilism.

Posthumanism, as I will define it here, is not an overcoming of the human but takes a similar form to the structure of nihilism. Here is Nietzsche's diagnostic account if nihilism: a 'higher' world of truth is posited behind appearances, so that this actual world is given lesser value. When science fails to establish that greater foundational higher world, we fall into despair, left as we are this only this given world. If belief in a transcendent redemption negated the force of this world for a higher world, then a reactive nihilism responded to the loss of transcendence with despair, the horror that there might be nothing more than this world. Similarly, humanism affirms all value and being on the basis of the human logos: what is true and right is that which can be rendered rational. When that belief in a rational and grounding humanity falls away, what we are left with is a world *minus* man, a world in which there is no longer a truth or being, only observation. We subtract man's logical supremacy from the world and are left with the contingency of observation (Wolfe 1995). In this respect, the retreat to a world in which there is *only man*, not God, remains theological—for God has been subtracted but the world as God-less (abandoned to man) remains. The posthuman, similarly, renounces human privilege or species-ism but then fetishizes the posthuman world as man-less; 'we' are no longer elevated, separated, enclosed, detached from a man-less world, for there is a direct interface and interconnection—a mesh or network, a living system—that allows for one world of computers, digital media, animals, things and systems. There is a continuation of the humanities, which had always refused that *man* had any end other than that which he gave to himself, in the posthuman notion that man is nothing but a point of relative stability, connected to one living system that he can feel affectively and read. Not only have motifs such as 'affect,' 'posthuman,' living systems and digital media been explicit topics—giving the impression that 'the' humanities can survive criticisms of the illusions of a once-dominant (supposedly) Cartesian rationalism, these motifs have intensified and entrenched the strategies that have always marked the humanities. They allow for business as usual—in the same manner that nihilism allowed for a continued theologism; we have abandoned God and man, but now live this world as what is left *after* the subtraction of God and man. What we have are living interconnecting systems, with no point of exception, privilege or transcendence. If a world devoid of God and man continues a certain myopia of insisting that what is is that which can be observed, this ultra-human posthumanism is conducted in a reactive and resentful mode. For what have 'the posthuman,' 'affective' or 'ethical' turns licensed? There has been an avowed reaction against a supposed linguisticism or textual narcissism (also referred to as linguistic idealism), so that the God of language is dead, and we no longer believe that this world of ours is given order from without by 'a' system of language or structure which it would be the job of literary critics or cultural studies to decode. There has been a return to life, bodies, animals, ecology and the inhuman in general, as though we are once again liberated from the prison of our humanity, no longer distanced from the world and now able to find a truly post-theory, posthuman world of life. We turn back to history, contexts, things, bodies, life and nature.

The humanities would, through all its demarcation disputes, attacks, defenses and mutations be defined *not* by a normative notion of the human but by an anti-normative insistence that *man is not, for he has no positive being other than that which is given to him by virtue of his historical and living becoming.* The humanities would be primarily critical and interpretive, and would be entwined with a logic of negation and refusal. The sciences would be procedural, operating from within paradigms (however sophisticated, reflected upon or provisional) while the humanities would occur through self-distancing or reading: whatever life or system is given, it is the task of the humanities—because there is no such *thing* as the human—to open a space of conversation, legitimation, questioning or critique. Without such a space one would be reduced to the ruthless actuality of metrics or utilitarianism. 'Man' as given in the humanities is not the man of science (subjecting the world to so many repeatable, efficient and quantifiable functions). Nor is the humanity of the humanities the 'man' of the human sciences (whereby man's social and political being can be read as an expression of what Foucault refers to as his 'empirical density': man speaks and labors because of the needs of life, and it is this emergence from life that allows man to read himself in today's anthropology, social linguistics, evolutionary psychology and cognitive archaeology). The man of the humanities was already posthuman, possessing no being other than his reflexive capacity to read his own ungrounded and utterly flexible becoming. 'At the very moment that we are acting physically for the first time on the global Earth, and when it in turn is doubtless reacting on global humanity, we are tragically neglecting it' (Serres 1995, 29).

For Michel Serres humanity is not a concept that grounds the humanities, nor is 'man' a concept expressed by the various disciplines that comprise the humanities. Rather, 'humanity' is a meteorological impera-tive, a concept that needs to be created today in order to confront the change in techno-geological climates. Serres's work, despite its manifest humanism in *The Natural Contract*, does not take the form of a resistance to the technical reduction of man to systems. (What his work demands, in a manner similar to Deleuze's affirmation of differential calculus, is not an overcoming of calculation but a more subtle *differential* calculation: a reckoning of the quantities and systems produced by the relations among the bodies of the human species and the other forces upon which it is parasitic.) Serres's theorization of the human is not a posthumanism that would happily conflate human existence with life in general. Such post-humanisms are, as I have already suggested, ultimately *ultra-humanisms* insofar as they attribute all the qualities once assigned to man—quali-ties such as mindfulness, connectedness, self-organizing dynamism—to some supposedly benevolent life in general that needs to be saved from the death of merely calculative systems. Against this Rosalyn Diprose has re-asserted the role of human meaning, perception and value in provid-ing an opening of the event in an otherwise leveled world:

> Formulating an ethics for the posthuman world requires a more considered ontology to supplement that which is assumed in biopolitical analysis. The challenge is to bet-ter understand what kind of collective practices allow the emergence of the 'event' within assemblages of human, non-human, meaning, and technical elements without ignoring the mediating role of (historically conditioned) human per-ception, receptivity and responsiveness. (Diprose 2009, 13)

That is, supposedly, the value of the humanities today, lies both in its ideal resistance to a culture of economic rationalism and narrow utilitari-anism and its less pious claim to educate students with transferable skills or critical reasoning or rhetorical flexibility. The humanities of posthu-manism has happily abandoned species-ism and exceptionalism—man is no longer adjudicator or hermeneutic arbiter outside the web of life—for there is one de-centered, mutually imbricated, constantly creative mesh, system or network of life. According to Timothy Morton:

The ecological thought imagines interconnectedness, which I call the *mesh*. Who or what is interconnected with what or whom? The mesh of interconnected things is vast, perhaps immeasurably so. Each entity in the mesh looks strange. Nothing exists all by itself, and so nothing is fully 'itself.' There is curiously 'less' of the Universe at the same time, and for the same reasons, as we see 'more' of it. Our encounter with other beings becomes profound. They are strange, even intrinsically strange. Getting to know them makes them stranger. When we talk about life forms, we're talking about strange strangers. The ecological thought imagines a multitude of *strange strangers*. (Morton 2010, 15)

Morton's project differs both from the simple ecological affirmations that would reunite humans with a lost nature (for he aims to think ecology without grounding and unifying nature), and also from the strands of 'object oriented ontology' that would insist that not everything is connected (Harman 2012, 132). And it is this latter possibility of disconnection or detachment that is, I would suggest, productively inhuman. Yes, most avowed posthumanisms have celebrated the destruction of man as the ground of all reason, but what they have brought back is one grand whole of interconnected systems of observation (often readable in terms of some grander system of class, power or life). But it is the sacrifice of man as Cartesian subject in favor of a posthuman ecology of systems that allows the humanities to live on. If the human is assumed to be nothing more than an interface, already at one with a world that is one living system, then posthumanism is nothing more than the negation of a humanism that never was. It is an ultrahumanism precisely because once man is abandoned as a distinct system or inflection he returns to characterize nature or life in general, just as the death of God left an implicit and widespread theologism that no longer had a distinct or explicit logic. Posthumanism is an ultrahumanism and partakes of the same metaleptic logic of reactive nihilism. In nihilism, a higher world is posited to justify or grant worth to this world. This higher world is posited from a reaction against the force of this world. When that supposed transcendence is no longer affirmed, this world becomes a world *minus transcendence, godless, worthless, void and negated.* Humanism posits an elevated or exceptional 'man' to grant sense to existence, then when 'man' is negated or removed what is left is the human all too human tendency to see the world as one giant anthropomorphic self-organizing living body. Not surprisingly, there become increasingly shrill calls for human meaning (including a pragmatic or humanized religion, and a certain substitution of literature for God as the ground of human sense-making). 'Man' is effected as that animal who would be especially poised to read the logic of life, and this because of his capacities for speech and sociality; it is the creation of man that enables a certain concept of life. When man is destroyed to yield a posthuman world it is the same world *minus humans,* a world of meaning, sociality and readability yet without any sense of the disjunction, gap or limits of the human. Like nihilism, the logic is metaleptic: the figure of man is originally posited in order to yield a sense or meaning of life, and yet when man is done away with as an external power what is left is an anthropomorphic life of meaning and readability. A certain idea of man—Foucault notes—was intertwined with the possibility of the human sciences and of a concomitant notion of life. If, for Foucault, both 'man' and 'life' emerge in the eighteenth century this is because there is a new distribution in the table of knowledge, a new fold between inside and outside. Rather than examining the forms of living being in a world of analogies—with humanity being an expression of a broader cosmology, there is now something like life as such with its specific temporality and imperatives. Whereas humans had been privileged beings (blessed with reason) it is now *man* who is at once empirically constituted by life (required to speak, labor and constitute polities because of the needs of his species being) and yet also capable of reading that logic of life as transcendental: psychoanalysis, Marxism, ethnography, structuralism and (today's) evolutionary psychology or cognitive archaeology all account for the modus of the human organism according to a certain logic of life.

> [T]he end of metaphysics is only the negative side of a much more complex event in Western thought. This event is the appearance of man. However, it must not be supposed that he suddenly appeared on our horizon, imposing the brutal fact of his body, his labour and his language in a manner so irruptive as to be absolutely baffling as to our reflection. It is not man's lack of positivity that reduced the space of metaphysics

so violently. No doubt, on the level of appearances, modernity begins when the human being begins to exist within his organism, inside the shell of his head, inside the armature of his limbs, and in the whole structure of his physiology; when he begins to exist at the center of labour by whose principles he is governed and whose logic eludes him; when he lodges his thought in the folds of a language so much older than himself that he cannot master its significations, even though they have been called back to life by the insistence of his words. But, more fundamentally, our culture crossed the threshold beyond which we recognize our modernity when finitude was conceived with an interminable cross-reference with itself. Though it is true, at the level of the various branches of knowledge, that finitude is always designated on the basis of man as a concrete being and on the basis of the empirical forms that can be tied to his existence, nevertheless, at the archaeological level, which reveals the general, historical *a priori* of each of these branches of knowledge, modern man—that man assignable in his corporeal, labouring, speaking existence is possible only as a figuration of finitude. Modern culture can conceive of man because it conceives of the finite on the basis of itself. (Foucault 2003, 346)

Today, even though man as a privileged being has been incorporated into a posthuman plane of interacting living systems what remains is the reactive and ultrahuman logic of finitude: it is because there is *life* (or a being's relation to an ecology) that one can only know the world as it is given through organic conditions. A being is alive insofar as it maintains itself and does so in relation to a milieu that it perceives according to its own capacities; humans and animals have worlds, and *the* world is not so much data to be represented by an imposed order nor a book of life but an interactive and dynamic mesh of living systems. One can account for language, labor and life according to a single logic of man: a being emerges from the needs of self-maintenance (which in the case of man require language, the polity and labor), but it is man who has the capacity to read the enigmatic density of life. His empirical being is the sign of a broader logic (a transcendental logic of life).

If the humanities—for Foucault—had any value it would not be as an extension of this logic—such that we might see literature as emerging from evolving and self-furthering life, or as somehow the means by which the empirical being of man might be awakened to his proto-transcendental powers of critique. Rather what Foucault referred to as *literature* would evidence something like a force beyond life, a machinic power that could not be referred back to the self-furthering human organism (Deleuze 2006, 110). Language would not be the system through which we could read man's emergence from a general order of life as self-maintenance; it would not be world-disclosive, nor an extension of organic and organizing imperatives of life.

Now if it is *this* man (of finitude) that has been removed from exceptionalism in the posthuman landscape, and if the humanities disciplines have abandoned poetic assumptions of human speech as a special or privileged domain for revelation, what remains is a negative or reactive continuation of anthropomorphic projection by other means. Self-maintaining organicism and auto-poeisis are everywhere. In terms of theory this has led to a posthuman landscape in which there is one general dynamic system with animals, machines and digital codes all woven to constitute a single ecology; the knowledge procedures are generally *extensive*, subsuming more and more events within the domain of one evolving and efficient life. It is for this reason that Rosi Braidotti has marked out two distinct modes of posthumanism, one of which would draw attention to the ways in which lines of life and thought are 'topologically bound'—*not* considered to be one expressive aspect of one single system of life. The posthumanism of which Braidotti is critical is of a single-system where all observations can be grounded on a single self-expressive living whole (Braidotti 2006, 199). What is not considered in the posthumanisms of living systems are radically differing intensities, or intensive multiplicities, in which different speeds and economies open different and incompossible systems. I would suggest that it is no surprise, then, that certain Luddite modes of literary Darwinism have gained literary vogue. Despite the sophisticated achievements of Darwinism in philosophy and science (from thinkers as diverse as Elizabeth Grosz and Stephen Jay Gould) that have stressed a certain divergence from function in evolutionary life, there has been a proclamation of the return of literary studies to purposive and meaningful life. Not only have explicit versions of literary Darwinism led to a rejection of high theory (a high theory that had supposedly imprisoned thought in language [Carroll 2004,29]); there has also been a more general proclaimed posthumanism that considers the absence of man to be a license for a new literalism, with direct talk of life, affect, bodies and ethics/politics.

The ethical turn, like the affective turn, is a turn *back* away from a supposed human imprisonment within language to the real and collective conditions of existence. One might cite, as an example, Eva Ziarek's critique of Agamben. Agamben had already attacked the deconstructive attention to limits in order to retrieve the event of saying or opening of the political (Agamben 1999, 209). Ziarek, in turn, wants to take Agamben's general concept of potentiality, from which the polity would open, and locate this force in intersubjective communality: 'potentiality cannot be understood, as Agamben seems to suggest, in terms of the isolated subject and what 'he can or can not do,' because it is fundamentally a relational concept, emerging from the encounter with another 'you.'' (Ziarek 2010).

In a similar manner Hardt and Negri also want to turn away from the locatedness of centering points of view, and therefore from language and other constituting, inhuman and transcendent (to human life) systems, to the commons, the multitude—immanent political bodies that would have nothing outside or beyond themselves (and certainly not any imposed norm of humanity):

> The primary decision made by the multitude is really the decision to create a new race or, rather, a new humanity. When love is conceived politically, then, this creation of a new humanity is the ultimate act of love. (Hardt and Negri 2005, 26)

In addition to these general affirmations that would now return man to the one common life of which he is a political and benevolent, and ultimately productive, expression, new 'posthuman' objects of interest also return differential structures to purposive, self-maintaining, fruitful and generative life.

Digital media studies and animal studies affirm a continuous milieu of exchange in which there is neither a radical outside nor any limit to human comprehension. There has emerged in addition to a posthumanism that affirms a simple, continuous interface a *critical* posthumanism that affirms embodiment. In reaction to those who feel that humanity may extend or overcome itself through technology, there have been those who stress the resistance and significance of the embodied substrate, directly rejecting the 'substrate neutral' claims of those who stress computation (Dougherty 2001). Critical posthumanism reacts against the idea that the body is nothing more than contingent hardware or a vehicle for an intelligence or humanity that is primarily informational; this counter-technophilia is more critical of the residual humanist (or Cartesian, or rationalist) assumption that 'we' have now arrived at a point in history where technology might overcome the body. Critical posthumanism is nevertheless—like other affective, ethical, corporeal or post-linguistic 'turns'—a retrieval of the lived body that follows the same logic of reactive nihilism. That is, whether one uncritically affirms the capacity for humans and life to evolve to a point of posthuman freedom from all grounded biology, or whether one maintains an insistence on bodies and interests, one nevertheless grants the human (and the humanities) a continued critical role of reading and meaning. What is left out of play is the rigid separation or malevolence of the human that can neither be willed away in a mode of techno-vital euphoria, nor retrieved as some point of re-creating invention.

By contrast, both Serres and Deleuze focus on the inhuman multiplicities of systems: Serres's concepts of parasitism and pollution allow for an examination of what Deleuze and Guattari refer to as stratification (Deleuze and Guattari 2004, 176). While systems are relational, it is also the case that appropriations, overcodings and disturbances produce distinct registers. The human, as a concept, would be one way of thinking technological, meteorological or disciplinary thresholds that create intense ruptures. Humanity would be a disturbing outcome of systemic events, not an origin. Given that both Serres and Deleuze's concepts of humanity or 'the people' are futural—gestures towards how we might think the ways in which the human-sensory motor apparatus has intersected with and created new speeds for other systems—it is not surprising that both Serres and Deleuze and Guattari have a counter-interdisciplinary mode of linking discourses without commensurability. What occurs is cross-contamination or discursive germinal warfare rather than communication and a common life world.

It was the genius of Foucault to take the modern logic of life and show its direct consequences for human *disciplines*. It is the turn to *life*—the idea that social historical man can be explained by a more general process of species being (or man as a laboring political animal)—that enables social sciences. These disciplines are *reactive* because they no longer present norms as direct imperatives but as following on from the needs of life; there can only be biopolitical management of populations if there are human sciences that enable an ethics of knowledge, an organization of the human species according to broader requirements of existence. The humanities, if they react *against* this reduction of man to a material body and affirm either the capacity of man as a speaking, laboring being *not to speak or work* (Agamben's impotentiality) or more standard humanist affirmations of that which is *not* quantifiable because embodied, affective and lived, do nothing more than maintain the normative logic of life that would entail their redundancy. That is: let us say that the human sciences and bio-politics reduce 'man' to bare life, to being manipulable and manageable data. It follows that *either* the humanities becomes a supplement to this model—business ethics, bio-ethics, the production of transferable skills or critical reasoning—*or*, it argues that 'humanity' is never simply data, information, animality or bare life but has an excess of potentiality that remains unactualized. This would allow certain versions of posthumanism—those that argue for the ways in which animals or digital media complicate any simple Cartesian or rationalist model of the human—to keep the humanities alive. Man would not be mere biological mass, nor an information machine, and for this reason his 'rights' could neither be saved in themselves nor extended to animals and humans: on the contrary, the embodied interactions of humans, machines and animals would evidence a richness of the lived, of the affective, or suffering or lived body. So if man as a particular and exceptional being has been vanquished, what is saved is nevertheless a highly normative (theological-organic) logic of life in which the bounded and self-separating body with a world of its own is affirmed against various calculative reductivisms.

So what of the humanities, if anything at all, might we say is really worth saving? Stanley Fish's objection to the closing of humanities departments never makes quite clear just what mode of humanities he wishes to save, or why such survival would truly be worthy. He does refer to the horror of closing French departments when it was precisely French culture that was the breath of life for humanities departments in the 1980s. One might note as an aside the odd objection to losing French (French!!!!); Jean-Luc Nancy even protested, ironically, that it would of course be more efficient to learn 'Java' or Chinese (as the language of business). Was he really, in leaping to the defense of the humanities, suggesting that saving French was properly open and futural, while emphasizing Chinese was mercantile—akin to reduced 'languages' to 'Java'?

> Peut-être serait-il judicieux d'introduire à la place, et de manière obligatoire, quelques langages informatiques (comme java) et aussi le chinois commercial et le hindi technologique, du moins avant que ces langues soient complètement transcrites en anglais. (Nancy 2010)

Leaving aside what French might contribute to the twenty-first century, one needs to ask what aspect or consumed fragment of this mourned French theory yields a properly viable mode of humanities study. A certain strand of French thought—one highly suspicious not only of 'man' but of certain structures of knowledge in which the emergence of systems and idealities might always be returned to the lived—is precisely what has been occluded in so called posthumanism today. Indeed, the humanism that has been rejected is Cartesian computational or cognitive rationalism in favor of embodied, affective, distributed, emotional or subjective life. The humanities would somehow return disengaged logics and structures to the properly living or embodied plane of life from which they emerge. It is not only Habermas (1987), then, with his insistence that sciences always emerge *from* a lifeworld who domesticates and anthropomorphizes knowledge systems. It is what currently passes for French-inflected theory that celebrates the primacy of the lived. N. Katherine Hayles, one of the key figures of contemporary posthumanism, proclaims her distinction and theoretical sophistication from a naïve computationalism in a return to embodiment, and the lived. For Hayles:

> The computational universe becomes dangerous when it goes from being a useful heuristic device to an ideology that

privileges information over everything else. As we have seen, information is a socially constructed concept; in addition to its currently accepted definition, it could have been, and was, given different definitions. Just because information has lost its body does not mean that humans and the world have lost theirs.

Fortunately, not all theorists agree that it makes sense to think about information as an entity apart from the medium that embodies it. Let us revisit some of the sites of the computational universe, this time to locate those places where the resistance of materiality does useful work within the theories. From this perspective, fracture lines appear that demystify the program(s) and make it possible to envision other futures, futures in which human beings feel at home in the universe because they are embodied creatures living in an embodied world. (Hayles 1999, 244)

This 'critical' posthumanism is reactive in two inextricable senses, morally/politically and epistemologically. As Nietzsche described the logic of *ressentiment*: the lesser value of my life, the suffering or weakness I feel, is caused by some evil other—an other whose power and mastery proves their evil and my valued innocence. Like nihilism, which posits a higher world, diminishes the worth of actuality, and then falls into despair when the higher world is lost and there is nothing other than the actual, so *ressentiment* attributes all the world's ills and evils to the Cartesian man of rationalism and instrumental reason, and finds enchanted life and unified nature to be worthy because innocent and other than human. One posits a value outside life (humanity) that would render life meaningful or worthy, and when that value is no longer affirmed or believed in one lives on in a state of weak, mournful and enslaved subjection. Only the humanities can grant *meaning* to the world: in the absence of both God and man all we are left with is meaning. Various calls to save the humanities rely upon an asserted 'something' that must be irreducible to the quantitative materialism of economic rationalism. Methodologically or epistemologically this mystical 'x' can either be the return of the multitude as self-creating whole as event (Hardt and Negri), the human as bare potentiality witnessed in its impotentiality (Agamben), the affective or lived experience that is manifest precisely in its alienation, or just a general weak affirmation of meaning (Cottingham 2003, Wolf 2010; Eagleton 2007). Just as Foucault (1978) argued that man would be maintained by a process of enquiring into his hidden sexuality that must be the cause of his being, so the human and humanities survive by continually searching for that ultimate cause *from which* calculative and scientific reasoning must have emerged. One reacts against theory and disenchantment by a return to the lived. Mark Hansen, self-proclaimed new philosopher of new media, insists that it is precisely when digital media produces images with which I strive (but fail) to identify or empathize that 'my' lived and affective embodiment is, by default, re-affirmed:

> the shift of affective power here explored—from image to body—goes hand-in-hand, and indeed exemplifies, a larger shift currently underway in our incipient digital culture: from the preformed technical image to the embodied process of framing information that produces images. What this means, ultimately, is that we can no longer be content with the notion that we live in a culture of already articulated images, as philosophers and cultural theorists from at least Bergson to Baudrillard have maintained. ... Bluntly put, the processes governing embodied life in the contemporary infosphere are disjunctive from those governing digital information. Accordingly, in our effort to reconfigure visual culture for the information age, we must take stock of the supplementary sensorimotor dimension of embodied life that this heterogeneity makes necessary. Since there is no preformed analogy between embodiment and information, the bodily response to information—that is to say, affectivity—must step in to forge a supplementary one. In order for us to experience digital information, we must filter it through our embodied being, in the process transforming it from heterogeneous data flux into information units—images—that have meaning for us to the precise extent that they catalyze our affective response. (Hansen 2003, 225)

That is, the more inhuman, dehumanizing, replicating, alienating or simulating the image—the more the human appears as nothing more than appearance susceptible to inauthentic doubling—the more my alienated and impossible human feeling persists. It is as though the intensity of the despair I feel at your claims that God does not exist simply proves—through my very sense of loss and sadness—that really there must be a God or spirituality after all, known in His retreat or in my mourning. I feel a loss of meaning, *ergo* it is.

The second example of subjective recuperation comes from Žižek, who draws upon Rancière and Badiou to criticize a postmodern politics of a single domain of circulating opinions and tolerated identities in order to affirm the event of the subject. In a mode akin to St. Paul's universal Christianity in opposition to Greek sophistry or 'the Jewish discourse of obscurantist prophetism,' the subject is not an affirmed substance within the world, nor a messianic visitation from another world, but is given only in its act of break or disorder—again known only in its not being known:

> the way to counteract this remerging ultra-politics is not more tolerance, more compassion and multicultural understanding but the *return of the political proper*, that is, the reassertion of the dimension of antagonism that, far from denying universality, is consubstantial with it. Therein lies the key component of the proper *leftist* stance, as opposed to the rightest assertion of particular identity: in the equation of *universalism* with the militant, *divisive* position of engagement in struggle. True universalists are not those who preach global tolerances of differences and all-encompassing unity but those who engage in a passionate fight for the assertion of truth that engages them. (Žižek 1998, 1002)

The problem with humanism, so it seems, is that it is deemed to be rather inhuman. The Cartesian subject of calculative reason, along with computational theories of mind or representation, including both older humanisms of man as supreme moral animal and posthumanisms envisioning a disembodied world of absolute mastery, cannot cope with the complexity and dynamism of affective life. The humanities should, supposedly, be posthuman in this quite specific sense: the destruction of man—the being who represents a world to be known—would give way to one single domain of life as living system. There would no longer be a privileged center of knowing, nor 'a' world in general, just a web, network or mesh of multiple worlds. This would either yield a macro-organicism of Gaia and deep ecology along with a humanities oriented towards care, concern and eco-criticism or deep ecology, or—and these two paths are not mutually exclusive—a highly interdisciplinary mode of humanities in which words and texts are part of the same circulating web of things, bodies, technologies, images or any other event. It is not surprising then that philosophy has argued for connecting the mind back to the world (Clark 1997) or putting mind into life (Thompson 1997), and for thinking of societies and living bodies, as well as political systems and languages as assemblages of interconnected and immanent, but always realist and material, registers (De Landa 2006; Protevi 2009; Latour 2005). But if systems theory, assemblages and living systems approaches allow the humanities to live on, no longer as privileged decoders of culture but just as readers of systems alongside other (possibly more scientific) readers, then perhaps the most valiant posthuman ultra-humanist modes of humanities have been those that appeal to science for a grounding of their modes of reading; no longer are they seduced by the specialness of literary objects. It is in this manner that Brian Boyd neatly points out Derrida's ignorance of the scientific findings for language's emergence from life, a point that then allows Boyd to pursue a science-based literary Darwinism that, like the work of Joseph Carroll, corrects the 'high theory' notion of linguistic construction:

> If they had been less parochial, the literary scholars awed by Derrida's assault on the whole edifice of Western thought would have seen beyond the provincialism of this claim. They would have known that science, the most successful branch of human knowledge, had for decades accepted antifoundationalism, after Karl Popper's *Logik der Forschung* (*The Logic of Scientific Discovery*, 1934) and especially after Popper's 1945 move to England, where he was influential among leading scientists. They should have known that a century before Derrida, Darwin's theory of evolution by natural selection— hardly an obscure corner of Western thought—had made

anti-foundationalism almost an inevitable consequence. I say 'parochial' because Derrida and his disciples think only in terms of humans, of language, and of a small pantheon of French philosophers and their approved forebears, especially the linguist Ferdinand de Saussure. There was some excuse for Derrida in 1966, but there is none for the disciples in 2006, after decades of scientific work on infant and animal cognition. (Boyd 2006)

Like many other turns, returns or reassemblings Boyd's argument takes the form of a redemption narrative: we used to be Cartesian, computational, humanist, linguistically enclosed, but now we have discovered life. The humanities now takes everything in and in abandoning the closure of the literary object regains the world—the living, dynamic and interdisciplinary world. Manual De Landa also writes about materialism's capacity to save us from linguistic narcissism or idealism (De Landa 2006, 12-13), while Andy Clark specifically refers to putting the world back together *again* (although his culprit, as with Evan Thompson, is not French theory but Cartesianism and computationalism) (Clark 1998 xi-xii).

Mind is a leaky organ, forever escaping its 'natural' confines and mingling shamelessly with body and with world. What kind of brain needs such external support, and how should we characterize its environmental interactions? What emerges, as we shall see, is a vision of the brain as a kind of associative engine, and of its environmental interactions as an iterated series of simple pattern-completing computations. (Clark 1998, 53)

Would the humanities be worth saving in such a world? Would not humanities scholars be better replaced by journalists—reporting and disseminating findings from the sciences—or by scientists themselves? If, as Boyd claims, understanding literature really requires understanding evolution would you not rather trust someone with a rigorous training in that area? And if the body and its neural responses were really the basis for what goes on in digital media, who would you save, a critic who can correct Deleuze by looking back to Bergson or someone who just received a NSF grant for a new fMRI machine?

There is a definite historical sense and teleology here: language, literature and the objects of the humanities—including 'man'—emerge
from life. Man, unfortunately, made the mistake of regarding himself as
distinct from life, leading to Cartesianism and linguisticism, but science
has redeemed us. Neuroscience has returned the brain to affective emotional life, and evolutionary theory has returned that living affective life
to a broader narrative of the organism's efficiency. Interdisciplinarity will
save the humanities as will a sense of historical emergence or genesis. We
will become posthuman via consumption—absorbing information and
methods from the sciences—and extension: no longer limiting human
predicates such as thought, affect, pathos and signification to humans.

It might seem to follow, then, that a combination of the work of Gilles
Deleuze and Michel Serres would finally be in order. Consider the key
motifs of their works: an inter-weaving of different disciplinary registers
(mathematics and poetry), a refusal to isolate the human animal from
life, a sense of life as a multiplicity, a complex historical sense that would
destroy the history of man in favor of a history of bodies (where bodies
would include technological objects, words, languages, animals, polities,
cities and images) and an emphasis on *sense*. The latter term would not
be *meaning* or the way in which the world is for 'us' but would open out
onto a broader domain of interaction and relations (as well as that which
is devoid of relation and connection). What I would suggest, though, is
that there is an *inhuman* (rather than posthuman) approach to knowledge
offered by the ways in which Deleuze and Serres approach the problems
of history and sense, and that such an approach would not *extend* the life
of the humanities by melding it with a single interdisciplinary domain
of which the sciences would also be a part, but would intensify certain
dimensions of the humanities only by destroying certain majoritarian,
anthropomorphic or dominant components.

It is true that Deleuze and Guattari weave together insights from science linguistics, art, philosophy and the social sciences, not only in *A
Thousand Plateaus* but also in *What is Philosophy?* The latter volume poses
the question of philosophy as a genuine problem; it does not so much
define philosophy extensively (generalizing from what has already actually occurred) but rather creates an intensive plane: if we can see science,
art and philosophy as they are already given, what are the distinct forces

that make these lines of thought possible? On the one hand, philosophy art and science emerge from virtual powers (such as the capacity, in art, for sensations to be presented *as such*); on the other hand, Deleuze and Guattari also specify the economic, imaginary, geographical and historical conditions for something like the philosophical practice for creating concepts. They also locate art, not in human practice, but in animal life. However, it is precisely through the expansion of a disciplinary tendency beyond its *human* form that Deleuze and Guattari destroy a certain model of inter-disciplinarity. If one could think of concepts, affects and functions *not* as practices grounded in a self-maintaining human life, then one would not only have to rethink the supposed self-evident good of *inter*-disciplinarity and the unity of the humanities, but also the future and survival of disciplines and the dominant image of the (now highly humanized) humanities. Such a future would not assume the value of *living on* in its current form, either of humanity or the humanities, and it would abandon such assumed values precisely because of what we might refer to—after Serres—as climate change. If we could imagine the radical sense of climate, from *clima* and inclination, or the inflection that yields a certain patterning of what surrounds us, then we might say that now is the time to question the human and posthuman basis of thinking, especially when the posthuman has been a return of the human into one single life with one single inclination, that of ongoing self-maintenance. To conclude with a more positive—which is to say, destructive—approach to thinking beyond the interdisciplinarity of the humanities I will conclude with drawing upon two concepts from Serres—parasitism and pollution—and two concepts from Deleuze and Guattari: concepts/affects and higher deterritorialization. Assembled together these concepts can yield a new sense of *sense* and a new sense of history.

At its broadest the concept of parasitism would at first seem to place Serres's approach within a single and unified field of knowledge, as it yields a model not just for relations among living bodies, but for information systems and—one might say—life in general. But if *the relation* of parasitism, and its capacity to displace the illusion of predator-prey relations, is general , then what parasitism discloses are irreducible differences and ularities that require highly discerned cuts and judgments. Whereas a predator would be a vaguely self-sufficient body, capable of maintaining itself and using some other body as means of sustenance, the parasite would have no existence other than that of supplementarity: 'And that is the meaning of the prefix *para-* in the word *parasite*: it is on the side, next to, shifted; it is not on the thing, but on its relation. It has relations, as they say, and makes a system of them. It is always mediate and never immediate' (Serres 2007, 38-39).

To claim that man is parasitic, rather than a predator, and that this occurs in a life of parasitism in general entails several consequences for humanism, posthumanism and the 'disciplines' that might be adequate to thinking the inhuman. If one abandons the concept of predator then one also abandons the concept of the good and just relation: it would not be the case that a proper humanity would use 'its' natural milieu according to reasonable or ecological needs, maintaining a balance with a world he uses but towards which he could also contribute (by cultivating, re-planting, mitigating, adapting, capping, trading and offsetting). There would be no *good* humanity of reasonable predatory use that might be morally distinguished from a parasitic humanity that would be nothing more than a consumer or digester of energies not its own. For that is the nature of distinction and being: one is not a unified body that then might produce good (self-sustaining) or evil (ultimately short-term and destructive) relations to one's milieu.

Let us accept that humanity is and must be parasitic: it lives *only* in its robbing and destruction of a life that is not its own. Our current predicament of climate change, whereby we have consumed and ingested blindly—bloating and glutting our body politic through the constant destruction of resources without recompense—would not be a late accident, nor a misjudgment of a post-industrial age. To be a body is to be a consuming body, to be in a relation of destructive consumption with what is effected as other, as resource, through consumption. Climate change would be the condition of human organicism in general: for there would be no climate, only *clinamen,* an inclination, deviancy or parasitism that creates a supplemental body (of man) who would then retroactively imagine that he has an environment, a *klima,* for which he ought to have been more mindful. But if this places humanity as one aspect of a general parasitism, then it is also the case that 'man' occurs as a specific inclination or deviation, and it would be the task of thinking to examine each parasitic swerve (human and non-human) according to its own differential. The deviation that enables mathematical systems, for example, would occur when the counting procedure deflects from living praxis and becomes a formalized supplemental system. From here one could then examine the geneses of formalization and ideality. Similarly, one could see poetry as a specific parasite, taking the language of speech and action and developing a relation among sounds and rhythms of the voice and script, but with no benefit from the organic or living bodies and practices from which it emerged.

Attempts to *return* systems to the sense of their origin—to see literature as benefiting the bodies from which it emerged, to see digital media as grounded in affect and embodiment, or to see all disciplines as expressions of one self-maintaining life-world would be to suffer from the illusion that parasitism goes in two directions. Not only does Serres insist that it does not; this irreversibility can be evidenced by any semi-autonomous or parasitic system. A system develops its own laws of survival irrespective of its host, and this is so even if the complexity of relations often confuses—for observers—who is host and who is parasite. Not only could there be no general *inter*-disciplinary humanities, whereby each discipline recognized its place in the ongoing self-understanding of man; each declination or parasitism would have its own inflection. *As parasitic* it could not be grounded in 'the' body of a single life.

This leads to pollution, which cannot be seen as some late-industrial nor specifically human inclination. It would not be the deviation from proper inhabitation, for inhabitation as such involves not just added markers or territorial inscriptions but contributing something like *waste* or matter that elicits disgust or revulsion to an approaching outsider (Serres 2008, 29). There is a connection here with parasitism that further debilitates (or ought to debilitate) 'our' usual notions of ecology, environment and symbiotic interconnectedness. Pollution is not simply making a niche, having a world that would, in turn, contribute to other worlds; to pollute or mark a space as one's own habitus is to subtract, diminish and defile the origin's integrity. If there is *only* pollution, and if there is no clean or ethical living, or if ethos is entwined with abjection then one could not attribute climate change to man alone. That is another way of saying that climate change would not be recognizable as long as one remained in a human or posthuman mode of thinking: for such a mode would begin with man destroying his milieu (anthropogenic climate change would then require man to mitigate, adapt or trade in order to live on). And posthuman celebrations of a single ecology would not be able to face a condition of climate change *in general*. To live and inhabit is to be parasitic, to pollute, to alter the *clima*, to effect an inclination that cannot be remedied or mitigated by some return or retrieval of the proper.

This suggests several critical and positive conclusions. *Critically* one could no longer ground ethics on an understanding of a proper humanity: not only humanity in general but any living form—any being that marks or territorializes itself—must distinguish itself from its milieu. In the beginning would be neither mutual exchange nor symbiosis but theft (Deleuze and Guattari 2004a, 203). Survival and self-maintenance, or the creation of a specificity or identity, require deviation and distortion.

Where does this leave notions of ecology, symbiosis and Gaia? On the one hand Serres's focus on the *clinamen* reinforces the relational aspect of all being: there are not identities or terms that then enter into relation, nor a world of individuals or beings who must then somehow contract with or contact each other. But this is not to suggest either that there is one harmonious world, expressed each in its own way by each living form. On the contrary, as in Deleuze's monadology, Serres's Leibnizian world is one of *incompossibility*. Not only is each inclination or deviation an opening and disruption of a quite specific or singular differential—a quite singular creation of a field—it occurs always as disruption of other differentials and relations. The emphasis on parasitism and pollution precludes any nostalgia or restoration; in the beginning is defilement. This then yields a far more positive conception of a natural contract, which would not be man becoming one with nature as one living and symbiotic whole. Rather, it is precisely *the supposedly ethical* position of man as an interdisciplinary animal—man as assembler and negotiator of a single field of knowledges—that would give way to a natural contract that is a multiplicity, with divergent rather than harmonious lines of inflection. Climate change in a positive sense, following on from this parasitism and pollution, would occur as a negotiation or natural contract of the infinitely multiple. The contract is at once epistemological and legal, for it requires not only that *man recognize his natural milieu, but that the very concepts of milieu, environment and climate in their singular sense would have to be rendered obsolete if nature also 'contracts.' Nature also has its inflections, worlds, multiplicities and differentials.* We could not, then, imagine a grounding or ideal (even inaccessible) nature that is lost in the creation of technical systems. There has always been globalization; each event in the world is a disturbance or distortion that enables something like an inflection or inclination to occur from chaos. (A new threshold occurs with modern post-industrial humanity precisely because its inflections do not just radiate outward and create local distortions but *deterritorialize* or become inflections of the whole, capable of infecting or polluting every other line of system or parasitism.) The 'contract' of the natural contract is therefore not a signature (an act of the hand, inscribing a blank surface) but a contraction (the introduction of a noise or pollutant that ramifies throughout the open whole). Here is where Serres's work connects with Deleuze's similarly divergent Leibniz-ism. The world is a monadology, an infinitely divisible chaos in which smaller and smaller differentials will enable subtler and subtler relations and encounters—so that there is no nature in general outside or beyond the multiplicity of contractions: 'organs fully belong to matter because they are merely the contraction of several waves or rays: the nature of a receptive organ is to contract' (Deleuze 2006b, 111). If, today, networks of technology and techno-science have, in their parasitism, effected something like a totality of nature in general, this is not as an object of scientific knowledge so much as a field of implication:

> Classical Western philosophy never calculated the cost of knowledge or action but considered them to be free of charge. However, as soon as work appears, everything is subject to the martial law of price. The yield of work is never one on one; there are always residues and garbage. As long as work remains cold and local, price is calculated in terms of profit and loss. As soon as heat enters work, the productivity of the thermic machine is calculated. When world-objects are in operation, the cost becomes commensurable with a world

dimension. Local, negligible waste is succeeded by global pollution of the world. (Serres 2006)

In a manner that seems close to Hardt and Negri's positing of a new
global humanity effected through the immaterial networks of technology
Serres suggests that a global 'we' has emerged, requiring a reflexive discipline concerned with humanity's total polluting power. Here is where one
might note a disjunction between the affirmation of the people as 'missing' in Deleuze and Guattari (1994, 176) and Serres's almost mournful
lament of this new 'we' with unforeseen destructive powers that finally
produces nature as a totality (not so much as on object of knowledge but
as a consequence of destruction).

For Serres something like humanity has been rendered possible and
effective not because of knowledge as recognition but because of a
general polluting and parasitic power that has overtaken the locality
of systems and relative disturbances. If we align this new 'subject' with
Deleuze and Guattari's recognition of capitalism as an axiomatic then
this provides us with a new way of thinking about a positively destructive
'humanities.' This would be inhuman, rather than posthuman, precisely
because the creation of the single system or axiom where work and production overcode all other relations, including supposedly environmental or ecological imperatives of survival and adaptation, would need to be
annihilated to give way to differentials along a different axis.

Consider, here, Deleuze and Guattari's created concepts, in *What is
Philosophy?* which are not *extensive* insofar as they do not name or gener-
alize actually existing disciplines but are *intensive*: they create or mark out
speeds and rhythms for thinking. Consider concepts: although it is possible in a weak and general sense to locate concepts as one part of everyday
speech, Deleuze and Guattari create a concept of concepts. A concept,
considered philosophically, possesses a unique speed and rhythm. The
concept of the *cogito,* for example, did not label an already existing entity,
nor did it perform a move in an already practiced language game. Rather,
when Descartes creates the concept of the cogito he slows thought
down, retreats from action and efficiency, and from practical communication and institutes a thoroughly new, virtual and philosophic terrain.
Doubt is oriented to a perception of the world as calculable, of 'a' subject
as self-present, of philosophy as a mode of questioning and of bodies as

suspended or placed in parentheses. Similarly, Deleuze and Guattari also create the concept of affects/percepts and functions. The former do not describe already existing art practices, nor what art always is. Like the concept of philosophy and its capacity to create concepts, the concept of art (as the production of affects/percepts) intuits a potentiality that may exist in a mixed or impure form in thinking as it currently is, but that can be intimated and gestured to *futurally* in what thought might be. What would it be to create a percept that would not be the perception *of* some observer, or an *affect* that would be neither the affection of an author nor an affection produced in the reader/viewer?

By creating the concept of the concept in *What is Philosophy?* Deleuze and Guattari allow for a new mode of philosophy: if democracy is a *concept* then the problem of democracy is not so much what it *is* (what social systems are really democratic) but the orientation it creates in thinking. What would it be to develop a socius with no other power than its own capacity for decision? Similarly, by creating the concept of affects and percepts they enable a new mode of art theory: how might we imagine a work, not as the communication of an author, nor as the representation of a world, nor as the meaning it yields for its readers, but as a 'stand alone' or monumental detachment of percepts and affects from the lived? The affect or percept would yield color as such, melancholy as such: one might think here of the attempt to capture light in paint, to capture the sounds of the earth in synthesizers, or the striving to sculpt courage in stone. Deleuze and Guattari's concepts—the concept of philosophy as the creation of concepts, of art as the production of affects—allow us to think beyond 'the humanities,' beyond 'interdisciplinarity,' and they do so in ways that intersect fruitfully with Serres's concepts of parasitism, pollution and a new humanity.

For Serres a threshold is reached with current extensions of pollution that create a difference in kind. Humanity is no longer one pollutant or polluter among others, creating a territory, milieu or inclination. Humanity effects a climate change of climates; there are no longer multiplicities of inclinations, but an inclination or clima that has extended to such a *degree* that is constitutes a difference in kind—a pollution of such intensity that it now precludes the dynamisms, systems and disturbances of anything outside its own terrain. Serres argues that this *calls for* a concept of humanity. Such a concept would not be a reflection upon man as he is or has been, would not be a critical uncovering of the specific life of man. As a futural concept it would, like Deleuze and Guattari's created concepts of philosophy, art and science, require and enable an interrogation into humanity as inclination. How is it possible that in a life or earth that is nothing other than a multiplicity of inclinations and parasitisms one specific line or disturbance has taken over the whole, at the very expense of its own tendency? If all life is improper, noisy, disturbing and deprived of any grounding or proper form—if, in the beginning, is the swerve—then how might one account for both the overtaking of the plane of disturbances and the emerging desire for a survival *not* of man as he is—a humanity that would manage its polluting tendencies—but that might create a new concept of itself?

The very concept of the humanities in its dominant form—as critical and interdisciplinary—would need to be destroyed in a productive manner. This is because the idea of man that underpins the humanities as an interdisciplinary problem has been extensive: disciplines are activities, achieved by a division of labor, with man examining himself as a historical animal whose life creates him as a social and linguistic being capable of self-reflection and communication. It is not surprising that *this* man of reflexive knowledge and moral self-management confronts climate change as an extensive and managerial problem: how might we use less in order to live longer, how might we act more frugally in order to survive? But if we accept that there are capacities or potentialities that are not those of managerial man—either Serres future humanity or Deleuze and Guattari's 'still-missing people'—then we would have to abandon the idea of earth as environment to which we might bear our proper and restorative relation, along with *the* humanities as some domain of communication that might return us to our better selves. A futural approach to disciplines would embrace and intensify the distinct inclinations of thinking—the differences of thinking in concepts, colors, sounds, affects—and would not assume precisely what climate change forces us to question: Why, if information regarding our polluting and parasitic existence is so extensive, are we so incapable of thinking intensively, of imagining a different inclination beyond that of the adaptation and survival of man?

Why Saying 'No' to Life is Unacceptable

Just what counts as acceptable or unacceptable is obviously a cultural, social and historical variable. That being so it might still be possible to make claims regarding broader structures of unacceptability, and certain motifs that, within epochs, dominate cultural production. We can perhaps begin by asking—today—just what might count as unacceptable *in general*. That is to say, one can imagine all forms of socially refused content, ranging from prohibited actions and lifestyles to censored content. But on what grounds or by what logic is the border between the acceptable and the unacceptable drawn? The problem can be given some generality and purchase today if we ask what the rationale for accepting or refusing something might be, and—further—what forms the limit of acceptability today. I would suggest that despite dispute over what counts as acceptable the governing rationale for dispute is the concept of *life*: one either argues for an intrinsic 'right to life' or one asserts one's rights to choose on the basis of the autonomy of one's own life. The logic of normativity is grounded on life, which is to say that norms are not—as they once might have been—given transcendently (as what is dictated by God or social propriety)—but are immanent to life. One either argues against gay marriage, single parenting or other alternative lifestyles on the grounds that it threatens 'our way of life' (including the family, reproduction, maintaining humanity as it is), *or* one insists on the right to determine one's life. Cultural production also reinforces this unquestioned affirmation of life: from lifestyle channels, to reality television's display of life, to celebrity culture to legal and medical dramas and the increasingly close-angled camera work displaying the minutiae of life, all external criteria give way to the value of *life itself*. At first glance it appears that the enlightenment project of removing all forms of transcendent justification—Church,

State, privilege and prejudice—has been achieved, and now there is nothing other than life. And yet, such a frenzied surge in an unquestioning insistence on the value of life is accompanied both by an inability to confront the imminent demise of life (whether that be by way of accelerated extinction due to climate change, or disaster scenarios resulting from terrorism, nuclear warfare, viral pandemic or bio-weapons and resource depletion—or, the inevitable panic that would follow on from and exacerbate the appearance of any of these threats.) In addition to the shrill insistence on the primacy of life, and alongside the deluge of information regarding increasing and exponentially accelerating threats to life, there has been a strange incapacity to ask the question of life. That is: now that life appears to be in danger of disappearance, diminution or mutation beyond recognition, living humans indulge both in greater and greater insistence on the sanctity of life, *and* seem incapable of directly confronting the intensifying threats that menace the present.

The hinge of the acceptable is life, both because acceptability is negotiated on the basis of life, and because any *question* of life is evidently unacceptable. This inadmissibility of the question is most clearly the case precisely when the question of life *seems* to have been posed. That is, when cultural production turns directly (as it does occasionally) to the problem of life, it is precisely at that point that the question of life refuses to be asked. The question of what we accept and do not accept, what we can consider or question and what remains beyond question, is probably always a query of some interest. But the question of the value of life should gain in interest (if not urgency) for us now, and for three reasons. First, the question or problem of life is now an actual question that is everywhere being asked (and yet also deferred in the very mode of the question's formation.) We are no longer simply confronted with the 'meaning' of life, or the enigma of existence, for it is quite possible, probable or increasingly certain that we will begin to witness the beginning of the end of life (mass extinctions, resource depletion threatening human order, climate change that is moving at a pace beyond predictions of exponential acceleration, and even the strange mutation of the human brain via digital technologies and visual culture that may spell the 'end' of cognitive man). Yet, oddly enough, despite the urgency of this problem the question of life has—more than ever—been articulated in terms of *meaning*, with a flurry of supposedly deeply philosophical accounts of the unavoidable horizon of meaning when approaching what appears as life (Wolf 2010; Cottingham 2003; Eagleton 2007). Further, and despite recent academic and philosophical insistence upon life's meaning, there has been a surge of cultural production focusing on life's termination—ranging from disaster fiction and cinema to survival guides for end-of-the-world scenarios. In addition to a flourishing genre of post-apocalyptic cinema and literature, there have also been documentaries and non-fictional thought experiments about the world without humans, the aftermath that would follow catastrophes, and other human-witnessed posthuman scenarios. In sum, the problem of the continuation of life *ought* to be at the forefront of reflective inquiry (and is indeed played out in a series of fictional and semi-fictional scenarios) but the problem is (in that very process of being played out) displaced. It is as though cultural production, at least in its dominant mode, is indulging in Freud's grandson's *Fort-Da* game: we play and replay the disappearance and reappearance of life, and do this to anticipate and master an event that concerns our (in this case, very real and possible) non-existence. Third and finally, even in its barely articulated, suggested, but not fully posed mode, the form of the question of life has altered in the twenty-first century. Until recently, if the problem of life were posed it took the form of theodicy, or justification: of how 'we' can explain life's utter cruelty and seeming disregard for human suffering. It is this question that is played out in Job, in Greek tragedy, in Milton's *Paradise Lost* and even perhaps in modern novels, such as William Godwin's *Caleb Williams,* where inscrutable injustice is now politicized (and can be attributed to corrupt and therefore remediable institutions). A pre-modern form of tragedy would, in pre-Christian mode, confront the tragic contingency and inhumanity of life (and it was Nietzsche who admired this noble capacity of Greek tragedy's encounter with the brute force of existence); in Christian thought, especially in its modern Miltonic mode, the seeming tragic senselessness of life will ultimately be redeemed in a regained paradise. In works such as Godwin's *Caleb Williams* the experience of tragic desperation and the inhumanity of life is historicized and seen to be symptomatic of a social system that may (and should) be transformed. These modern novelistic explorations of life's cruelty are tales of fortitude, and of the nobility and dignity of withstanding the force of existence. The endpoint of this tradition might be Kafka or Beckett, in which the individual confronts a life that is tragically void of all sense and (for that individual at least) hope. One can either interpret Kafka and Beckett existentially (as writers who face the void of non-meaning) or regard that experience of the void as a (potentially) political hope for a world of non-damaged life. It is perhaps thoroughly modern to shift from a tragic acceptance of the brute contingency of life to some sense that the struggle itself is one of personal meaning. (This was why Nietzsche so admired the ancient Greeks, for having the capacity to experience the violence and 'festive cruelty' of life's force, without moralizing [Nietzsche 2000]. Today, and for some time, the tragic mode has become less acceptable *as tragic*. Some form of resolution or compensation usually closes narrative form. The forces of good triumph in the end, or suffering itself is given meaning: Hollywood cinema rarely allows itself a conclusion void of redemption, while tales of suffering—from *Born on the Fourth of July* (1989) to *The Pursuit of Happyness* (2006) and *127 Hours* (2010) are morality plays of individual triumph rather than an exploration of cosmic indifference.) Even so, and despite a refusal to confront the limits of life just when the historical actuality of life's end is becoming apparent, though not witnessed, it is possible to note a shift of genre away from human-to-human adversity to, at least initially, something like a war between humans and the cosmos (and this despite all the deep ecology proclamations of our oneness with life).

A new mode of the question of life has come to dominate cultural production: not, 'Why are humans subjected to the brutal force of existence?' but: given human brutality and life-destructiveness, by what right will humans continue to survive? It is no longer life that needs to be justified, but the human species' malevolent relation to life. Nietzsche had already charted the ways in which 'man' as a moral animal had been effected from an inability to accept the violence of the forces of life. Whereas Ancient Greek tragedy was initially akin to a theater of cruelty, not yet indulging in justification, the positing of a 'higher world' that would justify life created man as a slavish animal (Nietzsche 2007). When that higher world was turned inward, it was not God who enslaved man, but 'humanity': we are now always already guilty, chastened and humiliated by an ideal of our own making, and fall into nihilistic despair if the once imagined higher world seems no longer real. Freud made a similar observation: once we move from a tribal competitiveness and warring aggression and take on the command to love one's neighbor as oneself we can only react neurotically: in my failure to love my fellow man I will turn that guilt back upon myself in damaging self-aggression. Both Freud and Nietzsche diagnosed the twentieth century's incapacity to face up to the inhuman contingency of existence; if life is horrific then someone must be guilty, and why not both attribute that guilt to man as he has been, while insisting on a proper humanity that will emerge from the human wreckage?

We simply cannot live existence without granting it some sort of meaning. That, itself, is not the problem. As Adorno and Horkheimer described the dialectic of enlightenment: the 'shudder' of existence prompts a magical projection of our own anthropomorphic limits on the world. If enlightenment destroys the mimesis or doubling of the world that has reconfigured life in order to render it acceptable to humans, this process of enlightenment nevertheless achieves 'disenchantment' by containing and mastering the world—silencing all the sounds of damage and suffering. The horrors of twentieth-century atrocities did much to destroy our forms of meaning, allowing high modernism and the art of the absurd to emerge. For Adorno, modern art's refusal to grant the world harmonious order was a sign that we might be able to move beyond our inability to confront disjunction. We need to move beyond an absurd abandonment of all hope without falling back into kitsch resignation with art acting as the promise of happiness. Yet today it is not nihilistic despair in the face of non-meaning that seems to be the dominant affect. On the contrary, not only is *meaning* now the seemingly unquestionable horizon of human existence—ranging from 'philosophical' studies to the Oprah Winfrey Network and projects of individual self-development—cultural production reaches its points of tragic despair by questioning the rampant violence of humans in relation to life rather than life's lack of concern for humans. It is not humanity that is cruelly placed in an inhuman world, so much as an inhuman humanity that has become unjustifiable in an anthropomorphized world.

The Post-Apocalytpic

The opening of the twenty-first century is marked by a supposedly new genre (or the efflorescence of an old genre) of the post-apocalyptic. However this term is used, one way we can make sense of the *post*-apocalyptic is to note that scenes of near-destruction of the human milieu are followed by an exploration of what will survive or remain, or what ought to survive or remain, after the absence of humanity as we now know it. The post-apocalyptic is best read as a question posed: just as the human species starts to approach the real possibility of its actual non-existence (whether through climate change, viral pandemic, terrorist use of nuclear or bio-weapons, wars on the terror aiming to avert the latter, resource depletion, panic, or any conjunction of the foregoing) there is a barely perceived and half-articulated problem of how and whether humans ought to survive. What is it about humanity that one would want to accept? Further—as the very use of the word 'post-*apocalyptic*' indicates—the genres and modes in which this problem is articulated preclude the problem from being posed. There is a constitutive inability to confront the very content that 'we' are nevertheless constantly replaying.

According to Freud art is primarily a rendering acceptable of otherwise indulgently unacceptable private content (Freud 1908). Jokes, similarly, allow otherwise unacceptable content to circulate, allowing what can be thought but not *really* said to find some outlet (thus explaining, for Freud, the body's explosion in laughter). Beyond Freud, and in a line that runs at least from Adorno to Jameson, there is a commitment to the idea of narrative and form as processes that render the intolerable tolerable. Despite its debt to Marx, this strand of what I would refer to as existential or Hegelian Marxism problematizes a Marxist concept of 'the political' that has tended to dominate whatever is left today of ideology critique: according to this basic Marxist imperative of politicizing or denaturalizing whatever appears as simple, inevitable, universal or irrevocable, one ought to historicize the present, and account for the genesis of the social and political world on the basis of 'man's' transformation of that world. What appears as intolerable should not be seens as inevitable but re-read as an outcome of the division of labor and the conditions of production. Nothing should simply appear as transcendent, inhuman and inscrutable. For Adorno, working against theodicy, there is an imperative to maintain an irresolvable negativity or disjunction between the sense we make of the world and a 'world itself' that can only be given as other than the human (Adorno 1983, 361). The shudder of existence, or the brute otherness of life that simply cannot be lived, is tempered in general by the projective processes that form the world. What appears today in the form of 'the aesthetic' enables us to have some sense of a historical trajectory in which the radically alien and contingent force of life has passed through a process of animism, or a mythologizing reduction of the world, through enlightenment (or the reduction of the world to so much calculable and 'disenchanted' matter) through to modernism (Adorno and Horkheimer 2002). Modernism, for Adorno, is counter-bourgeois and counter-kitsch, an experience of form in its deadness, in its incommensurability with life. Without endorsing Adorno's high modernist resistance to the easily consumed and already circulating forms that render the world always already amenable, it is nevertheless worthwhile to pursue this crucial insight: art can be seen as having a *humanizing* function, a rendering of the world into some form of manageable order. In quite different ways Paul de Man, also indebted to Hegel in some respects, and also less ready to see language's ordering of the world as a process of meaning or familiarity, sought to draw attention—however impossibly—to language and form as radically *inhuman* (Cohen, Colebrook and Miller 2011). For both Adorno and De Man, the text or art operates as a disjunction, negation or instance of 'deadness' or 'afterlife.' It is the lure of 'the aesthetic' to imagine that art is somehow an expression of 'life.'

If art in general is a formalizing process that grants the raw violence of life some moralizing structure, then certain modes of narrative would seem to intensify what Fredric Jameson (writing after Adorno) has summarized as the ideological transformation of existential horror into social symbolization. Science fiction, for example, codes otherness as such into the delimited and opposed figure of the alien or invader (Jameson 2005, 141). (Spy fiction has its different narrative modes of discerning or reading just who or what counts as a threatening other, or just where the limits and readability of self and other lie). In so doing narrative parses into a temporal project—an overcoming of adversity—what could not be confronted as such: our subjection to life. The novelistic imagination tends to personalize, or even render familial, the symbolizing order that had once—in epic or tragic modes—required a confrontation with forces that required more than 'life management.' If one examines cultural production today the manifest content that seems at first to confront radically threatening forces is ultimately returned to the genres of family drama and romance, as though even the end of human existence could be Oedipalized. That is, there is an efflorescence of disaster and post-apocalyptic narrative, but always with a narrative resolution that restores a basic human binary (such as the romance ending that allows humanity to triumph in *The Adjustment Bureau* [2011] or the victory of New Age humanoids over corporate and military greed in *Avatar* [2009].) Even a story as bleak as Cormac McCarthy's *The Road* (especially in its cinematic adaptation of 2009), devolves around a father-son relation: the man and boy wander a landscape while struggling for survival against remaining humans; the journey concludes with a sense of the possible renewal of the family-maternal bond as the son is taken in by a potential new family. In blockbuster entertainment, the 2008 film *Traitor* figured the 'war on terror' and the conflict between fundamental Islam and US security and espionage as ultimately a problem of fraternal misunderstanding: the warring individuals ultimately find common cause in the discovery of their underlying humanity. It is as though terrorism and militarism could be overcome if only we could return, once again, to face-to-face encounters. One might add to this continual anthropogenicism any number of disaster epics that are organized into human-human agonistics: it is never the earth, the climate, contingency or catastrophe as such that is presented as the intruding force of destruction; rather, it is some identifiable face that allows the sheer violence of adversity to be translated into a resolvable and symbolized other.

Occasionally, however, within narrative trajectories there have been moments when the *question* of life reaches articulation. If life—or the idea of a body that goes through time, manages an external world, and then arrives at its own end—has always been figured through some narrative imaginary that renders stark contingency into a mastered and acceptable *sense* (Brooks 1984), then the question of life seems to destroy narrative. I want to cite two pre-contemporary examples before looking at the different ways in which the question of life's acceptability has changed its structure in the twenty-first century.

Narrative Life

In Milton's *Paradise Lost*, which is a self-proclaimed theodicy or justification of the apparent intolerability of life, Adam asks God why he (Adam) was made so unfairly and impossibly free. If we accept that man deserves to be expelled from paradise because he chose to transgress the order of Eden, it does not follow that man deserved to be given this task in the first place. Adam's lament cries out against the burden of human freedom, or man's capacity to act against life. Why did God make him thus?

> Did I request thee, Maker, from my Clay
> To mould me Man, did I sollicite thee
> From darkness to promote me, or here place
> In this delicious Garden? as my Will
> Concurd not to my being, it were but right
> And equal to reduce me to my dust,
> Desirous to resigne, and render back
> All I receav'd, unable to performe
> Thy terms too hard, by which I was to hold
> The good I sought not. To the loss of that,
> Sufficient penaltie, why hast thou added
> The sense of endless woes? inexplicable
> Thy Justice seems; yet to say truth, too late,
> I thus contest; then should have been refusd
> Those terms whatever, when they were propos'd:
> (*Paradise Lost* 10: 742-757).

God responds by unfolding a vision of history: Adam will see increasing violence and destruction, but will eventually see man benefit from grace and forgiveness. If, after all this evil, God will still sacrifice his son, allowing man to receive a law that is now internalized and accepted from a condition of forgiven fallenness, then life once more makes sense. Human life, for all its apparent perversity is ultimately a higher good, all the better for having turned away from, and then re-found, itself. One might say that all narratives are theodicies, or ways in which the seemingly senseless destruction of existence is given redemptive form. The unacceptable is rendered acceptable, not just in the sense of what is socially frowned upon being presented as more palatable—but in a more radical sense in which something like *the social* is formed. Narrative creates the lure of a world in common, an order of sense and humanity, in which otherness is personalized and rendered familial and familiar.

This has specific purchase today: it is almost as though the more unimaginable the possible forces of destruction appear to be, the more local our narrative imagination becomes. In addition, though, to the process of narrative as social symbolization—in which order as such is constituted—the problems, intolerable conflicts or disjunctions to which narrative responds are varied. One can imagine the ways in which race, sex, social disintegration, internecine conflicts, historical transitions and so forth, all need to be worked through by narrative (Jameson 214). What is suggested by Adorno's approach, and in Jameson's concept of ideology, is that these 'political' figures are ideological precisely because they give a binary and humanized form to existential conflict as such:

> The fantasy level of a text would then be something like the primal motor force which gives any cultural artifact its resonance, but which must always find itself diverted to other, ideological functions, and reinvested by what we have called the political unconscious. (Jameson 129)

On the one hand, then, there is an ordering or meaning-producing function of narrative, a function that answers what might be referred to in general as the problem of existence. On the other hand, there are historically specific ways in which the modes of this question or conflict are formed; the ways in which intolerable life is reconfigured and rendered acceptable vary according to just what the horrific other of humanity is deemed to be.

In *Paradise Lost*, and theodicy generally, the problem is the burden of human freedom in relation to a God and life that *must be* conducive to harmony. In Mary Shelley's *Frankenstein* the similarly formed question is now directed to man (Victor Frankenstein) by his monstrous progeny. Here the question is not so much human freedom as humanity's creation of a world in which its offspring are then abandoned. What duty do we owe to the future? If Victor Frankenstein plays God he does so not only in his creation of a living being who is at once a mirror of his own being and yet deemed by him to be lesser, but also in his tyrannical laying down of terms the monster cannot accept. Allegorically, Shelley can be seen to be posing Milton's question again, somewhat blasphemously: what sort of God creates a being and then leaves it wandering in a world of despair? Or, as the monster accuses Victor, 'You, my creator, abhor me; what hope can I gather from your fellow creatures, who owe me nothing? They spurn and hate me? The desert mountains and dreary glaciers are my refuge.' (Shelley, 94.)

The creature's plea to his maker is also an allegorical questioning of humanity's relation to production: how can we leave a populace of the future so miserably orphaned? In Shelley's case this is sharpened by the fact that the monstrous being of the future promises to be less rapacious than man (even though he still is refused by his creator):

> My food is not that of man; I do not destroy the lamb and the kid to glut my appetite; acorns and berries afford me sufficient nourishment. My companion will be of the same nature as myself, and will be content with the same fare. We shall make our bed of dried leaves; the sun shall shine on us as on man, and will ripen our food. The picture I present to you is peaceful and human, and you must feel that you could deny it only in the wantonness of power and cruelty. (Shelley, 128-9)

Shelley's novel is a play of mirrors (directly re-writing *Paradise Lost*), in which 'man's' plea against existence is at once given a political-allegorical form (so that the monster appears to be a disenfranchised other who could, in theory, be redeemed and included), at the same time as the monster's creator and pseudo-God also feels the utter horror of what it had intended to create as a free, productive and world transforming being. The maliciously and thoughtlessly reproductive Victor poses the same question to himself: how can one go on living when existence is intolerable, when one's free actions yield such monstrous outcomes: 'Cursed, cursed creator! Why did I live? Why, in that instant, did I not extinguish the spark of existence which you had so wantonly bestowed?' (121). Shelley's formulation aims to give some political purchase to the existential question, suggesting that it is Victor's theological imaginary that prompts him first to play God and then to hold on to proper notions of man and morality in the face of the monster's rather ecological and reasonable request. Even so, Shelley—like Milton—begins by posing the question of the intolerable terms of life *for man*. If Milton seeks resolution in grace, a 'paradise within' and a future when the world shall be 'all in all,' Shelley suggests a more radical response: the truly human future does not close itself off to the non-carnivorous generations who will live in the glaciers and deserts. Something like the 'properly human' functions as Shelley's political answer to the question of life. Like Marx, Adorno and Jameson after her, Shelley will suggest that the existential shudder of existence should properly be understood not as a relation between man and world, but among men. To varying degrees all these writers—from Milton and Shelley, to Marx, Adorno and Jameson—recognize that it is ideological and hasty to present adversity as a simple problem in the form of an isolated and humanized other, but it is also insufficient to abandon thinking and fall into an existential despair with regard to the brute violence of existence.

Criticism, in this tradition, has as its task to hold on to the notion that damaged life might be redeemed, while avoiding the easy fantasy solution that would lie in attributing evil to some binary other. To this end Shelley undertakes a genealogy of the self: she describes the genesis of Victor's monster, who first encounters the sensations of life and then becomes humanized by overhearing a reading of Milton's *Paradise Lost* (and then Volney's *Ruins of Empire*). After this basic training in humanity the monster is, however, spurned by those he encounters, primarily because of his visible difference from the humans with whom he feels such kinship. Shelley's politicization of what seemed for Milton to be a problem of human freedom (or the relation between life and law) is— if we accept Jameson's definition of ideology—a counter-ideological gesture. What appears as the pure horror of life, or what for the moralizing Victor can only be the menacing threat of beings who are radically other, is seen ultimately by Shelley to be a problem of critical enlightenment. What appears as existentially unacceptable should be transformed through social and political revolution. If recognition were granted to the potential hordes of the future one would be faced not with violence but sympathy and pity. *Political* solutions are therefore akin to the formalizing procedures of art: what appears as intractable, unacceptable, intolerable or horrifically other can be given resolution by transforming torment as such into an anthropogenic problem. If Jameson argues that ideology is the way in which politically unacceptable structures are given imaginary resolution, and that the social symbolism of narrative completes a redistribution that should properly be revolutionary, then this is because of his post-Marxist commitment to transforming seemingly natural, universal or intractable problems into human-to-human struggles.

Minus the Political

An entire genre of what has come to be known as post-apocalyptic film and literature currently and repeatedly, with ever increasing verve, plays out a fantasy of human near-disappearance and redemption, and does so precisely when our energies ought to be focused on what humans have done to the planet and how they might desist from so doing. In response to this deluge of cultural production, we would need to adjust the Marxist approach to politics and humanization. Marxist critique aims to humanize and historicize—the two gestures being the same: what appears to be simply and universally intolerable needs to be recognized as having a history, where history is a history of labor and human relations. When those human relations are naturalized or 'frozen'—when the family or the male-female couple appears as the fantasy frame through which all horrors can ultimately be resolved—then, for Marxism, it is the figure of bourgeois man that needs to be criticized and historicized. The problem is deemed to be intra-human and intra-historical: we should be able to imagine forms of collective, non-exploitative and historically transformative modes of life—not resign ourselves to the apparent 'natural' injustices of the present. But what if the problem today were not that of a justice among humans? What if social political revolution among human beings were still to leave the relation between the human species and life in the same place? Today's frequently cited Marxist cry—it is easier to imagine the end of the world than the end of capitalism—should be read as symptomatic. Should we not be more concerned with the world's end than the relations among markets and individuals? The Marxist premise that we cannot save the world ecologically until capitalism is dealt with, should be questioned, and reversed: as long as we imagine life and the

world to be primarily anthropogenic, or emerging from human meaning and history, we will not confront the disjunction between the human
species (in all its modes) and the life that it regards as its own. A new
mode of critique that would *not* be political would be required. Indeed,
it is the *political* gesture, or the understanding of conflicts as ultimately
intra-human, that needs to be questioned. One needs a hypo-Marxism
or counter-Marxism whereby the very premise of Marxism—man as a
laboring animal who furthers his own life—needs to be recognized as the
limit of thinking. For what 'we' cannot accept is the obvious counter to
this assumption: man is not an animal who furthers his own survival.

For Milton and Shelley the problem was that of the violence of life
for an ill-equipped human. Whereas Milton will respond theologi-
cally—arguing that God's grace and the unfolding of human history will
justify the seemingly unjustifiable torments of life, Shelley will adopt a
more modern and political approach: humanity is capable of living well,
living in a humane manner, if only social and political structures were
transformed to be conducive to sympathy and recognition. If we came
into existence like Frankenstein's monster—through sensations, reading and a dwelling with loving others—rather than through doctrines of
piety, then we would be capable of living without the torments of impla-
cable injustice. Shelley diagnoses human despair and regards its genesis
as human, but for that very reason also resolvable. And this is in accord
with the critical tradition that I have already and that culminates in an
Adorno who regards the violence of existence to be something humanity
finds intolerable and will thereby *either* mythically project onto an ani-
mated other, or 'rationally' subject to its own order. Critique or dialectics recognizes that the sense or acceptability we have projected onto the
world is at once *not* the world's own and yet—politically—demands to
be brought into being.

Things have changed. The overwhelming question that presses itself
upon us—requiring incessant repression and working through—is not
the question of how we humans were placed in a world in which the task
was too hard, the conditions too bleak or the burden of freedom too confronting. The question is not one of how we humans can justify hostile
life, but how we can possibly justify ourselves given our malevolent relation to life.

The current vogue for what is misleadingly called post-apocalyptic fiction seems to indicate that we are now feeling (if not thinking) a new relation between the human species and time. More accurately, we are experiencing humanity *as a species,* not just a humanity that emerged from the depths of time but a specified mode of organism that will one day have had its time. Just as post-Darwinian nineteenth-century literature had a sense of deep time—feeling some alarming presage of a time before humans and adjusted its plot structures accordingly, literary and cinematic form is struggling with forms of expression that might capture a new mode of inhuman time. We rehearse over and over again our near annihilation, playing a cosmic version of Freud's grandson's *fort-da* game, in which we replay our disappearance (semi-traumatically) and then stage our return and redemption (Freud 1961). *This* problem now focuses not on creation—why was man created given the hard terms of his existence?—but on extinction: what reasons might we fathom for wanting our survival? (Here it is not a question of justifying the life that man must face, but of justifying the man who has done so much to deface life). Humanity has been violent all too violent; it is not the horror of existence that tortures humanity but a humanity that can do nothing other than destroy itself and its milieu, and all—perversely—for the sake of its own myopic, short-circuited and self-regarding future.

Living Extinction

In 2008 *The Day the Earth Stood Still* featured a deadpan alien (played appropriately by Keanu Reeves) who informed humanity that its violence and destructive modes of consumption no longer entitled it to life on earth. The narrative of the film proved this judgment and diagnosis to be peremptory: Keanu is given the chance to see the benevolent side of humanity through the eyes of a young boy, and the annihilation of the human species is delayed. A common motif in science fiction narratives of alien invasion, the judgment of humanity as life-denying and life-unworthy is neither refuted nor answered, but simply set aside as the plot hurtles toward redemption. Humanity is split in two: the worthless, violent, historical and life-denying humans perceived by the judging aliens, and the proper (futural) humanity that is created and revealed by the morality tale of the narrative. In *The Adjustment Bureau* of 2011, human freedom—that which makes us human and therefore supposedly worthy—is judged to be the cause of sufficient destruction to the point where man's free existence can no longer be permitted. This adaptation of a Philip K. Dick story features a team of intervening agents whose task is to allow humanity to run its proper and seemingly free course while making minor corrections if events appear to stray from their appropriate end. The heart of the film concerns a love story that is at odds with the prescribed order of events. Despite a series of more and more complex adjustments, and in the face of all adversity, the lovers—even with one of them knowing about the 'adjustments'—remain committed to their love. They stand firm, despite the warnings of the catastrophes that follow. The tale is heroic and Promethean, but not tragic. In the end it is this miniscule and possibly disastrous granting of human love and freedom—against the 'adjustments' of the angelic guardians—that wins the day. One of the adjusters had already explained to the male lead (Matt Damon) that human freedom, when given free reign, has led to the dark ages and (among other things) the first and second world wars (including the Holocaust). Even so, narrative sympathy is with the love and freedom that asserts itself against such bureaucratic calculation, and this is in accord with a common motif of science fiction's postulates of the end of man. There is something pernicious, evil or *apolitical* in simply denying the right to existence of humanity; such diagnoses appear as unacceptably ruthless, as having no feeling for the love and passion that makes us human. This is so much the case that dystopian visions of the world need be no different from the present other than presenting the absence of human passion, even if that absence creates a world of peace and happiness. The classical statement of this malaise is *Brave New World* (Huxley 1932) where a manufactured happiness is presented as horrifically inhuman, but the reasoning is the same in *The Adjustment Bureau*; there is something insidious about a world that might be managed, for our benefit, or in which it had been decided that we ought to be guided away from our freedom to be violent.

As I have already suggested, the once common question of theodicy that challenged the goodness of life and man's tragic subjection to a violence beyond that of his own comprehension, has been reversed into a problem of human destructiveness towards an otherwise neutral, if not benevolent, milieu. In the 2007 Oliver Hirschbiegel film *The Invasion*, the central character played by Nicole Kidman faces a world in which a virus is released when a space shuttle crashes to earth. The virus causes its hosts to become inhumanly robotic, void of all passion. Despite the absence of war and violence that would ensue, the narrative has a typical redemptive trajectory that sees the virus vanquished with the world returned to its human order. (Or disorder: the film concludes with newspaper headlines of war and other returns of violence.) Why, we might ask, do *Brave New World* scenarios of passionless peace seem so objectionable, and why—precisely when we do indeed face a future of possible human nonexistence (and sooner rather than later)—is present discourse focused on *how we might survive*, rather than whether we ought to survive? Or, if we accept the parochial desire to survive why can we not hear all the voices that accuse us of an existential worthlessness? The present seems to be split between two myopias of the future: the first is evidenced by climate change policy's discourse of managerialism. We speak of adaptation, mitigation, sustainability, cap and trade and even—despite cataclysmic game-changers—of recovery and renewal. Given the stark facts, how could 'our' survival possibly be adjusted in terms of using slightly less, or consuming at a slower rate, or with one part of the globe trading its destructive emissions with another? Even beyond the crises of climate change, other disaster scenarios—ranging from terrorism and viral pandemic to panic and systemic collapse—seem to require something that is a difference in kind, not degree. It could not be a question of either adjusting our desires and expectations to a diminished future, or finding *other* resources of energy and maintenance. For the problem lies not in the substance of energy—of what, if you like, we accept as our milieu— but the mode of acceptance as such. As long as there is something like *life* that presents itself as that which must be sustained, or—worse—as that by which we value sustainability (such that the good is what allows life to continue as it is), we have failed to ask the question that is being repeatedly articulated and yet never addressed.

I want to conclude by looking at the new dominant mode of reaction formation questions: these are questions that at first glance appear to face forward to the future but that are ultimately ways in which the reality of the future is covered over. In short, one may say that it is precisely at the point in humanity's history when the question of the acceptability of the species ought to be asked that this very question mutates into a defense mechanism. By asking *how* we will survive into the future, by anticipating an end unless we adapt, we repress the question of whether the survival of what has come to be known as life is something we should continue to admit as the only acceptable option.

The Violence of the Question

Before looking at the culturally dominant modes of the question I want to consider a philosophical example, for it brings the flagrant self-delusion of humanity into sharp focus. For quite some time the philosopher Peter Singer has posed a rather uncomfortable thought experiment: I am wearing a pair of designer shoes and I pass by a child drowning in water that is deep enough to kill the child but insufficiently deep to pose any risk to me. I decide not to save the child because doing so would damage my shoes (2009). (In an earlier version [1972] Singer simply set saving the child against allowing our clothes to become muddy.) Singer suggests that few, if any, of us would accept this decision. We would save the child. And yet, he goes on to argue, we continually choose small and not highly significant or necessary material pleasures over the minor and barely noticeable material sacrifices it would require to save the lives of distant others. If we faced up to the real situation of our choices—which Singer suggests we ought to do by extending the range of our consideration beyond the immediate sympathies of those who are present to us—then we would conclude that we ought to give up a not too significant portion of our material wealth for the sake of benefiting an other in a way that is far more life-preserving than the minor life-enhancement of a pair of designer shoes. In response to this provocation Richard W. Miller (2010) starts to assess the degree to which sympathy and sacrifice for others diminish what is integral to the self. He argues that it might make sense, in terms of a person's self-definition and the duty they owe to themselves, to act more kindly to those closer at hand (including one's children and one's self). Singer's case is already thoroughly (but perhaps disturbingly) reasonable. He is not asking us to sacrifice all inequalities or benefits for the sake of saving other lives, just those that would not diminish our own pleasures and happiness significantly. Singer accepts a limitation of sympathy and an apparently non-negotiable selfishness, such that his argument—for all its audacity as a thought experiment—is really quite compatible with a world in which some people just do have more than others. The critical responses to Singer's principles of sympathy and charity disclose the degree to which human selfishness or self-maintenance is not only the accepted principle of living well, but lies at the heart of moral philosophy. Morality is deemed to be a question of doing what is required in order to *be the being that I am* (Wolf 2010). There is, it seems, a sense in which either acting without principle *or* giving up too much of one's wealth would threaten my self-identity. What is scandalous, I would suggest, is not that humans have placed their own survival as more valuable than other lives, but that at the heart of moral philosophy is an assumption that nothing is more valuable or definitive of value than human life's capacity to maintain and define itself. We ground value on life, either the sustainability of life, or our capacity to give our lives form and definition, or—to really face up to the circularity—we value life because it is life that makes value possible.

Life is, properly considered (which is to say, always considered in terms of what defines humanity), selection: we say that something is living if it maintains or strives to maintain itself through time. The dispersed, the haphazard, the inert, the contingent, the diffuse and the unformed—these are not living. They are therefore not only not *valuable* but also (significantly) not valuing. We value what values: we defend animal life because it too makes its way in the world, possesses a degree of choosing this rather than that, and is therefore on its way to something like meaning or sense. We seem to think not only that the prima facie value of life lies in its modes of flourishing, but that something like destruction and annihilation are *other than life and therefore unacceptable.*

This brings us back to the new mode of the existential question: how can humanity be at once the figure of that which renders life self-evidently valuable (because humanity is that animal that values) and yet be the being that has—through valuing itself—annihilated not only others of its own kind, but precipitated the end of all modes of life, valuing and otherwise? How is it that humanity defines itself as that being that inevitably chooses life, and yet has done so by saving only its own life? Why is it that the increasingly shrill affirmation of life—not just human life, but life as a living that furthers and values itself—occurs precisely at the moment in the history of life when it is at its most destructive and at its most evident end?

In series three, episode nine, of *True Blood* (2010), the villainous anti-hero Russell Edgington appears suddenly on live National News to tear out and chew the spine from the broadcasting newsreader. Edgington announces an end to vampire-human reconciliation—the seeming motif of *True Blood*'s ongoing elegy to the desirability of human passion—and declares that a vile, destructive, violent and planet-destroying humanity must give way to another more worthy species. The question is not so much answered as deflected. The narrative trajectory of *True Blood*, its romantic propulsion, lies in the desirability of being human: while the villainous vampires embrace their immortality, the heroic central figure seeks the love that is only possible with human finitude. Despite this, of course, the vogue for vampire fiction and the fanzine embrace of Edgington as the twenty-first century's 'mad, bad and dangerous to know' type suggests that the manifest yearning for being human covers over a deeper flirtation with a sense of the end of man. If humanity has always asked questions about its predicament, it has—as I have suggested—begun to consider the violence of its being in relation to the very figure of life that has rendered the human exemplary of life as such.

Now, when the actual end of man approaches, when it seems necessary to ask what mode of the human—if any at all—should live on, the discourse of life can apparently only consider questions of degree rather than questions of kind. We ask *how* we might survive, adapt, mitigate or even trade our way into the future; we do not ask whether there is a future *for us,* and we cannot ask this because the 'we' of the question is at once that which has defined life *and* that which is essentially hurtling towards its own extinction. What disturbs us today is not theodicy, or how human life can live with the violence of its milieu, but anthropodicy, or how human life can avoid asking how it might justify itself.

Finally

How has the common figure of the self-evident value of human life given way to an increasing sense of species guilt and preliminary mourning? Why, just as humanity begins to have some sense of its end, are policies of survival, adaptation, mitigation and climate *change,* accompanied by a wide sense and figuration of the unacceptable nature of human life? Nothing defines the concept of reaction formation better than the present: everywhere there is evidence of the nonviable and unacceptable modus of human life, and yet the one notion that is unacceptable—incapable of being heard—is that human life has no value. This is not to say that—being without value—what has come to be known as humanity ought to extinguish itself, but rather to say that what is left of the human needs to confront the absence of value. (Some arguments, such as those of David Benatar (2006) that 'prove' that coming into human existence is always a harm—for all its provocation—remain thoroughly within the axiology of life: Benatar argues that human lives are more likely to be dominated by suffering rather than joy and are therefore not to be chosen. He therefore considers human life as something that humans choose or do not choose—when it is perhaps more probable that life is thrown at humans, and humans are thrown into life. It is perhaps more provocative not to ask about the value of human life *for humans* but of human life *for life.*) For it is value and the holding on to that which saves itself, preserves itself, values itself and maintains itself that has precluded confrontation with the question that we are at once screaming out and yet also not hearing.

One way to pose the question of the unacceptable is to consider what we, as a species, might affirm as our own or reject as inhuman. This is a standard and complex border, played out in the thought experiments of monstrosity and the genre of the supposedly post-apocalyptic. If we imagine a future where certain aspects of humanity take over then we may adjust ourselves accordingly. Dystopias are warnings or cautionary tales in which a tendency of the present may be averted. (This is perhaps why many post-apocalyptic dystopias have considered unacceptable solutions to the problem of energy (ranging from the cannibalism of *Soylent Green* [1973] and Kenneth Cook's *Play Little Victims* [1978] to the faux humans bred for maintaining the rest of us in *Brave New World* and *Moon* [2009].)

Such dystopias would, presumably, act as salutary cautions against us following the course of our current actions to the nightmarish conclusions that would follow. If we imagine another species—vampires—who are defined by a certain inhumanity that has manifested itself in the human species, then the battle for humanity *as life* becomes a figural war against the future. The vampiric or zombied other is an allegory for humanity gone awry, the bad humanity from which we can save ourselves in order to emerge as properly and justifiably human. That is: we imagine what it might be for the inhumanity within ourselves—a rapacity, ruthlessness and consuming rage—to become a species in its own right (figured as the dystopian man of the future). Rather than deal with humanity's war on itself we have narrativized and figured the horror of humanity into some distant other. We imagine that it is *in the future* that man becomes cannibalistic, void of empathy, ruthlessly calculative, and so dependent on technology that he ceases to think; in this exercise of the imagination we preclude considering all the ways in which this 'other' dystopian 'man' has already (and has always already) arrived.

The supposedly future narratives of the post-apocalyptic are counter-futural. We represent the future as *possibly* overtaken by destruction, cannibalism, zombies, violent technocracy or the invasion of mindlessness; in so doing we present as *possibly futural and counter-human* just those tendencies that have marked the species to date. In so doing—for all our *post-apocalyptic or techno-utopian* posthuman imaginings—we remain tied to a nostalgia for the properly human that has supposedly been threatened by an inhumanity that may appear from without. We remain in a state of denial or reaction towards the future in two senses: humanity's end presents itself to us, and rather than ask the question this poses we instead imagine external threats to the species that are then warded off in a clear species-species agonistics. (One would not want to read too much, or perhaps anything at all, into the current vogue for vampire fiction, except perhaps to note that like late eighteenth-century gothic it occurs alongside the frenzied affirmation of the life of man against various forms of threatening transcendence.) We also war against the future by presenting the world of the present—a world of species self-annihilation and global rapacity—as a future dystopia, or as a possibility that may occur unless humanity saves itself. What we do not ask, and herein would lie a possible acceptance of the future, is not whether man ought to survive, but why this question is so unacceptable as to be constantly displaced and dis-figured.

Chapter 10

The Joys of Atavism

A single duration will pick up along its route the events
of the totality of the material world; and we will then be
able to eliminate the human consciousness that we had at
first laid out at wide intervals like so many relays for the
motion of our thought: there will now only be impersonal
time in which all things will pass (Bergson 1965, 47)

Every living being borders on death; or perhaps it might be more accurate to say that every being has one side turned towards the non-living. Without that border between life and non-life, without the living being closing itself off to some extent from the fullness of life, there would be a pure influx, intensity or becoming without any resistance or stasis. If there were to be something like pure life, then it would be akin to Bergson's 'pure perception': in its purest mode perception would be an unmediated capture of what is given, without the distinguishing and forming marks of memory:

> we ask that perception should be provisionally understood to
> mean not my concrete and complex perception—that which
> is enlarged by memories and offers always a certain breadth of
> duration—but a *pure* perception, I mean a perception which
> exists in theory rather than in fact and would be possessed
> by a being placed where I am, living as I live, but absorbed in
> the present and capable, by giving up every form of memory,
> of obtaining a vision of matter both immediate and instanta-
> neous. (Bergson 2007 [1912], 26)

'Pure life' would be something like an unimpeded becoming, a bursting forth of energy, or what Bergson describes in the beginning of

Creative Evolution as a force of explosive power that is not yet divided into an exploding or differentiating power and an exploded matter that is differentiated. But a living being is never 'pure life,' for a living being closes itself off, to some extent, from the world's energies; a being is in part its open engagement with the world, but also a certain refusal of the dynamic life of the world, a selfsameness that remains unto itself and limits relations and stimuli. To say that every being borders on the non-living is to acknowledge a certain inertia that is intertwined with what it means for a being to become. Life can be considered as a double tendency, an explosive power of creative difference, and a counter-tendency of resistance: 'it is probable that life tended at the beginning to compass at one and the same time both the manufacture of the explosive and the explosion by which it is utilized. In this case, the same organism that had directly stored the energy of the solar radiation would have expended it in free movements in space. And for that reason we must presume that the first living beings sought on the one hand to accumulate, without ceasing, energy borrowed from the sun, and on the other hand to expend it, in a discontinuous and explosive way, in movements of locomotion' (Bergson 1911 A, 115-16).

But, like Bergson's 'pure perception,' this pure life of explosive/exploded force is speculative: what we encounter are mixtures, which we can intuit by seeing each composed being as in part dynamic and open, in part closed and stable. Rather than refer to this counter-tendency of resisting creative difference as death, it is perhaps more accurate to say that the condition of any ongoing sameness is some capacity to resist the differentiating fluxes of time—a certain non-living or material fixity. This way of thinking about the fold between life and non-life would allow us to think about texts and their relation to a counter-vitality without assuming that texts were living beings (or it would allow us to think of living beings as texts, as in some part detached from the life from which they emerge and distinguish themselves). Today, more than ever, it might appear to be fruitful to mark a distinction between texts and life, for there is currently an efflorescence of theories seeking to explain writing and other technical systems as extensions of the living organism's will to survive. Various evolutionary Darwinisms have reacted against the modernist insistence on the force of writing and disembodied voices and have sought to see literature as primarily adaptive and cognitive (Boyd 2009; Zunshine 2006). Insisting on a certain and necessary lifelessness in all beings, including texts, is perhaps one of the great ideas we can take from a Bergsonian/Deleuzian tradition of modernism. On the one hand we would need to insist on a certain lifelessness of the letter, but to do so would not be to mark a simple binary distinction between texts and living bodies, but to see all bodies as both living and non-living (and perhaps at their most alive when exposed to annihilation).

Perhaps a text, to be a text (or to be read), must at least in part be considered alive. When John Milton made a case for allowing books to circulate freely he suggested that one would destroy *more* life (or spirit) by annihilating a book than would be lost by murdering a human:

> unlesse warinesse be us'd, as good almost kill a Man as kill a good Book; who kills a Man kills a reasonable creature, Gods Image; but he who destroyed a good Booke, kills reason it selfe, kills the image of God as it were in the eye. Many a man lives a burden to the Earth; but a good Booke is the pretious life-blood of a master spirit, imbalm'd and treasur'd up on purpose to a life beyond life. (Milton 1905 [1644], 9)

A book has the capacity to extend the spirit or sense from which it emerged well beyond the author's life; but it is also because of that afterlife that a book is always potentially dead, not only because it lives on by taking a material form that could be destroyed, but also because that same materiality has a force of its own that cannot be contained by the organic life of authors, readers or even the world from which it emerged. The condition for any being's survival, its 'living on,' is that it take on some distinct and repeatable form: but it is that very distinction, ipseity or separateness that also cuts the text or body off from an ongoing life that will necessarily outlast the living. If there can be something like 'a' life then this is only because there is a difference and distinction between a specified being and the milieu from which it draws its sustenance. In the case of literary texts: a book can survive and be read if it is incarnated or given a material support that is not reducible to the animating intention of author or reader, but it will also therefore have a life or force distinct from any animation or sense.

In the case of literary modernism we can be even more specific: modernism could emerge and have being only because it made a claim *to life*, but this claim was destructive of life in its actual self-maintaining modes and appealed to another life, beyond organic survival. Key to this joyous atavism was a disdainful attitude towards the textual archive, alongside a recognition of deep archival forces. As a literary movement, modernism needed at once to regard the textual archive as so much noise and dead weight; at the same time, modernism could only take hold *not* by producing more literary life but by deadening the textual corpus that was at its disposal. One would read texts *not* as extensions or expressions of life, but as detached fragments with an odd afterlife. There is, I will argue, something to be gained—today more than ever—by reading modernism not as vitalism but as murderous textual annihilation. Further, this counter-vital modernism of the dead letter is best read through the supposedly vitalist work of Henri Bergson. If modernism were to be reread not as a lament on the infertility and deadening of the West, with the implied goal of revitalization of the word, but as a creatively destructive movement of willed extinction, then several consequences would follow. First, we would need to rethink both postmodernism and post-structuralism, given that both these movements are rendered possible by a certain response to modernism. Second, a new sexuality of modernism would emerge that would be essentially queer. (That is, it would be by deflection, divergence, deviation and dehiscence—and not reproduction—that modernist writing would operate: at once destroying the archive while allowing new archival forces to emerge.) To make this second point more clear and specific, I'd like to begin with the counter-thesis of modernism as a vitalism, with the underlying sexual (and racial) normativity that any vitalism or privileging of life would entail (Jones 2010).

Modernism and vitalism: responding to the mechanized, industrial, rationalized, quantifying, capitalist and reifying forces of an increasingly reductive world of homogeneous time and space, modernism sought to inject life into a desiccated western tradition by giving blood to the voices of the past. Descending into Hades where all the voices of history and becoming had been reduced to so much noise, the modernist artist would once again experience the opening or genesis of culture, retrieving life's original, animating and fertile voice. (Pound's first Canto begins with just such due homage to the prophetic souls of the past, with the task of finding voices other than the 'impetuous impotent': 'Poured we libations unto each the dead ... I sat to keep off the impetuous impotent dead, / Till I should hear Tiresias' [1987].) Such a theme of revitalization could be figured in profoundly sexual, and intensely heterosexual terms. Joyce's *Ulysses* returns to the murmur of Molly Bloom's body— ironically distancing itself from the novel's long series of feminine/maternal oceanic motifs (such as Stephen's early figurations of his mother's image as 'Ghoul! Chewer of corpses,' or Leopold Bloom's recollection of Palestine as the 'grey sunken cunt of the world' [Joyce 2000, 8, 50]). Although *Ulysses* is in tune with so much of modernism in its depiction of a series of failed and infertile sexual encounters, it nevertheless ends with an affirmative, fluid, embodied, feminine and open return to life. It is as though the novel's narrative trajectory, from Bloom's urination and defecation, through the city of Dublin and a funeral—interspersed with the disembodied voices of newspapers, advertisements, fragments of the past and Stephen Dedalus's scholarly musings—can be opened towards a future, however fragile and ironic, of purely potential (not yet embodied or actualized) life. It is possible to read the canonical texts of literary modernism as all addressing the problem of an infertile archive by imagining some act of (hetero)sexualized and unselfconscious redemption. Such a claim is easy to make in the case of Yeats, Lawrence, Pound, and Eliot. Yeats's 'Leda and the Swan' presents the involuntary and inhuman event of sexual coupling as a violently creative force, and this could be contrasted with the personal and immobilizing passions that are elicited by women caught up in the petty and historical plays of politics. ('The Circus Animals' Desertion' laments: 'I thought my dear must her own soul destroy / So did fanaticism and hate enslave it' [Yeats 2011, 212].) Lawrence also contrasted a dark, disruptive, and counter-bourgeois sexual force with the 'human all too human' (paralyzingly infertile) love of marriage. In 'The Ladybird,' Count Dionys tells the very English Daphne: 'The true living world of fire is dark, throbbing, darker than blood. Our luminous world that we go by is only the white lining of this" (Lawrence 2002,180). Eliot's *The Waste Land* diagnoses the inertia of the modern city by contrasting the mechanical and neither voluntary nor violent sex between 'the typist' and the 'young man carbuncular' with the absent and mourned softly flowing Thames. Pound situates bankers, journalists and homosexuals in the same infertile circle of hell. Like the other modernists, redemption is not gained by any form of Romanticisms's 'spousal verse'; classic muse figures are, if anything, ironized. But there is something akin to a distant oceanic feminine that would seem to offer life beyond the limits and disenchantments of actual women. That this non-reified, flowing, dynamic and pre-systemic life is feminine is clear in literary modernism (allowing the artist in turn to be something like a creator giving form to the formless).

There is a tension, then, in the vitalist strategy of modernism: on the one hand, literary revitalization takes the form of a critique of already actualized and bounded forms (and is implicitly powered by a drive to overcome already constituted norms of 'man' and gender); on the other hand, this shockingly new vitality is figured via a highly sexualized metaphorics of the force of life infusing passive matter. The vitalist philosophers of modernism—including Bergson—would seem to be so focused on a critique of human and bounded figures of life that nothing like a gendered or sexual normativity could be valorized. And yet if we take the accepted reading of Bergson as a vitalist who was critical of 'man' into account, it seems hard to avoid the problem of sexual difference in two senses: Bergsonism would be set against a static norm of man and yet would affirm all those masculine figures of active, forceful, creative, incisive, penetrative and productive life that have marked gendered thinking (Hill 2008). Why, we might ask, has sexual difference been such a rigid and persistent figure in questions of life? Apart from narrowly psychoanalytic answers, which have their legitimacy, it seems obvious that questions about life would take their cue from the image of the living being, and that sexual reproduction—despite being one mode among many of reproduction—would be a ready figure for considering not only the emergence of bounded living forms from an otherwise not-yet-specified matter, but also the living being's relation to the life that it expresses. What psychoanalysis contributed to the understanding of the imaginary conditions of life was that the border between living and non-living was sexual. That is, the living being, in order to live, must be open to what is not itself—must bear a relation of desire (or of attaining what is not yet the case) towards its milieu. Life must be open to influx from the outside.

But in order to be a living *being*, the organism must also close itself off, in part, from the full force of the life from which it emerges: full overcoming of desire or difference would annihilate the being's individuation. Sexual difference figured as gender allows this strange border between living being and life to be negotiated imaginatively or (following Bergson), intellectually, for the intellect is that faculty that allows the complexity of life to be managed through concepts that reduce intensive difference. Life would be imagined as some fluid, oceanic, maternal plenitude from which the bounded form of a distinct and representing body would emerge. To think of mind as a camera that cuts the world into assimilable units of information: this, according to Bergson, is at how the intellect manages and imagines itself. An 'image of thought' is formed in which mind is a picturing machine. This capacity of the intellect to reify itself via some image of detached mind could only be countered by retrieving an intuition of life that would be at odds with all our figures of 'man.'

In many ways this Bergsonian appeal to life beyond the bounds of the already formed organism is in line with a broader modernist critique of the figure of man as a Cartesian subject. Anti-Cartesianism generally has proceeded by appealing affirmatively—against *man*—to qualities that had once been figured as feminine but that now seem to offer ways of thinking about the vital order as such. Life would not be rational, bounded, logical, efficient and progressive, but dynamic, open, fluid and affective. One would move from gender—or older motifs of man as subject relating to formless but potential matter—to sexual difference. Fecund, creative, explosive, fluid, unbounded, potential, and intensive life would be that from which the desiccated and disenchanted intellect would emerge. All those predicates that had once been attributed to a chaotic femininity opposed to male reason would now characterize life as such, and the modernist-vitalist critique of the subject would be a critique of man. Man would, through an intuition of vitality, destroy the gendered binary that had locked him into an affectless, lifeless, disembodied Cartesian prison; he would become one with—and not simply the medium for—all that had been projected onto the feminized figures of life. Whereas other modernists used scenes of *jouissance* to overcome the miserable pleasures of bounded male-female coupling, figuring a form of un-self-conscious depersonalization achieved through sexual boundlessness, Bergson contrasted the joy of transcending intuition with the self-serving consumption of bourgeois pleasure:

> There is a difference of vital tone. Those who regularly put into practice the morality of the city know this feeling of well-being, common to the individual and society, which is the outward sign of the interplay of material resistances neutralizing each other. But the soul that is opening, and before whose eyes material objects vanish, is lost in sheer joy. Pleasure and well-being are something, joy is more. For it is not contained in these, whereas they are virtually contained in joy. They mean, indeed, a halt or a marking time, while joy is a step forward. (Bergson 2002, 325)

Bergson's vitalism—like modernism more generally—could be considered as a passage to impersonality via something like 'becoming-woman.' Not surprisingly, then, Bergson's way of thinking about thought's overcoming of its own imprisonment in the image of man takes on a phallic mode: penetrating what is not itself, emerging with ever more nuanced, distinct, differentiating and dynamic forms (Hill 2008).

Imagine, though, another Bergsonism, another modernism and—in turn—another twenty-first century (another way of proceeding after modernism that would not be the usual—if multivalent—postmodernism). What if modernism were not a vitalism? How would a different reading of Bergson create a different present, after a different, non-vital, and essentially queer modernism? Before exploring what this might mean I want to put forward the following claim: post-modernism, especially as it ceases to theorize a dynamic relation to modernism and becomes a form of proclaimed posthumanism, becomes an ultra-humanism. This is especially so if we take note of the turns towards affect, literary Darwinism, and cognition, all of which seek to explain complexity and systems as *extensions* of life rather than pursuing Bergsonian notions of splitting, bifurcation, and the branching out into differences in kind (rather than degree). If we reverse today's vitalisms and then trace a genealogy of a counter-vital post-modernism, we can find another Bergsonian modernism. Such a historical move would be in accord with a Bergsonian method of retracing the path of evolution in order to explore certain bifurcations, at once finding an explosive origin that would yield the force from which distinction emerges, while also finding a more profound difference. To revisit a tired question: what then is/was modernism, and how did post-modernism mark its difference from the former?

Modernism—against notions of revivification and the vitalist critique of technology—can be considered as a profound attention to the force of *the dead* (Goldman 2004). We should not, I would suggest, see James Joyce's most explicit presentations of the dead voice—the newspaper lines, malapropisms, clichés and mechanical voices of the city—as points of inertia to be overcome by the life of writing. We could consider a transition from the paralysis of *Dubliners,* where the dead letters of cliché and script seem to immobilize life, such that the absence of expression leads to a detachment between bodies and their desires, to a liberation of proliferating voices in *Finnegans Wake.* But I would suggest that there is already a counter-vital, counter organic, and lifeless (pro-paralysis) celebration of the word in *Dubliners.* Consider, here, Bergson's theory of both laughter and dreams. For the most part the body's energies are organized towards survival, focused on the efficient and productive present; when that organization breaks down, and the body appears less as organism and more as machine, the body convulses in laughter (Bergson 1911 B). Similarly, when the body is asleep, no longer oriented to tasks at hand, the images of dreams surge forth. In *Dubliners* it is the functional, embodied, practical, and seemingly expressive relation to language that operates through a unified, rigid, and organic image of life. In the 'easy' flows of conversation and banter, life moves on, steadily, progressively, automatically—and it is perhaps this ongoing life that is the real paralysis of *Dubliners.* By contrast, it is when language appears as dead, when the body is no longer given expressive passage to the word, that there is a break with the line of time; something like the perception of 'time in its pure state' emerges. It is, for example, when writing is seen as a proper and personal extension of the self—when writing is organic—that Joyce describes the same dull round of suburban normality: it is only when writing is liberated from life, when one no longer grounds systems of inscription on the supposedly self-maintaining organism, that one disrupts the normalizing figure of bodily life.

Bergson laid the grounds for formulating a counter-vitalist approach to system and techne. Consider his key thesis of creative evolution: in the beginning is an explosive force of differentiation, with no distinction yet between differentiating force and differentiated matter. If this original explosive power or potentiality *to differ* could be considered to be life, then we would have to redefine life beyond its bounded forms, and beyond organic notions of self-maintenance. Certain vitalist moralisms would have to be rethought. We could not, for example, hold the standard narrative that begins with an organism or relatively stable form, with bodies then becoming enslaved to and alienated by the systems it created for its own efficiency; nor could we conclude from such a narrative of life-alienated-by-techne with the resulting imperative to revitalize the raison d'etre of life from which all systems emerged and towards which they ought to return. Reading Bergson and Modernism against this normalizing mode would open a new counter-politics.

It is no surprise, perhaps, that Derrida—commenting on Heidegger's theory of time—makes a brief remark pertinent to today's renewed interest in Bergson and life: the problem, Derrida argues, with *any* attempt to avoid a 'vulgar' (spatialized, quantified, punctuated) notion of time is that in order to think about time or have a *concept* of time we must have some notion of *time in general*. The very nature of cognition or conceptualization must render any supposedly proper, fluid, pre-articulated or originating temporality into some repeatable mode. In so far as one thinks and experiences time *as time* there will always be a reduction of time to what cannot be considered as some pure temporality of difference. For Derrida, then, Bergsonian notions of intuition or of creating a concept adequate to every perception would be typical of a logocentric metaphysics of presence (Derrida 1982, 60). Rather than appeal to a proper temporality before the 'fall' into techne, language and quantification, Derrida suggests that one can might think forward to the promise of the concept. It is not the case that there is some proper origin of life belied by language; for it is the idea created by language that offers something like a time 'to come,' a future beyond any of the actualized forms of the present. This promise of concepts—or the difference of concepts from any already given life—yields a politics of futurity. We do not look back to a lost life, a lost democracy, a belied justice or a mourned origin. We allow the concept to open 'justice to come,' or 'democracy to come,' via a messianic promise without the full body of the messiah (Derrida 2005, 86). Not surprisingly, then, Derrida reverses a Marxist ethics of alienation and the proper: it is not the case that one could or should 'exorcise' all the phantoms and ghosts that have deflected life from its original and purposive striving. The condition of 'life'—some ongoing self-sameness—is death; some technical system that is not the body itself allows for a stable bounded form. The lived body is possible because of systems of labor, action, language, society and relation that are not the body's own. Thus, Derrida's 'Marxism' focuses on the double bind of spirit: on the one hand, the future, reading and 'living on' require some notion of spirit, of what life would or should be beyond its already actualized forms; at the same time, that appeal to spirit will always haunt and alienate the very life it supposedly fulfils (Derrida 1994). Not surprisingly, Derrida, exploring the difference and distance of the 'letter' from anything like a bodily or originating life, increasingly focuses on the 'word' in modernist writing, especially the writing of Joyce. Whereas in his early work, Derrida (1978 A) had questioned the Joycean project of the book and its claims to equivocity—adopting all the languages of the world and time—he increasingly celebrated Joyce and literature as offering a mode of deconstruction and democracy. The word in Joyce would not be grounded in sense, and—as in all literature—the detachment of word from the presence of voice would allow the word as such, in itself, to circulate freely in a democratic opening that would not anchor language back to some putative origin. Democracy would not be some return of all systems (such as language) to the expressive life of man; democracy is the free circulation of anything that can be said, the open right to 'say anything.'

One might say, then, that post-structuralism is indebted to a certain counter-organic vitalist reading of modernism: the word is not an extension of the body, and cannot be returned back to the living voice without remainder. The word itself has force or life, creating relations and events that are generated neither by bodies nor subjects. Close to this post-structuralist counter-organic vitalism of the word or trace—and yet importantly different—would be an attention to the power (if that is the correct word) of explosive destruction or atavism. Recall that Derrida's philosophy is, on his own insistence, radically open and futural. It is the power, not of life, but of the word, trace, concept or idea that generates an open promise: there can be no actuality that can exhaust the idea or concept of justice, and it is the force of the concept—as that which would insist on a sense above and beyond any actual instance—that will yield a 'justice to come,' allowing us to conclude that deconstruction 'is justice.' For Bergson, rather than moving from the ideal promise of the concept to an open future, intuition would destroy what has come to be assembled by concepts. Intuition of differential movements would fracture ongoing sameness and the forward movement of concepts, and would 'retrace' the path from which concepts emerged. This would ultimately allow for the emergence of ever finer differences that would be destructive of the word, and would explode the forward propulsion of organic striving. Life is at war with itself: it is at once an explosive differentiation that would preclude anything like a line of time in which a past would be retained in order to organize a future, while life also harbors a tendency towards quiescence that diminishes the force of the differential for the sake of self-sameness.

Bergson's criticism of organicism traces a different path from what would become the post-structuralist elevation of writing, not only in Derrida but also in Foucault. Despite Deleuze's celebration of Foucault's corpus, he criticized Foucault for focusing on language as the locus of deterritorialization (Deleuze 1988): yes, literary writing would detach writing and the word from 'man' as a reasoning and communicating animal, but one could also imagine life, and not just writing, in a deterritorializing mode. Here, Deleuze cited the force of silicon to produce syntheses that would not be organic. We can look at the genealogy of this remark to assess its consequences for thinking about Bergson and modernism. First, looking back we can see that Deleuze (unlike Foucault, Derrida and other post-structuralists) took his departure not only from phenomenology but from Bergson. Whereas for Husserl the thought of time would require us to think of something like pure synthesis, not a subject *who* *synthesizes* but synthesis as such or a transcendental subjective power, Bergson would regard subjects as effects of an impersonal, dispersed, and synthetic power that would have various rhythms and tendencies ranging from the matter of rocks to the expansive memory of the minds of saints and mystics. Derrida, always more in the phenomenological tradition than Deleuze, would extend the phenomenological theory of temporal syntheses to see language itself as a power to create forces or ideas beyond intentionality and life. Not surprisingly, then, Derrida would turn frequently to Joyce, the futural force of the word, the promise of spirit along with all the ghosts, hauntings, and spectres that could not be grounded in anything like life.

The modernism of this post-structuralism would be critical of the closed efficiency of the organism, and would focus on the release of the word into a future that could be neither contained nor regarded as an extension of life as it actually is. One could cite, here, beyond the free indirect and stream of consciousness styles of Joyce (and the tendency of the word to operate beyond intentionality and to open up networks and systems of its own), the mournful mode of Eliot's *The Waste Land* where the bourgeois self-interest of bodies is at odds with the fragments of literary tradition, and where words indicate a lost lyricism or deeper meditative time in contrast with urban efficiency. One could also include Pound's emphasis on the machinic qualities of texts, on non-phonetic script, on the autonomy of the image and the *force* of text. By contrast, although he was also indebted to phenomenology, Deleuze took up Bergson's task of intuition and—though he referred to a modernist range of texts including Joyce—made more of the work of Woolf and Lawrence. If one does not focus on the synthetic and futural force of concepts and their power to open up to an ideality that cannot be grounded in life, and if one does not regard time as tradition or history (as a panorama or wasteland of dead voices) but takes up Bergson's challenge of destroying concepts to go back to the explosive power of life, then this might open up the importance of pre-linguistic forces and a radically geological atavism.

Bergson allows us to think of a modernism that is pre- or counter-linguistic, but this is so not because language is returned to organic or vital life but because, for Bergson, vitality is only one of the tendencies of life. Other tendencies, such as those in conflict with the organism, are not found in concepts—which are thoroughly organic and synthesizing—but in intuitions or the tendency towards pure perceptions, which are fragmenting and dispersing. It is true that Bergson wrote of a human potential of spirit to open life beyond the closed forms of 'man.' If morality is enabled by bodies gathering together to maintain themselves against others, then one can take that capacity for bodies to extend their interests into communities and moral groupings, and release that capacity from any actual body and open an intuition of what it might be to act selflessly as such, not self-sacrifice now for the sake of gain later, but self-sacrifice or self-annihilation (becoming-imperceptible as such) (Bergson 1935). Contrast, again, with Derrida: Derrida recognizes that if we can operate with a comportment of justice or ethics towards this other here and now, then this is because there is something like the concept of 'the other' in general, which might be opened by a face to face encounter but always exceed that presence (Derrida 1978B, 102). The concept of the other in general, of hospitality in general, or democracy in general would liberate thought to move beyond actuality towards futurity. By contrast, even though Bergson (1935) does write of the saint or mystic who can think beyond any actual 'humanity' towards spirit in general, this power is *not* achieved through language and it is the same power that will operate in the smallest of intuitions. It is neither a futural move nor a nostalgic return but an explosive atavism that then allows for an inhuman future— *not a posthuman future, which would be man's capacity to think beyond himself, but a thought of a world without man that is released from the orbit of evolving time.*

Here I would suggest that we take our cue from Deleuze and Guattari's reading of Woolf and Lawrence in *A Thousand Plateaus* in order to open a modernism of inhuman time—not a modernism of either stream of consciousness or stream of text (Deleuze and Guattari 2004, 278). This atavistic modernism might in turn allow for a re-reading of other modernists and post-modernism. Rather than posit something like tracing, marking, writing, text, *differance* or the word that would disperse and fragment any supposed grounding life, Bergson makes a direct claim about life as that which creates difference. Life is neither psyche, nor organism, and certainly not an inchoate chaos that is repressed by the order of psychic and organic wholes; life is an organizing power that operates in part by reducing the proliferation of intensive difference to allow for ongoing selfsame wholes, but life operates also by creating complexities and relations that cannot be contained by the human logic of organic efficiency. A modernism that followed this positively destructive atavism of intuition would not look beyond man to some higher human promise, but would allow the human to be invaded by the forces of the cosmos that he has all too efficiently silenced.

Consider D.H Lawrence's poem, 'The Shadow of Death,' which opens with a description of the earth's movement ('again,' so that we are already adopting a planetary duration). The point of view is initially not that of any human observer; a space, rhythm and 'seeing' that is non-human— 'the sun stands up to see us'—precedes the poetic 'I,' and when the 'I' enters, it is as though the human is an emergence and intrusion from a far deeper time:

> The earth again like a ship steams out of the dark sea over
> The edge of the blue, and the sun stands up to see us glide
> Slowly into another day; slowly the rover
> Vessel of darkness takes the rising tide.
>
> I, on the deck, am startled by this dawn confronting
> Me who am issued amazed from the darkness, stripped
> And quailing here in the sunshine, delivered from haunting
> The night unsounded whereon our days are shipped.
>
> Feeling myself undawning, the day's light playing upon me,
> I who am substance of shadow, I all compact
> Of the stuff of the night, finding myself all wrongly
> Among the crowds of things in the sunshine jostled and racked.

The human voice, far from being the word through which the world is mediated, seems to be nothing more than a deathly silence, incapable of viewing what is other than itself other than in terms of death ('What are they but shrouds?'):

> I with the night on my lips, I sigh with the silence of death;
> And what do I care though the very stones should cry me unreal,
>   though the clouds
> Shine in conceit of substance upon me, who am less than the rain.
> Do I know the darkness within them? What are they but shrouds?

As in most of Lawrence's poetry, there is a transition from a sense of deathly struggle with a world of inhuman forces, towards a sense of the perception of inhuman durations followed by a joyous sense of the minor resistance or rhythm of one's own existence at odds with a complex time of the planet:

> The clouds go down the sky with a wealthy ease
> Casting a shadow of scorn upon me for my share in death; but I
> Hold my own in the midst of them, darkling, defy
> The whole of the day to extinguish the shadow I lift on the breeze.

The defiance of voice emerges as perception overcomes the sense of haunting and disjunction to intuit a 'virility' of life that is not that of man and that—more importantly—gives itself in the form of a 'bright' 'living darkness':

> And I know the host, the minute sparkling of darkness
> Which vibrates untouched and virile through the
>   grandeur of night,
> But which, when dawn crows challenge, assaulting the vivid motes
> Of living darkness, bursts fretfully, and is bright:

The poem then shifts from the relation between perceiving speaker and perceived world, to a perception of a 'conflict' of light, as though intuition had somehow passed from point of view and observation to something like the force of life as light:

> Runs like a fretted arc-lamp into light,
> Stirred by conflict to shining, which else
> Were dark and whole with the night.
>
> Runs to a fret of speed like a racing wheel,
> Which else were aslumber along with the whole
> Of the dark, swinging rhythmic instead of a-reel.
>
> Is chafed to anger, bursts into rage like thunder;
> Which else were a silent grasp that held the heavens
> Arrested, beating thick with wonder.
>
> Leaps like a fountain of blue sparks leaping
> In a jet from out of obscurity,

Which erst was darkness sleeping.

Runs into streams of bright blue drops,
Water and stones and stars, and myriads
Of twin-blue eyes, and crops

Of floury grain, and all the hosts of day,
All lovely hosts of ripples caused by fretting
The Darkness into play.
(Lawrence 1993, 132-33).

If there is a vitality here it is not one of self-furtherance and homeostasis, but one of splitting, bifurcation, recombination and multiple paths. From here it follows that concepts do not open life to some ideal and non-actualized future, but anchor perception into known forms; those forms can, though, be pulverized beyond human recognition and point of view, to achieve something like a 'fretting' of darkness. It is as though our usual notion of perception as illuminating representation, passes over into illumination as a fleeting 'fretting' of a deeper geological plane of darkness.

The waning of light and the increasing absence of human conceptual order is not presented by Lawrence's poem as some descent into lifeless chaos, for the absence of light as we know it—light as cognizing illumination—gives way to light as the play of darkness, as though our perceived illuminated world were a fragment of a broader life, time and cosmos beyond the man of reason. Lawrence takes the great motif of man's gaze into the cosmos ('wonder') and attributes it to the heavens, 'arrested, beating thick with wonder.' Far from this inhuman world being a negation or absence of life and order, the poem discloses rhythms ('swinging rhythmic'), durations, and even 'myriads / Of twin-blue eyes.'

Virginia Woolf's To the Lighthouse also describes a familial, gendered, historical and thoroughly archived world in the first section of the novel: Mr. Ramsay and his philosopher friends are concerned both with 'subject, object and the nature of reality,' and with their possible legacy and reputation in the maintained tradition of philosophy. Mrs. Ramsay is caring, nurturing, primarily concerned with overseeing the marriages of the next generations and largely devoted to maintaining social cohesion. In this first section of Woolf's novel, the younger Lily Briscoe aims to paint Mrs. Ramsay, even though she is told by Charles Tansley (an aspiring philosopher) that 'Women can't paint, women can't write....' At the level of narrative, this section of the novel, 'The Window' ostensibly concerns whether or not a journey towards light—a trip to the lighthouse—will be take place. As in the first stages of Lawrence's poem, a human world of love and filiation is set over against a world of what can broadly be referred to as climate—forces that play havoc with human intentionality and cannot be mastered by either a philosophy of subjectivism or an art of representation. Accordingly the middle section—'Time Passes'—shifts away from a human temporality of expectation and calculation to the falling of darkness. Here the point of view shifts from the novel's characters, with their desires and expectations, to rhythms, durations, and interactions of the earth's forces entering the house. Narrated in third person, the subject of the journey through the house is not even the single personified wind, but 'airs' that question the stability and steadfastness of the human world (again, an inversion of the human observer looking into a cosmos):

> Nothing stirred in the drawing-room or in the dining-room or on the staircase. Only through the rusty hinges and swollen sea-moistened woodwork certain airs, detached from the body of the wind (the house was ramshackle after all crept round corners and ventured indoors. Almost one might imagine them, as they entered the drawing-room questioning and wondering, toying with the flap of hanging wallpaper, asking, would it hang much longer, when would it fall? (Woolf 2007, 337)

These 'airs' interacting with the human world of objects are directed by 'some random light.' Eventually the narration moves towards what I would refer to as the geological sublime: a sublime that is *not* that of the world appearing *as if* in accord with our intentionality, a world that is *not* that of harmonious order, but that is destructive of the anthopomorphic sense we make of things:

> The nights now are full of wind and destruction; the trees plunge and bend and their leaves fly helter skelter until the lawn is plastered with them and they lie packed in gutters and

choke rain pipes and scatter damp paths. Also the sea tosses itself and breaks itself, and should any sleeper fancying that he might find on the beach an answer to his doubts, a sharer of his solitude, throw off his bedclothes and go down by himself to walk on the sand, no image with semblance of serving and divine promptitude comes readily to hand bringing the night to order and making the world reflect the compass of the soul. The hand dwindles in his hand; the voice bellows in his ear. Almost it would appear that it is useless in such confusion to ask the night those questions as to what, and why, and wherefore, which tempt the sleeper from his bed to seek an answer. (Woolf 2007, 339)

Here, in conclusion, I would suggest that we take our line of thinking from Woolf's Bergsonian modernism—destructive of concepts, order, and any notion of a single illuminating light of reason—towards Deleuze and Paul De Man. De Man, discussing the sublime, insisted that going beyond the order and human harmony of beauty would allow for a thought, always resisting figuration, of a blank and inhuman materiality: 'The dynamics of the sublime mark the moment when the infinite is frozen into the materiality of stone, when no pathos, anxiety, or sympathy is conceivable; it is, indeed, the moment of a-pathos, or apathy, as the complete loss of the symbolic' (De Man 1996, 126). Deleuze, writing on Bergson, also focused on the power of intuition to arrive at inhuman durations: 'To continue Bergson's project today, means for example to constitute a metaphysical image of thought corresponding to the new lines, openings, tracings, leaps, dynamisms, discovered by a molecular biology of the brain: new linkings and re-linkings in thought' (Deleuze 1991, 117).

That is, to be after Bergson's modernism, would be to continue the two tendencies of life: both the durations of matter, and the capacity—from those durations—to produce 'a metaphysical image of thought.' Art and writing in their human modes are neither mutations of a single archive of man (for the archive is in concert with times and rhythms not its own), nor would art and writing be simple extensions of the planet's rhythms. Art and writing are pulsations that are irreducible to the cosmos, but also in vibration with the cosmos—the chaosmos. Those modes of writing, today, that are responding to the new rhythms of the earth—writing that aims to imagine what it might be to perceive a world without humans—are provocatively postmodern. I would conclude, then, by contrasting various posthumanisms that aim to imagine one life of interweaving and interacting powers—where man overcomes his distinction to merge with digital technologies, animal life, or the ecology of the planet—to a more radical atavism, suggested by Bergson, where humans intuit rhythms that are distinct, inhuman, and beyond the time of the present. A post-modernism of this mode can be discerned, not only in a range of texts that are concerned with life after the end of humans, but in new modes of writing that aim to take point of view beyond that of man as a speaking animal. One example might be Don DeLillo's *Point Omega,* which takes the novel form but adopts the point of view of a man viewing an art installation (Douglas Gordan's *24 Hour Psycho*), with the art installation, in turn, being a slowed down scene from Alfred Hitchcock's *Psycho*. It is as though DeLillo is at once writing in language in the genre of the novel, and yet tracing the temporality and distributed rhythms of non-literary visual and cinematic forms. Just as Woolf concludes her novel *To the Lighthouse* with Lily Briscoe painting a single dark line down the center of a canvas, DeLillo opens *Point Omega* with sentences that follow the path of an eye following the slowed down frames of a section of film. DeLillo writes of the movements of light and the display of unseen images before turning to the perceiving eye and its relation to the screen, as well as the screen's capacity to produce cadences that alter the relation between eye and cognition. Eyes, screens, light, and images: all harbor their own tendencies, and yet all enter into contingent relations, generating distinct rhythms and lines of becoming. The sentences of the novel's opening double the repetitive rhythm of the gaze and the different angles the screens are able to produce of the same scene; the simple syntax and shift to present tense empties the point of view of any mental content, affect or interiority—'Anthony Perkins is turning his head':

> The gallery was cold and lighted only by the faint shimmer on the screen. Back by the north wall the darkness was nearly complete and the man standing alone moved a hand toward his face, repeating, ever so slowly, the action of a figure on the screen. When the gallery door slid open and people entered,

there was a glancing light from the area beyond, where others were gathered, at some distance, browsing the art books and postcards.

[...]

The man at the wall watched the screen and then began to move along the adjacent wall to the other side of the screen so he could watch the same action in a flipped image. He watched Anthony Perkins reaching for a car door, using the right hand. He knew that Anthony Perkins would use the right hand on this side of the screen and the left hand on the other side. He knew it but needed to see it and he moved through the darkness along the side wall and then edged away a few feet to watch Anthony Perkins on this side of the screen, the reverse side, Anthony Perkins using the left hand, the wrong hand, to reach for a car door and then open it.

But could he call the left hand the wrong hand? Because what made this side of the screen any less truthful than the other side?

The slightest camera movement was a profound shift in space and time but the camera was not moving now. Anthony Perkins is turning his head. It was like whole numbers. The man could count the gradations in the movement of Anthony Perkins' head. Anthony Perkins turns his head in five incremental movements rather than one continuous motion. It was like bricks in a wall, clearly countable, not like the flight of an arrow or a bird. Then again it was not like or unlike anything. (DeLillo 2010, 1)

It is true that Bergson regarded the cinematic camera as the ill of the modern eye: we carve the world into so many snapshots, and then regard the world as nothing more than a collection of unified images, forgetting that the frozen image is a lesser cut in a complex and intensive 'open whole' that cannot be reduced to a collection of distinct atoms or moments. But DeLillo's style here takes a certain strand of modernism and carries it forward into the perceptual power of the machine; the slowed down frames of Hitchcock's *Psycho* allow the human eye to experience durations and angles not its own. That perceiving eye, in turn, allows for a mode and style of writing that is not the linear narrative of a novel, but closer to a haiku, as if composed forces yield a certain meter that allows writing to form. If Bergson's modernism challenged the human point of view of subjects representing objects and did so by suggesting that intuition might find other durations, he also opened a tradition of writing that would not rest easily with its own structures and systems but would—through encounters with other perceptions—strive to think, from within language, of rhythms beyond language.

I would suggest that Bergson's formal method of intuition, whereby perception in the present decomposes the evolved forms of experience to disclose the tendencies from which bounded and organic life has emerged, enables a genealogy of the future. If we slow down the frames through which the world is given—*not* assuming one whole life of interconnected unity, but an open whole of divergent and incompossible potentials—then what has taken to be posthuman (or the vanquishing of our own being to perceive life as such in its full reality) may be surpassed by the counter human. Living beings are at once emergent from life and at war with life *if life is defined as temporal progression towards complex and self-maintaining systems.* If, however, there is no such thing as life as such—if there is only an ongoing war between bounded complexity and unbounded dissolution—then we will be compelled to confront the human stain: 'man' cannot erase himself, for he has always composed himself *as self-erasure,* as a being who can become nothing more than a life and world that he properly perceives. It is precisely this stain of non-erasure or the awareness of our geological mark on the time of life that may enable us to think a future that is neither posthuman nor human so much as superhuman. If humans exist it is through a deflection of survival, a strange torsion of being at once closed off from life while at the same time claiming to be nothing more than life: this history of the human as an oscillation between self-formation and self-destruction rather than the joyous and blind declaration of the posthuman provides a thought for the future beyond our assumed right to life.

Works Cited

Adorno, Theodor and Max Horkheimer. 2002. *Dialectic of Enlightenment: Philosophical Fragments.* Trans. Edmund Jephcott. Stanford: Stanford University Press.

Adorno, Theodor. 1983. *Negative Dialectics.* Trans. E.B. Ashton. London: Continuum.

Adorno, Theodor. 1984. *Aesthetic Theory.* Trans. C. Lenhardt. Ed. Gretel Adorno and Rolf Tiedemann. London.

Adorno, Theodor. 1991. *The Culture Industry: Selected Essays on Mass Culture.* Ed. J.M. Bernstein. London: Routledge.

Agamben, Giorgio. 1998. *Homo Sacer: Sovereign Power and Bare Life.* Trans. Daniel Heller-Roazen. Stanford: Stanford University Press.

Agamben, Giorgio. 1999. *Potentialities: Collected Essays in Philosophy.* Trans. Daniel Heller-Roazen. Stanford: Stanford University Press.

Agamben, Giorgio. 1999B. *The Man Without Content.* Trans. Daniel Heller-Roazen. Stanford University Press.

Agamben, Giorgio. 2004. *The Open: Man and Animal.* Stanford, CA: Stanford University Press.

Ansell-Pearson, Keith. 1997. *Viroid Life: Perspectives on Nietzsche and the Transhuman Condition* London: Routledge.

Apel, Karl-Otto. 2001. *The Response of Discourse Ethics to the Moral Challenge of the Human Situation as Such and Especially Today* Leuven: Peeters.

Appiah, Anthony Kwame. 2006. *Cosmopolitanism: Ethics in a World of Strangers.* New York: Norton.

Arendt, Hannah. 2005. *The Promise of Politics.* Ed. J. Kohn. New York: Schocken.

Attridge, Derek. 2004. *The Singularity of Literature.* London: Routledge.

Ayala, Franciso J. 2010. 'The Difference of Being Human: Morality.' *PNS* 107.2: 9015-9022.

Badiou, Alain. 2001. *Ethics: An Essay on the Understanding of Evil.* Trans. Peter. Hallward. London: Verso.

Baldick, Chris.1983. *The Social Mission of English Criticism, 1848-1932*. Oxford: Oxford University Press.

Bate, Jonathan. 1991. *Romantic Ecology: Wordsworth and the Environmental Tradition*. London: Routledge.

Bate, Jonathan. 2000. *The Song of the Earth*. Cambridge, MA.: Harvard University Press.

Baudrillard, Jean. 1994. *Simulacra and Simulation*. Trans. Sheila Faria Glaser. Ann Arbor: University of Michigan Press.

Beer, Gillian. 1983. *Darwin's Plots: Evolutionary Narrative in Darwin, George Eliot, and Nineteenth-Century Fiction*. London: Routledge and Kegan Paul.

Benatar, David.2006. *Better Never to Have Been: The Harm of Coming into Existence*. Oxford: Clarendon Press.

Benjamin, Walter. 2008. *The Work of Art in the Age of Mechanical Reproduction*. Harmondsworth: Penguin.

Benn Michaels, Walter. 2001. 'The Shape of the Signifier,' *Critical Inquiry* 27.2: 266-83.

Benn Michaels, Walter. 2009. 'What Matters,' *London Review of Books*. August.

Bergson, Henri. 1911A. *Creative Evolution*. Trans. Arthur Mitchell. New York: Henry Holt.

Bergson, Henri 1931. *Creative Evolution*. Trans. Arthur Mitchell. New York. H. Holt and Company.

Bergson, Henri. 1965. *Duration and Simultaneity*. Trans. Leo Jacobson. Indianapolis: Bobbs Merrill.

Bergson, Henri. 2002. *Henri Bergson: Key Writings*. Ed. Keith Ansell-Pearson and John Mullarkey. London: Continuum.

Bergson, Henri. 1911B. *Laughter: An Essay on the Meaning of the Comic*. London: Macmillan.

Bergson, Henri. 1912. *Matter and Memory*. Trans. Nancy Margaret Paul and William Scott Palmer. London: G. Allen; New York: Macmillan.

Bergson, Henri. 1913. *Matter and Memory*. Trans. Nancy Margaret Paul and W. Scott Palmer. London: George Allen.

Bergson, Henri. 2007. *Matter and Memory*. Trans. Nancy Margaret Paul and W. Scott Palmer. New York: Cosimo.

Bergson, Henri. 1935. *The Two Sources of Morality and Religion*. Trans. R. Ashley Audra and Cloudesley Brereton. London. Macmillan.

Bergson, Henri. 1977. *The Two Sources of Morality and Religion*. Trans. R. Ashley Audra and Cloudesley Brereton. Notre Dame: University of Notre Dame Press.

Bérubé, Michael and Nelson, Cary. Ed. 1995. *Higher Education Under Fire: Politics, Economics, and the Crisis of the Humanities*. New York: Routledge.

Bloom Howard. 2000. *The Global Brain: The Evolution of Mass Mind from the Big Bang to the 21st Century*. New York: Wiley.

Bostrom, Nick. 2005. 'The Fable of the Dragon Tyrant.' *Journal of Medical Ethics* 31.5: 273–277.

Boyd Brian. 1998. 'Jane, Meet Charles: Literature, Evolution, and Human Nature.' *Philosophy and Literature* 22.1: 1-30.

Boyd, Brian. 2006. 'Getting it All Wrong,' *The American Scholar*. http://www.theamericanscholar.org/getting-it-all-wrong/

Boyd, Brian. 2009. *On the Origin of Stories: Evolution, Cognition, and Fiction*. Cambridge, MA.: Belknap Press of Harvard University Press.

Braidotti, Rosi. 2006. 'Posthuman, All Too Human: Towards a New Process Ontology.' *Theory, Culture & Society* 23. 7-8: 197-208.

Brassier, Ray. 2008. *Nihil Unbound: Naturalism and Anti-Phenomenological Realism*. New York: Palgrave Macmillan.

Brennan, Timothy. 2001. 'Cosmo-Theory,' *The South Atlantic Quarterly* 100.3: 659-691.

Brooks, Peter. 1984. *Reading for the Plot: Design and Intention in Narrative*. New York: A.A. Knopf.

Bryant, Levi, Nick Srnicek and Graham Harman Eds. 2011. *The Speculative Turn: Continental Materialism and Realism*. Re: Press.

Butler, Judith. 1990. *Gender Trouble: Feminism and the Subversion of Identity*. New York: Routledge.

Butler, Judith. 1993. *Bodies that Matter: On the Discursive limits of 'Sex,'* New York: Routledge.

Butler, Judith. 1997. *The Psychic Life of Power: Theories in Subjection*. Stanford: Stanford University Press.

Butler, Judith. 2004. *Undoing Gender*. New York, London: Routledge.

Butler, Judith. 2005. *Giving an Account of Oneself*. New York: Fordham University Press.

Butler, Judith. 2006. *Precarious Life: The Powers of Mourning and Violence*. London: Verso.

Carr, Nicholas. 2009. In the Shallows: What the Internet is Doing to Our Brains. New York: Norton.

Carr, Nicholas. 2010. *The Shallows: What the Internet is Doing to Our Brain*. New York: Atlantic.

Carroll, Joseph. 2004. *Literary Darwinism: Evolution, Human Nature, and Literature*. London: Routledge.

Clark, Andy. 1997. *Being There: Putting Brain, Body, and World Together Again*. Cambridge, MA.: MIT Press.

Clark, Andy. 2003. *Natural-Born Cyborgs: Minds, Technologies, and the Future of Human Intelligence*. Oxford: Oxford University Press.

Clark, Andy. 2008. *Supersizing the Mind: Embodiment, Action, and Cognitive Extension*. Oxford: Oxford University Press.

Clark, Timothy. 2010. 'Some Climate Change Ironies: Deconstruction, Environmental Politics, and the Closure of Ecocriticism.' *Oxford Literary Review* 32.1: 131-49.

Clough, Patricia Ticineto with Jean Halley. 2007. *The Affective Turn: Theorizing the Social*. Durham: Duke University Press.

Cohen, Tom, Claire Colebrook and J. Hillis Miller. 2011. *Theory and the Disappearing Future: On De Man, On Benjamin*. London: Routledge.

Colebrook, Claire. 2012A. *Blake, Deleuzian Aesthetics and the Digital*. London: Continuum.

Colebrook, Claire. 2012B. 'On the Spectacle of Financial Collapse: Beyond (Good) Investment and (Evil) Speculation. *Loaded Subjects: Psychoanalysis, Money and the Global Financial Crisis*. David Bennett ed. London: Lawrence and Wishart.

Cottingham, John. 2003. *On the Meaning of Life*. London: Routledge.

Crutzen, Paul. 2000. 'The Anthropocene.' *Global Change Newsletter.* 41.1: 17-18.

Damasio, Antonio R. 2000. *The Feeling of What Happens: Body and Emotion in the Making of Consciousness*. New York: Harcourt.

De Landa, Manuel. 2002. *Intensive Science and Virtual Philosophy*. London: Continuum.

De Landa, Manuel. 2006. *A New Philosophy of Society: Assemblage Theory and Social Complexity*. London: Continuum.

De Man, Paul. 1972. 'Genesis and Genealogy in Nietzsche's, *The Birth of Tragedy*.' *Diacritics* 2.4: 44-53.

De Man, Paul. 1996. *Aesthetic Ideology*. Ed. Andrzej Warminski. Minneapolis: University of Minnesota Press.

Debord, Guy. 1973. *Society of the spectacle*. Detroit: Black & Red.

Deleuze, Gilles. 1988A. *Bergsonism*. Trans. Hugh Tomlinson and Barbara Habberjam. New York: Zone Books.

Deleuze, Gilles. 1994. *Difference and Repetition*. Trans. Paul Patton. New York: Columbia.

Deleuze, Gilles. 2006B. *The Fold: Leibniz and the Baroque*. Trans. Tom Conley. London: Continuum.

Deleuze, Gilles. 1988B. *Foucault*. Trans. Seán Hand. Minneapolis: University of Minnesota Press.

Deleuze, Gilles. 2006A. *Foucault*. Trans. Seán Hand. London: Continuum.

Deleuze, Gilles. 2004. *Francis Bacon: The Logic of Sensation*. Trans. Daniel W. Smith. Minneapolis: University of Minnesota Press.

Deleuze, Gilles and Félix Guattari. 1977. *Anti-Oedipus: Capitalism and Schizophrenia*. Trans. Robert Hurley, Mark Seem, and Helen R. Lane. New York: Viking Press.

Deleuze, Gilles and Félix Guattari. 2004. *Anti-Oedipus*. Trans. Brian Massumi. London: Continuum.

Deleuze, Gilles and Félix Guattari. 2004A. *Anti-Oedipus: Capitalism and Schizophrenia*. London: Continuum. Trans. Helen Lane and Mark Seem.

Deleuze, Gilles. and Guattari, Félix. 1986. *Kafka: Toward a Minor Literature*. Trans. R. Bensmaïa. Minneapolis: University of Minnesota Press.

Deleuze, Gilles and Félix Guattari. 1987. *A Thousand Plateaus: Capitalism and Schizophrenia*. Trans. Brian Massumi. Minneapolis: University of Minnesota Press.

Deleuze, Gilles and Félix Guattari. 2004B. *A Thousand Plateaus*. Trans. Brian Massumi. London: Continuum.

Deleuze, Gilles and Félix Guattari. 1994. *What is Philosophy?* Trans. Hugh Tomlinson and Graham Burchell. New York: Columbia University Press.

Derrida, Jacques. 1997. *Deconstruction in a Nutshell: A Conversation with Jacques Derrida*. Ed. John D. Caputo. New York: Fordham University Press.

Derrida, Jacques. 1978A. *Edmund Husserl's Origin of Geometry: An Introduction*. Trans. John P. Leavey, Jr. Nebraska: University of Nebraska Press.

Derrida, Jacques. 2002. 'Force of Law: "The Mystical Foundation of Authority."' in G. Anidjar Ed. *Acts of Religion*. London: Routledge.

Derrida, Jacques. 1977. *Limited Inc*. Trans. Samuel Weber. Ed. Gerald Graff. Evanston: Northwestern University Press.

Derrida, Jacques. 1982. *Margins of Philosophy*. Chicago: University of Chicago Press.

Derrida, Jacques. 1984. 'No Apocalypse, Not Now (Full Speed Ahead, Seven Missiles, Seven Missives).' Trans. C. Porter, P. Lewis. *Diacritics*,14.2 Nuclear Criticism: 20-31.

Derrida, Jacques. 2001. *On Cosmopolitanism and Forgiveness*. Trans. Mark Dooley and Michael Hughes. London: Routledge.

Derrida, Jacques. 1994. *Specters of Marx: The State of the Debt, the Work of Mourning, and the New International*. Trans. Peggy Kamuf. New York: Routledge.

Derrida, Jacques. 2005. *Rogues: Two Essays on Reason*. Trans. Pascale-Anee Brault and Michael Naas. Stanford: Stanford University Press.

Derrida, Jacques. 1978B. 'Violence and Metaphysics.' *Writing and Difference*. Trans. Alan Bass. Chicago: University of Chicago Press.

Diprose, Rosalyn. 2009. 'Toward an Ethico-Politcs of the Posthuman: Foucault and Merleau Ponty.' *Parrhesia* 8: 7-19.

Donne, John. 2000. *John Donne: The Major Works*. Ed. John Carey. Oxford: Oxford University Press.

Dougherty, Stephen. 2010. 'Culture in the Disk Drive: Computationalism, Memetics, and the Rise of Posthumanism.' *Diacritics* 31.4: 85-102.

Dreyfus, Hubert L., Stuart E. Dreyfus and Tom Athanasiou. 1986. *Mind over Machine: The Power of Human Intuition and Expertise in the Era of the Computer*. New York: Free Press.

Dunbar, Robin. 1996. *Grooming, Gossip and the Evolution of Language,* London: Faber.

Eagleton, Terry. 2007. *The Meaning of Life*. Oxford: Oxford University Press.

Emerson, Ralph Waldo. 1982. *Nature and Selected Essays*. Ed. Larzer Ziff. Harmondsworth: Penguin.

Esposito, Robert. 2008. *Bíos: Biopolitics and Philosophy*. Trans. T. Campbell. Minneapolis, MN: University of Minnesota Press.

Feinberg, Todd E. and Julian Paul Keenan. 2005. *The Lost Self: Pathologies of the Brain and Identity.* Oxford: Oxford University Press.

Felman, Shoshana. 1987. *Jacques Lacan and the Adventure of Insight: Psychoanalysis in Contemporary Culture.* Cambridge, MA.: Harvard University Press.

Felski, Rita. 2011. "Context Stinks!" *New Literary History* 42.4: 573-591.

Fink, Eugen. 1970. 'The Phenomenological Philosophy of Edmund Husserl and Contemporary Criticism.' In *The Phenomenology of Husserl.* Ed. R. O. Elveton. Chicago: Quadrangle Books. 73-147.

Fish, Stanley. 2010. 'The Crisis of the Humanities Officially Arrives.' *New York Times.* October 11, http://opinionator.blogs.nytimes.com/2010/10/11/the-crisis-of-the-humanities-officially-arrives/?emc=eta1

Flanagan, Owen. 2007. *The Really Hard Problem: Meaning in a Material World.* Cambridge. MA.: MIT Press.

Foucault, Michel. 1978. *The History of Sexuality: Volume One.* Trans. Robert Hurley. New York: Pantheon Books.

Foucault, Michel. 1977. *Language, Counter-Memory, Practice: Selected Essays and Interviews.* Ed. Donald F. Bouchard . Trans. Donald F. Bouchard and Sherry Simon. Ithaca: Cornell University Press.

Foucault, Michel. 1970. *The Order of Things: An Archaeology of the Human Sciences.* London: Tavistock.

Foucault, Michel. 2002. *The Order of Things: An Archaeology of the Human Sciences.* London: Routledge.

Freud, Sigmund. 1961. *Beyond the Pleasure Principle.* Trans. James Strachey. New York: Norton.

Freud, Sigmund. 2011. *Beyond the Pleasure Principle.* Ed. Todd Dufresne. Trans. Gregory C. Richter. London: Broadview Press.

Freud, Sigmund. 1908. 'Creative Writers and Day-Dreaming.' *The Standard Edition of the Complete Psychological Works of Sigmund Freud, Volume IX* (1906-1908): *Jensen's 'Gradiva' and Other Works.* Trans. James Strachey. London: Hogarth Press. 141-154.

Gallagher, Catherine and Greenblatt, Stephen. 2001. *Practicing New Historicism.* Chicago, IL: University of Chicago Press.

Gallagher, Shaun. 2005. *How the Body Shapes the Mind.* Oxford: Clarendon Press.

Gallagher, Winifred. 2008. *Rapt: Attention and the Focused Life.* New York: Penguin.

Gardiner, Stephen. 2006. 'A Perfect Moral Storm: Climate Change, Intergenerational Ethics and the Problem of Moral Corruption.' *Environmental Values* 15: 397–413.

Gibbs, Raymond R. Jr. 2006. *Embodiment and Cognitive science*. Cambridge: Cambridge University Press.

Goldman, Jane. 2004. *Modernism, 1910-1945: Image to Apocalypse*. New York: Palgrave Macmillan.

Greenfield, Susan. 2000. *The Private Life of the Brain: Emotions, Consciousness, and the Secret of the Self.* New York: John Wiley & Sons.

Greenfield, Susan. 2008. *I.D.: The Quest for Meaning in the 21st Century*. London: Sceptre.

Gregg, Melissa and Gregory J. Seigworth. 2010. *The Affect Theory Reader*. Durham: Duke University Press.

Grosz, Elizabeth. 1994. *Volatile Bodies: Toward a Corporeal Feminism*. Sydney: Allen and Unwin.

Grosz, Elizabeth. 2011. *Becoming Undone: Darwinian Reflections on Life, Politics, and Art*. Durham: Duke University Press.

Grusin, Richard A. 2010. *Premediation: Affect and Mediality After 9/11*. New York: Palgrave Macmillan.

Habermas, Jürgen. 1987. *The Philosophical Discourse of Modernity: Twelve Lectures*. Trans. Frederick Lawrence. Cambridge, MA.: MIT Press.

Habermas, Jürgen. 1991. *The Structural Transformation of the Public Sphere: An Inquiry Into a Category of Bourgeois Society*. Cambridge. Trans. Thomas Burger with Frederick Lawrence. MIT Press.

Hansen, Mark B. N. 2003. 'Affect as Interface: Confronting the Digital-Facial Image.' *Journal of Visual Culture* 2.2: 205-228.

Hansen, Mark B.N. 2004. 'The Time of Affect, or Bearing Witness to Life.' *Critical Inquiry* 30: 584-626 .

Hardt, Michael and Antonio Negri. 2000. *Empire*. Cambridge: Harvard University Press.

Hardt, Michael and Antonio Negri. 2004. *Multitude: War and Democracy in the Age of Empire*. New York: The Penguin Press.

Harman, Graham. 2005. *Guerrilla Metaphysics: Phenomenology and the Carpentry of Things*. Chicago, IL: Open Court.

Harman, Graham. 2012. *The Quadruple Object*. London: Zero Books.

Hartman, Geoffrey H. 1970. *Beyond Formalism; Literary Essays, 1958-1970.* New Haven: Yale University Press.

Hayles, N. Katherine. 1999. *How We Became Posthuman: Virtual Bodies in Cybernetics, Literature, and Informatics.* Chicago: University of Chicago Press.

Hayles, N. Katherine. 2007. 'Hyper and Deep Attention: The Generational Divide in Cognitive Modes.' *Profession.* 13: 187-199.

Heidegger, Martin. 1996. *Being and Time.* Trans. Joan Stambaugh. Albany: SUNY Press.

Heidegger, Martin. 1969. *An Introduction to Metaphysics.* Trans.Ralph Manheim. New Haven: Yale University Press.

Heidegger, Martin. 1998. *Pathmarks.* Ed. William McNeill. Cambridge: Cambridge University Press.

Heidegger, Martin. 1968. *What is a Thing?* Trans. W. B. Barton, Jr., and Vera Deutsch. Chicago: H. Regnery Co.

Hill, Rebecca. 2008. 'Phallocentrism in Bergson: Life and Matter.' *Deleuze Studies* 2: 123-136.

Husserl, Edmund. 1965. *Cartesian Meditations.* Trans. Dorion Cairns. The Hague: M. Nijhoff.

Huxley, Aldous. 1932. *Brave New World.* New York: Doubleday.

Jackson, Maggie and Bill McKibben. 2008. *Distraction: The Erosion of Attention and the Coming Dark Age.* New York: Promethues.

Jameson, Fredric. 2005. *Archaeologies of the Future: The Desire Called Utopia and Other Science Fictions.* London: Verso.

Jameson, Fredric. 1977. 'Imaginary and Symbolic in Lacan: Marxism, Psychoanalytic Criticism, and the Problem of the Subject.' *Yale French Studies* 55/56 Literature and Psychoanalysis. The Question of Reading: Otherwise: 338-395.

Jameson, Fredric. 1981. *The Political Unconscious: Narrative as a Socially Symbolic Act.* Ithaca: Cornell University Press.

Jameson, Fredric. 1991. *Postmodernism, or, The Cultural Logic of Late Capitalism.* Durham: Duke University Press.

Jones, Donna V. 2010. 'Bergson and the Racial *Elan Vital*,' in *The Racial Discourses of Life Philosophy.* New York: Columbia University Press.

Joughin, J. and Malpas, S. Eds. 2003. *The New Aestheticism.* Manchester: Manchester University Press.

Joyce, James. 2000. *Ulysses*. Ed. Declan Kiberd. Harmondsworth: Penguin.

Kane, Joanna. 2008. With Duncan Forbes and Roberta McGrath. *The Somnambulists*. Stockport: Dewi Lewis.

Kant, Immanuel. 1991. 'Idea for a Universal History with a Cosmopolitan Purpose.' In *Kant: Political Writings*. Ed. Hans Reiss. Trans. H.B. Nisbet. Cambridge: Cambridge University Press. 41-53.

Kant, Immanuel. 1991. *Political Writings*. Ed. H.S. Reiss. Cambridge: Cambridge University Press.

Kant, Immanuel. 1999. *Practical Philosophy*. Ed. Mary J. Gregor. Cambridge: Cambridge University Press.

Kirby, Vicki. 1997. *Telling Flesh: The Substance of the Corporeal*. New York: Routledge.

Knapp, Steven and Benn Michaels, Walter. 1982. 'Against Theory,' *Critical Inquiry* 8.4: 723-42.

Korsgaard, Christine. 2008. *The Constitution of Agency: Essays on Practical Reason and Moral Psychology*. Oxford: Oxford University Press.

Korsgaard, Christine. 2009. *Self-Constitution: Agency, Identity, and Integrity*. Oxford: Oxford University Press.

Korsgaard, Christine.M. and Cohen, G.A. 1996. *The Sources of Normativity*. Ed. O. O'Neill. Cambridge: Cambridge University Press.

Kronick, Joseph, G. 1999. *Derrida and the Future of Literature*. Albany: SUNY Press.

Lacan, Jacques. 1977. *Ecrits: A Selection*. Trans. Alan Sheridan. New York: Norton.

Lakoff, George and Mark Johnson. 1999. *Philosophy in the Flesh: The Embodied Mind and its Challenge to Western Thought*. New York: Basic Books.

Langton, Rae. 1998. *Kantian Humility: Our Ignorance of Things in Themselves*. Oxford: Oxford University Press.

Latour, Bruno. 2005. *Reassembling the Social: An Introduction to Actor-Network-Theory*. Oxford: Oxford University Press.

Lawrence, D.H. 1993. *The Complete Poems*. Ed. Vivian de Sola Pinto. Harmondsworth: Penguin.

Lawrence, D.H. 2002. *The Fox, The Captains Doll, The Ladybird: Volume 2 of the Cambridge Edition of the Works of D.H. Lawrence*. Ed. Dieter Mehl. Cambridge: Cambridge University Press.

LeDoux, Joseph E. 1996. *The Emotional Brain: The Mysterious Underpinnings of Emotional Life*. New York: Simon and Schuster.

LeDoux, Joseph. 2002. *Synaptic Self: How our Brains Become Who We Are*. New York: Viking: 2002.

Lenneberg, Hans. 1958. 'Johann Mattheson on Affect and Rhetoric in Music (I).' *Journal of Music Theory* 2.1: 47-84.

Levinas, Emmanuel. 1979. *Totality and Infinity*. Trans Alphonso Lingis. The Hague: Martinus Nijhoff.

Levitt, Steven D. and Dubner, Stephen J. 2005. *Freakanomics: A Rogue Economist Explores the Hidden Side of Everything*. New York: Harper Collins.

Ligotti, Thomas.2010. *The Conspiracy Against the Human Race: A Contrivance of Horror*. New York: Hippocampus Press.

Lovelock, James. 1979. *Gaia: A New Look at Life on Earth*. Oxford: Oxford University Press.

Lyotard, Jean-Francois. 1994. *Lessons on the Analytic of the Sublime*. Trans. Elizabeth Rottenberg. Standford: Stanford University Press.

Macpherson, C. B. 1962. *The Political Theory of Possessive Individualism: Hobbes to Locke*. Oxford: Clarendon Press. 1962.

Mann, Michael. 2009. 'Defining Dangerous Anthropogenic Interference.' *PNAS* 106.11: 4065-4066.

Massumi, Brian. 1995. 'The Autonomy of Affect,' *Cultural Critique* 31, The Politics of Systems and Environments, Part II: 83-109.

Maturana, Humberto R. and Francisco J. Varela 1980. *Autopoiesis and Cognition: The Realization of the Living*. Dordrecht: Reidel.

Maturana, Humberto R. and Francisco J. Varela. 1987. *The Tree of Knowledge: The Biological Roots of Human Understanding*. Boston: New Science Library.

McCarthy, Cormac. 2006. *The Road*. New York: Alfred A. Knopf.

Meillassoux, Quentin. 2008. *After Finitude: An Essay on the Necessity of Contingency*. London: Continuum.

Mignolo, Walter D. 2000. 'The Many Faces of Cosmo-polis: Border Thinking and Critical Cosmopolitanism,' *Public Culture* 12.3: 721-748.

Miller, Richard. 2010. *Globalizing Justice: The Ethics of Poverty and Power*. Oxford: Oxford University Press.

Milton, John. 1905. *Areopagitica*. Ed. C.W. Crook. London: Ralph Holland.

Mitchell, Juliet. 1975. *Psychoanalysis and Feminism*. Harmondsworth: Penguin.

Mithen, Steven. 2006. *The Singing Neanderthals: The Origins of Music, Language, Mind, and Body*. Cambridge: Harvard University Press.

Montag, Warren. 2009. 'Imitating the Affects of Beasts: Interest and Inhumanity in Spinoza.' *differences* 20.2-3: 54-72.

Morton, Timothy. 2007. *Ecology without nature: rethinking environmental aesthetics*. Cambridge, MA.: Harvard University Press.

Morton, Timothy. 2010. *The Ecological Thought*. Harvard University Press.

Naas, Michael. 2008. *Derrida From Now On*. New York: Fordham University Press.

Nancy, Jean-Luc. 2010. 'Let Them Speak Java? Jean-Luc Nancy in Defense of the Arts and Humanities.' http://defendartsandhums.blogspot.com/2010/12/let-them-speak-java-jean-luc-nancy-in.html

Negri, Antonio. 2008. *Empire and Beyond*. Trans. E. Emery. Cambridge: Polity.

Negri, Antonio, Michael Hardt and Danilo Zolo. 2008. *Reflections on Empire*. Cambridge: Polity.

Nietzsche, Friedrich Wilhelm. 1968. *Twilight of the Idols; and the Anti-Christ*. Trans. R. J. Hollingdale. Harmondsworth: Penguin Books.

Nietzsche, Friedrich. 2000. *The Birth of Tragedy*. Trans. Douglas Smith. Oxford: Oxford University Press.

Nietzsche, Friedrich. 2007. *On the Genealogy of Morality*. Ed. Keith Ansell-Pearson. Trans. Carol Diethe. Cambridge: Cambridge University Press.

Overtveldt, Johan van. 2007. *The Chicago School: How the University of Chicago Assembled the Thinkers Who Revolutionized Economics and Business*. Agate Publishing.

Petito, J., Varela, F.J., Pachoud, B. and Roy, J-M. 1999. *Naturalizing Phenomenology: Issues in Contemporary Phenomenology and Cognitive Science*. Stanford, CA: Stanford University Press.

Pound, Ezra. 2002. *The Cantos*. London: Faber and Faber.

Protevi, John. 2009. *Political Affect: Connecting the Social and the Somatic*. Minneapolis: University of Minnesota Press.

Rancière, Jacques. 2009. *The Future of the Image*. Trans. Gregory Elliott. London: Verso.

Rifkin, Jeremy.2009. *The Empathic Civilization: The Race to Global Consciousness in a World in Crisis*. New York: J.P. Tarcher/Penguin.

Sartre, Jean-Paul. 1957. *The Transcendence of the Ego: An Existentialist Theory of Consciousness*. Trans. Forrest Williams and Robert Kirkpatrick. New York: Noonday Press.

Serres, Michel. 2008. *Le Mal Propre: Polluer Pour S'Approprier*. Paris: Le Pommier.

Serres, Michel. 1995. *The Natural Contract*. Trans. Elizabeth MacArthur and William Paulson. Ann Arbor: University of Michigan Press.

Serres, Michel. 2006. 'Revisiting The Natural Contract' http://www.ctheory.net/articles.aspx?id=515.

Serres, Michel. 2007. *The Parasite*. Trans. Lawrence R. Schehr. Minneapolis: University of Minnesota Press.

Shelley, Mary Wollstonecraft . 2000. *Frankenstein*. Ed. Johanna M. Smith. London: Palgrave Macmillan.

Singer, Peter. 1972. 'Famine, Affluence and Morality. *Philosophy and Public Affairs*. 1.1: 229-243.

Singer, Peter. 2009. *The Life You Can Save*. New York: Random House.

Smith, Adam. 1976. *An Inquiry into the Nature and Causes of the Wealth of Nations*. Ed. Edwin Cannan. Pref. George J. Stigler. Chicago: University of Chicago Press.

Stengers, Isabelle. 2000. *The Invention of Modern Science*. Trans. D. Smith. Minneapolis, MN: University of Minnesota Press.

Stengers, Isabelle. 2011. *Thinking with Whitehead: A Free and Wild Creation of Concepts*. Cambridge, MA: Harvard University Press.

Stiegler, Bernard. 2010. *For a New Critique of Political Economy*. Trans. Daniel Ross. Cambridge: Polity.

Stiegler, Bernard. 2010. *Taking Care of Youth and the Generations*. Trans. Stephen Barker. Stanford: Stanford University Press.

Stiegler, Bernard. 2009. *Technics and Time: Disorientation*. Trans. Stephen Barker. Stanford: Stanford University Press.

Susan Wolf. 2010. *Meaning in Life and Why It Matters*. Princeton: Princeton University Press.

Thompson, Evan. 2007. *Mind in Life: Biology, Phenomenology, and the Sciences of Mind*. Cambridge, MA: Belknap Press of Harvard University Press.

Thomson, Alexander John Peter. 2005. *Deconstruction and Democracy: Derrida's Politics of Friendship*. London: Continuum.

Varela, Francisco J., Evan Thompson and Eleanor Rosch. 1991. *The Embodied Mind: Cognitive Science and Human Experience.* Cambridge, MA.: MIT Press.

Welsh, Irvine. 2002. *Trainspotting.* London: Norton.

Wheeler, Michael. 2005. *Reconstructing the Cognitive World: The Next Step.* Cambridge: MIT Press.

Wilson, Elizabeth, A. 1998. *Neural Geographies: Feminism and the Microstructure of Cognition.* New York: Routledge.

Winterson, Jeanette. 1993. *Written on the Body.* New York: Knopf.

Wolf, Maryanne.2007. *Proust and the Squid: The Story and Science of the Reading Brain.* New York: HarperCollins.

Wolfe, Cary. 1995. 'In Search of Posthumanist Theory: The Second-Order Cybernetics of Maturana and Varela.' *Cultural Critique* 30.1: 33-70.

Woolf, Virginia. 2007. *Selected Works of Virginia Woolf.* London: Wordsworth.

Wordsworth, William. 1991. *The Prelude.* Ed. Stephen Gill. Cambridge:Cambridge University Press.

Worringer, Wilhelm. 1953. *Abstraction and Empathy.* New York: International Universities Press.

Wrathall, Mark A. and Jeff Malpas. Eds. 2000. *Heidegger, Coping, and Cognitive science.* Cambridge, MA: MIT Press.

Wright, Elizabeth. 1984. *Psychoanalytic Criticism: Theory in Practice.* London: Methuen.

Wright, Robert. 2010. *The Evolution of God: The Origins of Our Beliefs.* New York: Little, Brown Book Group.

Yeats, W.B. 2011. *Selected Poems and Four Plays.* Ed. M.I. Rosenthal. New York: Simon and Schuster.

Ziarek, Eva. 2010. 'Feminine 'I Can': On Possibility and Praxis in Agamben's Work.' *Theory and Event* 13.1 2010. *n.pag.*

Žižek, Slavoj. 1998. 'A Leftist Plea for 'Eurocentrism'' *Critical Inquiry.* 24.4: 998-1009.

Zunshine, Lisa. 2006. *Why we Read Fiction: Theory of Mind and the Novel.* Ohio State University Press.

Permissions

Earlier versions of some chapters appeared in the following publications.

'Extinct Theory' in *Theory After Theory*, ed. Jane Elliott and Derek Attridge (Routledge, 2011)

'The Sustainability of Concepts' in *Sustainable Design*, ed. Adrian Parr and Michael Zaretsky (Routledge, 2010).

'A Globe of One's Own: In Praise of the Flat Earth' as 'A Globe of One's Own,' *SubStance* 41. 1 (2012).

'Destroying Cosmopolitanism for the Sake of the Cosmos,' in *After Cosmopolitanism*, ed. Rosi Braidotti, Patrick Hanafin and Bolette Blaagaard (Routledge 2102);

'Time and Autopoiesis,' in *Deleuze and the Body*, ed. Joseph Hughes and Laura Guillaume (Edinburgh University Press, 2011),

'Face Race,' in *Deleuze and Race*, ed. Arun Saldhana and Jason Michael Adams (Edinburgh University Press, 2013).

'Post-Human Humanities,' in *Time and History in Deleuze and Serres*, ed. Bernd Herzogenrath (Continuum, 2012);

'Why Saying "NO" to Life is Unacceptable,' in *The Unacceptable*, ed. John Potts and John Scannell (Palgrave 2013).

'The Joys of Atavism,' in *Understanding Bergson, Understanding Modernism*, ed. S.E. Gotarski, Paul Ardoin and Laci Mattison (Bloomsbury 2013).

CPSIA information can be obtained
at www.ICGtesting.com
Printed in the USA
FSHW012048181121
86336FS